Algebra Connections
Version 3.1

W9-AOC-276

Managing Editors

Leslie Dietiker
Phillip and Sala Burton Academic High School
San Francisco, CA

Evra Baldinger
Phillip and Sala Burton Academic High School
San Francisco, CA

Contributing Editors

Carlos Cabana
San Lorenzo High School
San Lorenzo, CA

John Cooper
Del Oro High School
Loomis, CA

Mark Coté
Beaver Lake Middle School
Issaquah, WA

Joanne da Luz
The Life Learning Academy
San Francisco, CA

David Gulick
Phillips Exeter Academy
Exeter, NH

Patricia King
Holmes Junior High School
Davis, CA

Lara Lomac
Phillip and Sala Burton Academic
High School, San Francisco, CA

Bob Petersen
Rosemont High School
Sacramento, CA

Ward Quincey
Gideon Hausner Jewish Day School, Palo
Alto, CA

Barbara Shreve
San Lorenzo High School
San Lorenzo, CA

Michael Titelbaum
University of California
Berkeley, CA

Illustrator

Kevin Coffey
San Francisco, CA

Technical Manager

Bethany Armstrong
Davis, CA

Technical Assistants

Erica Andrews
Elizabeth Burke
Elizabeth Fong
Keith Lee

Eric Baxter
Carrie Cai
Rebecca Harlow
Michael Leong

Program Directors

Leslie Dietiker
Phillip and Sala Burton Academic High School
San Francisco, CA

Judy Kysh, Ph.D.
Departments of Mathematics and Education
San Francisco State University

Brian Hoey
Christian Brothers High School
Sacramento, CA

Tom Sallee, Ph.D.
Department of Mathematics
University of California, Davis

Consultants from San Lorenzo High School

Ashanti Branch	Laura Evans	Eric Price	Estelle Woodbury
Suzanne Cristofani	Lisa Jilk	Ana Ruiz	Dorothy Woods
Kristina Dance	Karen O'Connell	Hannah Witzemann	Lisa Wright

Assessment Contributors:

Evra Baldinger, Managing Editor
Phillip and Sala Burton Academic High School
San Francisco, CA

Carlos Cabana
San Lorenzo High School
San Lorenzo, CA

Mark Coté
Beaver Lake Middle School
Issaquah, WA

Leslie Dietiker
Phillip and Sala Burton Academic High School
San Francisco, CA

Laura Evans
San Lorenzo High School
San Lorenzo, CA

Judy Kysh, PhD
Departments of Mathematics and Education
San Francisco State University

Contributing Editors of the Parent Guide:

Bev Brockhoff
Glen Edwards Middle School
Lincoln, CA

Elizabeth Coyner
Christian Brothers High School
Sacramento, CA

Brian Hoey
Christian Brothers High School
Sacramento, CA

Patricia King
Holmes Junior High School
Davis, CA

Bob Petersen, Managing Editor
Rosemont High School
Sacramento, CA

Editor of Extra Practice:

Bob Petersen
Rosemont High School
Sacramento, CA

Technical Manager of Parent Guide:

Rebecca Harlow
Stanford University
Stanford, CA

5 6 7 8 9   10 09 08 07   ISBN-10: 1-931287-45-7

Printed in the United States of America   Version 3.1   ISBN-13: 978-1-931287-45-6

A Note to Students:

Welcome to a new year of math! In this course, you will be exposed to a powerful set of mathematical tools called algebra. As a set of tools, algebra is the foundation of higher mathematics. In fact, future courses will build from what you learn here. While you learn algebra, we also hope you become used to a new way of thinking: a way of investigating new situations, discovering relationships, and figuring  out what strategies can be used to solve problems. Learning to think this way is useful in mathematical contexts, other academic disciplines, and situations outside the classroom.

In meeting the challenges of algebra, you will not be working alone. During this course you will collaborate with other students as a member of a study team. Working in a team means speaking up and interacting with others. You will explain your ideas, listen to what others have to say, and ask questions if there is something you do not understand. In algebra, a single problem can often be solved several ways. You will see problems in different ways than your teammates do. Each of you has something to contribute while you work on the lessons in this course.

Together, your team will complete problems and activities that will help you discover mathematical ideas and methods. Your teacher will support you as you work, but will not take away your opportunity to think and investigate for yourself. Each topic will be revisited many times and connected to other topics. If something is not clear to you the first time you work with it, you will have more chances to build your understanding as the course continues.

Learning math this way has a significant advantage: as long as you actively participate, make sure everyone in your study team is involved, and ask good questions, you will find yourself understanding mathematics at a deeper level than ever before. By the end of this course, you will have a powerful set of mathematical tools at your disposal. You will see how these tools connect with each other so that you can use them to solve new problems. With your teammates you will meet mathematical challenges you would not have known how to approach before.

In addition to the support provided by your teacher and your study team, CPM has also created online resources to help you, including help with homework, a parent guide, and extra practice. You will find these resources and more at www.cpm.org.

We wish you well and are confident that you will enjoy learning algebra!

Sincerely,
The CPM Team

Algebra
Connections
Table of Contents

Student Edition

Chapter 9 Inequalities   373

Chapter 10 Simplifying and Solving   407

CHAPTER 1

Welcome to Algebra! What is algebra? This chapter will introduce you to many of the big ideas you will explore and the ways you will be working during this course. You will apply your current mathematical knowledge to solve problems, some of which you will revisit later in the course to solve using new algebraic tools.

This chapter will also introduce you to the five Ways of Thinking that are threaded throughout the course. They are: **justifying** (explaining and verifying your ideas), **generalizing** (predicting behavior for any situation), **making connections** (connecting your ideas to other ways of seeing or to past or future learning), **reversing thinking** (solving problems "backward and forward"), and **applying and extending** (applying your knowledge to new contexts and extending it to help solve new problems).

Guiding Questions

Think about these questions throughout this chapter:

What is algebra?

How can I solve a problem that I have never seen before?

How can I organize my work?

How can I describe my process?

Finally, this chapter is about problem solving. During this chapter, you will use a variety of problem-solving strategies that will remain useful throughout this course, including:

Guessing and Checking	Collecting Data	Finding Patterns
Drawing a Graph	Working Backward	

Chapter Outline

Section 1.1 This section will include several problems and activities that use many of the big ideas of algebra. Each one will require your study team to work together and use various problem-solving strategies.

Section 1.2 This section introduces another problem-solving strategy that will help you solve a complex problem called "The Apartment." You will also have opportunities to reflect on and write about your mathematical understanding by creating a Learning Log.

Algebra Connections

1.1.1 What stories can a graph tell?

Interpreting Graphs

You will focus on several challenges during this unit that will require you to use different problem-solving strategies. While all of the problems are solvable with your current math skills, some will be revisited later in the course so that you can apply new algebraic tools to solve them. Each problem also introduces you to an important concept of algebra that you will study in this course.

1-1.   GETTING TO KNOW YOU, Part One

How can a graph tell a story? Today you will find your team members and then will work together to write a story for a graph.

Your Task: Your teacher will give you one part of a graph. Find the students in the class who have the other pieces of the same graph. When you find all of the students whose graph parts belong with yours, sit down together as a team.

As a team, come up with a story that could be represented by your team's graph. Think carefully about each part of the graph. Once your team agrees on a story, make sure every member of the team can describe each part of the story and explain its connection to the corresponding part of the graph.

To help you work together today, each member of the team has a specific job, assigned by your first name (or by your last name if any team members have the same first name).

Team Roles

Resource Manager – If your name comes first alphabetically:

- Make sure that the team has tape.

- Ask the teacher when the **entire** team has a question. *"No one has an idea? Should I ask the teacher?"*

- Make sure your team cleans up by delegating tasks. You could say, *"I will put away the _____ while you _____ ."*

Facilitator – If your name comes second alphabetically:

- Start the team's discussion of the graph by asking, *"What could this graph be about?… What are some ideas?"*

- Help the team agree on a story: *"Do we agree on all of the parts of our story?"*

Recorder/Reporter – If your name comes third alphabetically:

- Tape the graph pieces together on a piece of paper to form the graph.

- Take notes for the team. The notes should include phrases like, *"For part one…"* and explanations like, *"Because part one is not so steep…"*

Task Manager – If your name comes fourth alphabetically:

- Remind the team to stay on task and not to talk to students in other teams. You can suggest, *"Let's move on to another part of the graph."*

- Listen for reasons and challenge your teammates to justify their thinking. *"But why do you think that?"*

Algebra Connections

1-2.   GETTING TO KNOW YOU, Part Two

Suppose the graph at right represents
something about the four students in your
team. But what is the graph about? Decide
what information the *x*- and *y*-axes could
represent so that each point represents a
different member of your team. **Justify** your
statements.

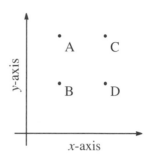

M ETHODS AND MEANINGS

MATH NOTES

The Perimeter and Area of a Figure

The **perimeter** of a figure is the
distance around the exterior (outside)
on a flat surface. It is the total length
of the boundary that encloses the
interior (inside) region. See the
example at right.

Perimeter = $5 + 8 + 4 + 6 = 23$ units

The **area** indicates the number of
square units needed to fill up a region
on a flat surface. For a rectangle, the
area is computed by multiplying its
length and width. The rectangle at
right has a length of 5 units and a width
of 3 units, so the area of the rectangle
is 15 square units.

Area = $5 \cdot 3 = 15$ square units

1-3.   MATHOGRAPHY

Write a letter about yourself that will help your teacher get to know you as an individual, addressing each of the general topics below (in bold). Choose a few of the suggested questions to get you started.

About You: By what name do you like to be called? What are your interests, talents, and hobbies? What are you proud of? With whom do you live? What languages do you speak? When is your birthday? What are you like as a member of a team? In what ways are you excited about working in a team? In what ways are you nervous about it?

You as a Math Student: Describe your memories as a math student from kindergarten until now. What experiences in math have you liked? Why? How do you feel about taking Algebra? Have you ever worked in a team in a math class before? What kinds of math do you imagine yourself doing in Algebra class?

1-4.   DIAMOND PROBLEMS

Finding and using a pattern is an important problem-solving skill you will use in algebra. The patterns in Diamond Problems will be used later in the course to solve other types of algebraic problems.

Look for a pattern in the first three diamonds below. For the fourth diamond, explain how you could find the missing numbers (?) if you know the two numbers (#).

Copy the Diamond Problems below onto your paper. Then use the pattern you discovered to complete each one.

a.   b.   c.   d.   e.

Algebra Connections

1-5. The area of the rectangle at right is 24 square units. On graph paper, draw and label all possible rectangles with an area of 24 square units. Use only whole numbers for the dimensions (measurements).

Area = 24 square units

    a. Find the perimeter of each of these rectangles. You may want to refer to the Math Notes box for this lesson for more information on the perimeter of a figure.

    b. Of these rectangles, which has the largest perimeter? Which has the smallest perimeter? Describe these shapes. Remember to use complete sentences.

1-6. CAR COMPARISON

The following three graphs describe two cars, A and B.

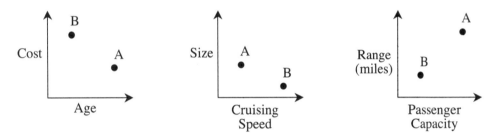

Decide whether each of the following statements is true or false. Explain your reasoning.

    a. The newer car is more expensive.

    b. The slower car is larger.

    c. The larger car is newer.

    d. The cheaper car carries more passengers.

1.1.2 How can I name a point?

. . . .

Using the (x, y) Coordinate Plane

Today you will use a **coordinate system** to refer to the locations of specific points in the form
(x, y). By the end of this lesson, be sure you and your teammates know the answers to the
following target questions:

> How can you plot a point using its (x, y) coordinates?
>
> How can you name a point on the graph?
>
> How can you describe a pattern formed by points?

1-7.   THE EUCALYPTUS GROVE

Some communities in Mozambique
plant eucalyptus tree farms because
their tall, straight trunks make great
poles for building homes. While
touring his farm, Etube (pronounced
"eh-**too**-bay") noticed that some of
the trees have a deadly disease. He created a coordinate system, shown in the diagram
below, to keep track of where the infected trees are. The farm's roads are shown as
the x- and y-axes in the diagram, and Etube's house is located where the two roads
intersect. Each section of the farm (known as a **quadrant**) has 12 rows of 12 trees.
The trees marked with a ✪ show signs of disease – the tops are turning brown!

a.   The tree marked A, located at
the point (–3, 6), is diseased.
In (x, y) form, list the locations
of all of the other diseased trees
shown on the diagram.

b.   On a piece of graph paper,
neatly draw and label x- and
y-axes to represent the roads
intersecting at Etube's house.
Place points or symbols on
your graph to represent the
diseased trees.

Etube just learned that the trees
at (–8, 2) and (5, –7) are also
diseased. Add these trees to
your diagram.

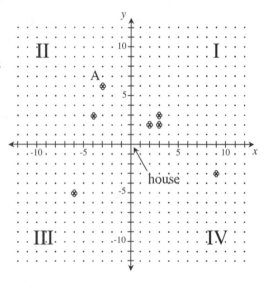

Problem continues on next page →

Algebra Connections

1-7.   *Problem continued from previous page.*

    c.   In (x, y) form, what is the location of Etube's house? This is also called the **origin** of a graph.

    d.   Etube is standing at the farmhouse looking out at Quadrant I and sees that the tree at $(3, 2)$ is diseased. However, he notices that he cannot see the tree at $(6, 4)$ because it is blocked by the tree at $(3, 2)$.

        In (x, y) form, write down the locations of two other trees that he cannot see from his house because they are hidden behind the tree at $(3, 2)$. What do the locations of these trees have in common? When looking at the coordinates, what pattern(s) do you notice?

    e.   While standing at his house, can Etube see the diseased tree at $(9, -3)$? If so, explain how you know. If not, name any trees that block its view. How can you be sure that these trees hide the tree at $(9, -3)$? Be sure to **justify** your team's conclusion.

    f.   The tree disease is passed each day when the leaves of a diseased tree touch the leaves of a healthy tree that grows next to it, as shown on the diagram at right. (Note that the disease cannot pass between trees on opposite sides of the road because their leaves do not touch.) Etube knows that the tree at $(-8, 2)$ is diseased. In (x, y) form, write the locations of four trees that will be infected by that tree on the first day.

    g.   In Quadrant I, three trees are diseased. Write the locations (x, y) of the trees that will be infected by these three trees by the end of the first day.

    h.   Etube noticed that there is one diseased tree in Quadrant III. The disease is spreading rapidly, and he is worried because the tree medicine will not arrive for four more days. How many trees in Quadrant III will still be healthy after the fourth day? How do you know? Use your diagram, keep track of the diseased trees, and **justify** your response.

1-8.   Reflect on how you used the coordinates (the x- and y-values) to find and refer to points on the graph during today's lesson. Revisit the target questions, reprinted below, and share your conclusions in a class discussion.

        How can you plot a point using its (x, y) coordinates?

        How can you name a point on the graph?

        How can you describe a pattern formed by points?

METHODS AND MEANINGS

MATH NOTES

Axes, Quadrants, and Coordinates

The *x*- and *y*-axes help define points on a graph (called a "Cartesian Plane"). The **x-axis** is horizontal, while the **y-axis** is vertical. The *x*- and *y*-axes divide the graphing area into four sections called **quadrants**. Written as an **ordered pair**, a point is named by its **coordinates** (x, y), with the *x*-coordinate written first.

4-quadrant graph:

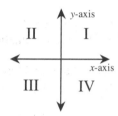

1st-quadrant graph:

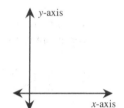

1-9.   In the graph at right, points A, B, and C represent three different students.

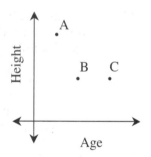

a.   Which student is oldest? Explain how you decided.

b.   What can you say about student B compared to students A and C? Tell as much as you can and **justify** your statements.

1-10.   Compute each of the following sums and differences.

a. $-7 + (-2)$ b. $3 + (-4)$ c. $-2 - 5$ d. $-1 + 5$

e. $4 - (-2)$ f. $-7 - (-8)$

1-11.   Using whole numbers only, draw every possible rectangle with an area of 18 square units on graph paper. Write $A = 18 \ un^2$ inside each figure. Label the dimensions (length and width) of each rectangle.

Algebra Connections

1-12.   Latisha is determined to do well in school this year. Her goal is to maintain at least an 85% average in all of her courses.

    a.   Latisha started with two scores: 72% and 89%. Confirm that the average of these two scores is 80.5%. Show your work.

    b.   Latisha's third score is 90%. Use her scores from part (a) to figure out her average now. Be sure to show your work.

1-13.   In Algebra, you will need to be able to work with numbers, words, and geometric representations. Use these representations to answer the following problems.

    a.   Draw and shade a figure that represents 100%. Label 100% below it. Then describe the figure in words.

    b.   Similarly, draw and shade figures that represent 50%, 25%, and 150%. Label each figure and describe it in words.

    c.   Draw and shade a figure that represents "one-third." How can this figure be represented with a number?

    d.   Describe what the diagram at right represents using words and numbers.

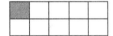

1-14.   Use the graph at right to answer the following questions about quadrants and coordinates of points.

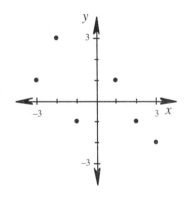

    a.   What are the coordinates of the two points in Quadrant II (where the x-value is negative and the y-value is positive)?

    b.   What are the coordinates of the two points in Quadrant IV (where the x-value is positive and the y-value is negative)?

1.1.3 How can I use data to solve a problem?

Collecting, Organizing, and Analyzing Data

Computing batting averages, performing scientific experiments, and polling people during elections are just a few examples of how data can provide useful information when it is collected and analyzed. In this lesson you will be collecting and organizing data to determine the potential danger of riding a roller coaster.

1-15. NEWTON'S REVENGE

Have you heard about Newton's Revenge, the new roller coaster? It's so big, fast, and scary that people are already starting to talk. Some people are worried about the tunnel that thrills riders with its very low ceiling.

The closest the ceiling of the tunnel ever comes to the seat of the roller-coaster car is 200 cm. Although no accidents have been reported yet, rumors have been spreading that very tall riders have broken their arms as they went through the tunnel with their arms raised over their heads. Unfortunately, due to these rumors, many tall people have stopped riding the coaster.

Your Task: Consider how you could determine whether the tunnel is actually safe for any rider, no matter how tall. Discuss the questions below with your team. Be ready to share your responses with the rest of the class.

Discussion Points

What is this problem about? What is it asking you to do?

What information can help you answer this question?

How can you get the information you need?

1-16.   One way to determine if the roller coaster is safe is to collect and analyze data.

a.   Collect data from each member of your team.

Each member of the team needs to be measured twice. First, have one team member stand and have another team member measure his or her height. Second, have the same student sit in a chair or desk, raise his or her arms so that they are stretched as far as possible above his or her head, and measure the distance from the seat of the chair to his or her fingertips. All measurements should be in centimeters.

Student Name	Height (cm)	Reach (cm)

Each person should record the team's data in a table like the one above.

b.   Send one person up to record your team's data on the class table. Then add the rest of the class data to your own table.

c.   Each person should put his or her initials on a sticky dot, then graph his or her own *height vs. reach* point on the class graph.

1-17.   Use the class graph to answer the questions below.

a.   Are there any dots that you think show *human error*? That is, are there any dots that appear to be graphed incorrectly or that someone may have measured incorrectly? Explain why or why not.

b.   Is a person's reach related to his or her height? That is, what seems to be true about the reach of taller people? Explain.

c.   Since a person's reach depends on his or her height, we call the reach the **dependent** quantity and the height the **independent** quantity. Examine the class graph of the data from problem 1-16. On which axis was the independent data represented? On which axis was the dependent data represented?

d.   Is there a trend in the data? How can you **generalize** the trend?

1-18. Everyone is complaining about how the teacher made the class graph!

a. Jorge is confused about how the teacher decided to set up the graph. *"Why is it a 1st-quadrant graph instead of a 4-quadrant graph?"* Answer Jorge's question. In general, how should you decide what kind of graph to use?

b. Lauren is annoyed with the *x*-axis. *"Why didn't the teacher just use the numbers from the table?"* she whined. *"Why count by twenties?"* What do you think?

c. Hosai thinks that the graph is TOO BIG. *"The dots are all mashed together! Why did the teacher begin both the x- and y-axes at zero? Anyone that short would never be allowed on the roller coaster. Why not just start closer to the smallest numbers on the table?"* she asked. What do you think?

d. Sunita says the graph is TOO SMALL! *"If we're supposed to be using this data to check if the coaster is safe for really tall people, the graph has to have room to graph tall people's dots too."* Do you agree? If so, how much room do you think is needed?

1-19. Using all of your ideas from problem 1-18, make your own graph that will help you determine whether the ride is safe for very tall people. For example, the basketball player Yao Ming is 7 feet 6 inches (about 228.6 cm) tall. Is the roller coaster is safe for him? Explain.

1-20. Is the roller coaster safe for all riders? Prepare a poster that shows and **justifies** your team's answer to this question. Every team poster should include:

- A large, clear graph.

- A complete, clear, and convincing explanation of why your team thinks the ride is or is not safe for all riders.

ETHODS AND MEANINGS

Adding and Subtracting Integers

An **integer** is any positive or negative whole number or zero. Look at the examples of integers and non-integers below:

$$-1001 \quad 56 \quad 0 \quad -2 \qquad \qquad \tfrac{1}{2} \quad 2.1 \quad \pi \quad 8.3$$

examples of integers   examples of non-integers

The diagram at right shows that $-1+1=0$. One way to think of this concept is to think of an elevator. If you start one floor below ground (-1) and travel up one floor $(+1)$, you end up on the ground floor (which can be represented with zero).

One useful strategy that works when adding and subtracting integers is to draw a diagram and eliminate zeros. Study the examples below:

Example 1: $5-8 = 5+(-8) = -3$

Example 2: $-2+7 = 5$

Example 3: $-6-1 = -6+(-1) = -7$

1-21.   Copy these Diamond Problems and use the pattern you
         discovered earlier, shown at right, to complete each of them.
         Some of these may be challenging!

a.   b.   c.   d.

e.   f.   g.   h.

1-22.   Compute without a calculator.

a. $-15 + 7$ b. $8 - (-21)$ c. $-12 - (-4)$ d. $-9 + (-13)$

e. $-50 - 30$ f. $3 - (-9)$ g. $-75 - (-75)$ h. $(-3) + 6$

i. $9 + (-14)$ j. $28 - (-2)$ k. $-3 + (-2) + 5$ l. $3 + 2 + 5$

1-23.   The area of each rectangle below is shown in the middle of the rectangle. For each
         figure, find the missing length or width.

a.   b.   c.

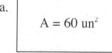   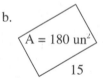

$A = 60$ un^2 $A = 180$ un^2 $A = 231$ un^2 14

      8   15

1-24.   Compute <u>without</u> a calculator.

a. $427 - (-3)$ b. $-50 + (-150)$

1-25.   In Algebra, you will need to be able to work with numbers, words, and geometric
         representations. Use these representations to answer the following questions.

a.   Write another fraction that is equivalent to $\frac{4}{5}$. Draw diagrams to show that
     they are equal.

b.   Find the equivalent decimal for both fractions. Was rounding your answer
     necessary?

c.   Find the equivalent percent for both fractions.

Algebra Connections

1-26.   On graph paper, draw all of the possible rectangles with an area of 16 square units. Use only whole-number lengths (no decimals). What are the dimensions of the rectangle with the smallest perimeter?

1-27.   The area of a rectangle is 450 square inches. If the length of the rectangle is 24 inches, what is the width?

1-28.   Latisha earned an 85% today. Her previous scores were 72%, 89%, and 90%. Calculate her new average.

1-29.   Estimate the areas of Montana and California using the grid below. Which state has the greatest area? Compare the area of Montana to the area of California. Explain how you estimated the area of each state.

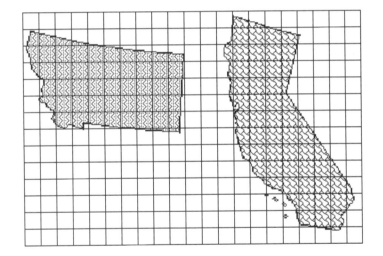

1-30.   The diamond at right represents the pattern you found in problem 1-4.

a.   Complete these Diamond Problems.

i.

ii.

iii.

iv.

b.   Create two new Diamond Problems of your own.

1.1.4 How can I generalize a pattern?

Finding and Generalizing Patterns

Often, mathematics is described as "the study of patterns." Today you will preview future work with patterns by studying two tile patterns and using them to make predictions. As you work on these patterns, consider the following questions:

How do I see the pattern?

How is it changing?

Is there another way to find a solution?

1-31.   GROWING, GROWING, GROWING

Copy the tile pattern shown below onto graph paper.

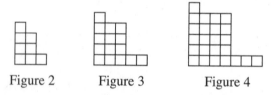

Figure 2   Figure 3   Figure 4

a.   Draw the 1st, 5th, and 6th figures on your paper.

b.   How is the pattern changing?

c.   What would the 100th figure look like? How many tiles would it have? How can you **justify** your prediction?

1-32.   Examine this new tile pattern. Copy it onto your paper.

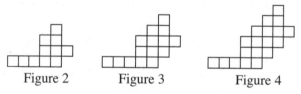

Figure 2   Figure 3   Figure 4

a.   Draw the 1st, 5th, and 6th figures on your paper.

b.   Michael knows that one of the figures in this tile pattern has 79 tiles. What is its figure number? There are <u>many</u> ways to figure this out – be sure to listen to each person's ideas about how to find a solution. Be prepared to explain how you answered this question.

Algebra Connections

1-33.   For either the pattern in problem 1-31 or the pattern in problem 1-32, prepare a team transparency or poster with your description of the pattern and your prediction. Every team transparency or poster should include:

- Clear drawings of figures from your pattern.

- An explanation of the pattern you found.

- Your prediction. (Make sure your reasoning is clear!)

METHODS AND MEANINGS

Fractions, Decimals, and Percents

Fractions, decimals, and percents are different ways to represent the same number.

Below are some ways to convert a number from one of these representations to another.

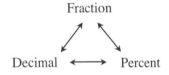

Percent to decimal:

Since "percent" means "out of 100," divide the percent by 100.

$29.6\% = 29.6 \div 100 = 0.296$

Decimal to percent:

Reverse the process: Multiply the decimal by 100.

$0.68 = (0.68)(100) = 68\%$

Fraction to percent:

Find an equivalent fraction that has 100 in the denominator. The numerator is the percent.

$\frac{3}{5} = \frac{60}{100} = 60\%$

Percent to fraction:

Since "percent" means "out of 100," place the percent in a fraction over 100. Simplify as needed.

$48\% = 0.48 = \frac{48}{100} = \frac{12}{25}$

Fraction to decimal:

Since a fraction implies division, divide the numerator by the denominator.

$\frac{7}{8} = 7 \div 8 = 0.875$

Decimal to fraction:

Write and reduce the fraction that has the same meaning of the decimal. For example, since 0.4 is "four-tenths":

$0.4 = \frac{4}{10} = \frac{2}{5}$

1-34.   Copy the axes below onto your paper. Place and
         label a point on the graph for each of the products
         listed below.

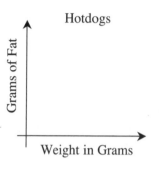

a.   Dog-Eat-Dog has a
      supreme hotdog
      that weighs 80
      grams and has 40
      grams of fat.

b.   Hot Doggies has a
      diet hotdog that
      weighs 50 grams and has only 9 grams of fat.

c.   Dog-alicious has a cheap hotdog that weighs 40
      grams and has 30 grams of fat.

1-35.   Copy and complete each sequence below. Using words, not numbers, describe how
         the patterns work. (For example, write, "Double the previous number.")

a.   1, 3, 6, 10, ___, ___   b. $1, \frac{1}{2}, \frac{1}{4}, \frac{1}{8}$, ___, ___

c.   1, 3, 9, 27, ___, ___   d.   8, 7, 5, 2, ___, ___

e.   49, 47, 52, 50, 55, ___, ___

1-36.   Recall the Diamond Problem pattern that you found in
         problem 1-4, which is represented in the diamond at right.
         Copy and complete the Diamond Problems below using the
         same pattern.

a.   b.   c.   d.

Algebra Connections

1-37. Copy the number line below onto your paper. Locate the following numbers by placing the lowercase letters *a* through *e* on the number line corresponding to the values given below. Part (a) is done for you.

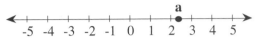

a. $2\frac{1}{3}$ b. -2.7 c. $\frac{1}{2}$

d. -0.2 e. $33\frac{1}{3}\%$ of 12

1-38. Draw and shade a diagram to represent $\frac{2}{3}$. Label your diagram with the fraction. Would 0.66 or 0.67 be a more appropriate decimal equivalent? Explain why.

1-39. Susan's apartment is shown at right. Assuming that all rooms are rectangular, find the quantities described below. All measurements are in feet.

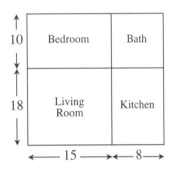

a. Find the area of her living room.

b. Find the area of her entire apartment.

c. How much larger than her bedroom is her living room?

1.2.1 How can I solve it?

Solving Problems with Guess and Check

In this lesson, you will work with your team to find a strategy for solving a complex problem. It will be important for you to find ways to organize your work so that other people can follow your process.

1-40.   THE APARTMENT

Your architecture firm has been hired to design an apartment building. Each of the apartments in the building will be laid out as shown at right so that each room is rectangular.

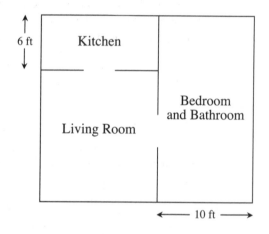

The building's owners have given you the following specifications.

*   The living room of an apartment must have an area of 180 square feet.

*   The shorter side of the kitchen must be 6 feet to make room for counter space.

*   The shorter width of the bedroom and bath must be 10 feet so that a dresser and king-sized bed will fit.

*   The entire area of each apartment must be exactly 450 square feet.

Your Task: Find the possible dimensions for every room in the apartment. Be prepared to **justify** your answer (show how you know it works), and show all of your work in a way that someone who is not in your team can read and understand it.

Discussion Points

How can you start?

How can you organize your work?

How can you use the results from one guess
to make your next guess better?

1-41.   Charles decided to start this problem by making a guess. He guessed that everything would come out right if one side of the living room were 10 feet.

   a.   Does it matter which side of the living room is 10 feet long? Why or why not? Find the area of the entire apartment twice: once if the base of the living room is 10 feet long, and again if the height of the living room is 10 feet long. Do the results come out the same?

   b.   Is Charles' guess correct? That is, can one of the sides of the living room be 10 feet long? Explain.

   c.   As you checked Charles' guess, did you organize your work so that anyone could read and understand your thinking? If not, try to find a way to reorganize your work to make it clear.

   d.   As a team, try another guess for a dimension of the living room. Organize your work to check if that guess is correct.

1-42.   One way to organize your work in this kind of problem is by using a table. The table can be structured something like this:

Length of _____	?	Total Area

   a.   Use this method to check the rest of your guesses for this problem.

   b.   Continue guessing and checking until you find correct room dimensions. Once you have an answer, organize your work so that it shows the dimensions of all of the rooms and can be read and understood by someone who is not in your team. Be ready to present to the class both your final answer and the different guesses that you tried along the way.

Further Guidance
section ends here.

1-43.   LEARNING LOGS

Throughout this course, you will be asked to reflect on your
understanding of mathematical concepts in a Learning Log. Your
Learning Log will contain explanations and examples to help you
remember what you have learned throughout the course. It is
important to write each entry of the Learning Log in your own
words so that later you can use your Learning Log as a resource
to refresh your memory. Your teacher will tell you where to write your Learning
Log entries. Remember to label each entry with a title and a date so that it can be
referred to later.

In this first Learning Log entry, describe what you know about the Guess and Check
problem-solving method. For example, what does a Guess and Check problem look
like? What does the solution look like? How does the method work? Title this
entry "Guess and Check" and include today's date.

METHODS AND MEANINGS

Multiplication and Division of Integers

MATH NOTES

When multiplying and dividing integers, an even number of
negative integers gives a positive result, and an odd number of
negative integers gives a negative result. Some examples:

$(-4) \cdot (-8) = 32$ $(-60) \div (-15) = 4$ $(-5) \cdot (-2) \cdot (-4) = -40$

$(-6) \cdot (5) = -30$ $(12) \div (4) = 3$ $(-3) \cdot (5) \cdot (-4) = 60$

Algebra Connections

1-44.   Copy and complete each of the Diamond Problems below.
          The pattern used in the Diamond Problems is shown at
          right.

a.

b.

c.

d.

e.

f.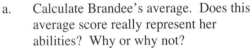

g.

h.

1-45.   Latisha's friend Brandee forgot to make up a
          test and had these scores: 80%, 92%, 91%,
          75%, 89%, 84%, 0%, and 85%.

          a.   Calculate Brandee's average. Does this
                 average score really represent her
                 abilities? Why or why not?

          b.   Brandee persuaded her teacher, Ms.
                 Juarez, to allow her to make up the
                 missed test. Brandee received a 78%.
                 Calculate her new average.

          c.   What difference did the 0% score make? Does this new average represent
                 Brandee's ability more accurately?

1-46.   While organizing his bookshelf, Michael noticed that he had eight more science-
          fiction novels than spy novels. If he owns 26 science-fiction and spy novels, how
          many of each type of novel does he own? Explain how you found your solution.

1-47.   Explain what the graph at right represents. What
          information does it convey?

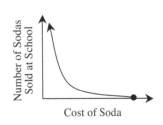

1-48.   Copy the axes at right and put a dot for each student
         described below.

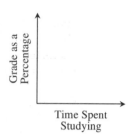

         a.   Student A, who studies hard but gets only
               average grades.

         b.   Student B, who studies little but gets good grades.

1-49.   Try these problems without a calculator first. Then use a calculator to check your
         answer.

         a. $-16 + 7$ b. $10 - (-24)$ c. $(3)(-9)$

         d. $-9 + (-11)$ e. $-49 - 36$ f. $-56 \div (-7)$

         g. $15 \div (-3)$ h. $-7 \div 7$ i. $(-6) \cdot 9$

         j. $(-5)(-5)$ k. $(-6) \cdot (43)$ l. $27 - (-3) - 4$

1.2.2 How can I organize my work?

· ·

More Guess and Check

As you continue your focus on Guess and Check today, organize your work so that you can find
your solutions methodically.

While you work, use the following focus questions to help guide your team's discussion:

                    What is the problem about?

            What is the relationship between the quantities involved?

            How can you use the results from one guess to make a better guess?

1-50.   BULL'S-EYE!

         Jaime was throwing darts at a target. When his dart landed in the
         center of the target (the "bull's-eye"), he earned 7 points. However,
         when his dart landed on the outside ring, he earned 2 points. After
         50 throws, his friend reported his score to be 160 points. Jaime
         wanted to know how many bull's-eyes he had hit, but his friend did
         not know. How many bull's-eyes did Jaime hit?

1-51.   Your teacher will assign your team one of the following problems. Use Guess and Check to solve your problem, and then prepare a presentation to share your solution and method with the class. Use the focus questions from the lesson introduction to help you get started.

   a.   Adele, Amanda, and Alisa are sisters who are raising funds to go on a scouting trip. Adele sold twice as many cookies as Amanda. Alisa sold the same number as Amanda. Their uncle also donated $15, but he did not want any cookies. Together they raised $655. How much money did each sister raise?

   b.   Rachel fenced off an area in the shape of a rectangle for her dog. She used 48 feet of fencing material, and the rectangle is 6 feet longer than it is wide. What are the dimensions (length and width) of the rectangle?

   c.   At track practice, each runner usually carries a lap counter. Hector and McQuisten want to make their coach think that they have run farther than they actually have, so they decide to share a lap counter. Hector runs twice as far as McQuisten does. When both are finished running, the lap counter reads 48 laps. How many laps did Hector actually run?

   d.   When the football game started, there were twice as many Philly students as Comstock students. Five minutes into the game, busses arrived, bringing an additional 600 Philly students to the game. Total attendance for the game was 3552 students. How many students attended from each school?

   e.   Shaunice has 36 feet of fence to put around her rectangular flowerbed. How long and how wide will the flowerbed have to be so that she has 72 square feet of area to plant flowers?

1-52.   Present to the class your team's method and solution to one of the parts of problem 1-51. As you listen to other teams' presentations, ask questions like, *"How did you know what columns to use?"*, *"How did you know what to guess?"*, and *"Does it matter which order the columns are in?"*

1-53.   Explain in your Learning Log how you can use the results of a guess to choose your next guess. How can you tell if you should make your next guess much different than or very close to your last guess? Title this entry "Choosing Good Guesses" and include today's date.

METHODS AND **M**EANINGS

MATH NOTES

Word-Problem Vocabulary

There are some vocabulary words that occur frequently in word problems. Examine these words and their meanings below.

Twice
• 2

This means "times two" or "double." For example, if Erica has *twice* as many dimes as she has quarters, then if she has 6 quarters, she has $6 \cdot 2 = 12$ dimes.

Sum
+

This is the result of adding. If a problem states that the *sum* of the number of pencils and pens is 10, that means that the number of pencils plus the number of pens is 10.

Product
( )( )

This is the result of multiplying. If a problem states that the *product* of two numbers is 96, that means that you multiply the first number by the second number to get 96.

More Than
+

This description tells you that something is a certain quantity greater than something else. This phrase is similar to phrases like "greater than" and "higher than." For example, if Erica has 8 *more* rabbits *than* pigs, and if she has 10 pigs, then she has $10 + 8 = 18$ rabbits. "More than" implies addition.

Less Than
−

This description works much like "more than" (above). This phrase is similar to phrases like "fewer than" and "shorter than." If Erica has 5 pounds *less* dog food *than* cat food, and if she has 11 pounds of cat food, then she has $11 − 5 = 6$ pounds of dog food. "Less than" implies subtraction.

Times More Than
( )( )

This description tells you that some quantity is a multiple of some other quantity. If Erica has 7 *times more* flour *than* sugar, and she has 3 pounds of sugar, then she has $7 \cdot 3 = 21$ pounds of flour. "Times more than" implies multiplication.

1-54. Solve the problem below using Guess and Check. State your solution in a sentence.

Todd is 10 years older than Jamal. The sum of their ages is 64. How old are Todd and Jamal?

1-55. Solve the problem below using Guess and Check. State your solution in a sentence.

Jabari is thinking of three numbers. The greatest number is twice as big as the least number. The middle number is three more than the least number. The sum of the three numbers is 75. Find the numbers.

1-56. Copy the pattern at right and continue the pattern for successive powers of 3.

a. In a sentence or two, describe a pattern formed by the units digits (the "ones") of the numbers in the pattern.

b. $3^1 = 3$. List the next three powers of 3 for which the ones place is a 3.

$3^1 = 3$
$3^2 = 9$
$3^3 = $ _____
$3^4 = $ _____
$\vdots$
$3^9 = $ _____

1-57. Copy and complete each of the Diamond Problems below. The pattern used in the Diamond Problems is shown at right.

a.

b.

c.

d.

1-58. The area of a rectangle is 24,396 square centimeters. If the width is 38 centimeters, what is the length? How do you know?

1.2.3 How can I solve it?

More Guess and Check

Today you will continue your work on solving word problems with Guess and Check. As you work with your teammates, use the following focus questions to help focus your team's discussion:

What is the problem about?

What is the relationship between the quantities involved?

How can you use the results from one guess to make a better guess?

1-59.   HELPING THE HOMELESS

A study team decided to volunteer at the local soup kitchen to help feed the homeless people in their neighborhood. While the team cooked the soup, Rose noticed that the number of cans of tomato paste was five more than twice the number of cans of noodles. Afterward, the team recycled 44 cans that were emptied into the soup.

a.   How many cans of each ingredient did the team use?

b.   Later, Rose learned that a can of tomato paste costs $0.70 while a can of noodles costs $0.50. How much did it cost to make the soup?

1-60.   Tamar was daydreaming during Social Studies class and only wrote down the following information: Mexico has 70 million more citizens than Canada; the United States has three times the number of citizens as Mexico; and there are 430 million citizens in Mexico, Canada, and the United States combined. Based on this information, how many citizens live in Canada?

1-61.   When setting the price of admission tickets for the amusement park, Tabitha wants the price for a two-child, two-adult family to be $100. She also wants the adult tickets to cost $8.00 more than twice the cost of a child's ticket. How much should a child's ticket cost?

Algebra Connections

1-62.   One side of a triangle is 3 inches shorter than twice the length of the shortest side. The third side is 5 inches longer than the shortest side. If the perimeter is 110 inches, find the lengths of all three sides.

1-63.   A pet shop has 15 animals, all cats and birds. If the animals have a total of 32 legs, how many birds are there?

1-64.   What questions do you still have about the Guess and Check solution process? In your Learning Log, write some questions you have about how to solve a word problem using Guess and Check. Title this entry "Questions about Guess and Check" and label it with today's date.

1-65.   Solve the problem below using Guess and Check. State your solution in a sentence.

The perimeter of a triangle is 76 centimeters. The second side is twice as long as the first side. The third side is four centimeters shorter than the second side. How long is each side?

1-66.   The pattern below is composed of nested squares.

a.   Draw the next figure in the pattern.

b.   Find the area of the shaded region for the figure you drew in part (a).

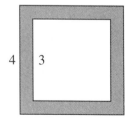

1-67.   Examine the tile pattern at right.

   a.   On your paper, sketch
         Figures 4 and 5.

   b.   How does the pattern grow?
         Explain how you know.

Figure 1   Figure 2   Figure 3

   c.   How many tiles will there be in Figure 100? Explain how you know.

1-68.   Look at each graph below and write a story or description about what each graph
         shows.

   a. 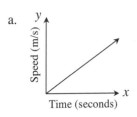   b. 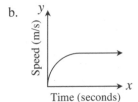   c.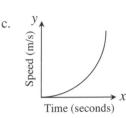

1-69.   Enrollment in math
         courses at Kennedy
         High School in
         Bloomington,
         Minnesota, is shown in
         the pie chart at right. If
         there are 1000 students
         enrolled in math
         courses, approximately
         how many students are
         enrolled in Algebra? In
         Geometry? In Calculus?

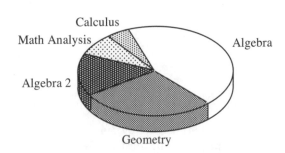

Algebra Connections

Chapter 1 Closure   What have I learned?

Reflection and Synthesis

The activities below offer you a chance to reflect on what you have learned during this chapter. As you work, look for concepts that you feel very comfortable with, ideas that you would like to learn more about, and topics you need more help with. Look for **connections** between ideas as well as **connections** with material you learned previously.

①   TEAM BRAINSTORM

With your team, brainstorm a list for each of the following three topics. Be as detailed as you can. How long can you make your list? Challenge yourselves. Be prepared to share your team's ideas with the class.

Topics: What have you studied in this chapter? What ideas and words were important in what you learned? Remember to be as detailed as you can.

Problem Solving: What did you do to solve problems? What different strategies did you use?

Connections: How are the topics, ideas, and words that you learned in previous courses are **connected** to the new ideas in this chapter? Again, make your list as long as you can.

MAKING CONNECTIONS

The following is a list of the vocabulary used in this chapter. Make sure that you are familiar with all of these words and know what they mean. Refer to the glossary or index for any words that you do not yet understand.

area	average	coordinates
dimensions	equivalent	graph
Guess and Check	integers	less than
more than	pattern	perimeter
product	quadrants	sum
table	twice	x- and y-axes

Make a concept map showing all of the **connections** you can find among the key words and ideas listed above. To show a **connection** between two words, draw a line between them and explain the **connection**, as shown in the example below. A word can be **connected** to any other word as long as there is a **justified connection**. For each key word or idea, provide a sketch of an example.

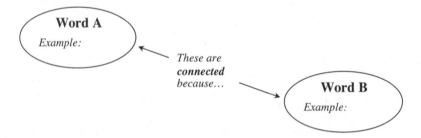

Your teacher may provide you with vocabulary cards to help you get started. If you use the cards to plan your concept map, be sure either to re-draw your concept map on your paper or to glue the vocabulary cards to a poster with all of the **connections** explained for others to see and understand.

While you are making your map, your team may think of related words or ideas that are not listed above. Be sure to include these ideas on your concept map.

③   SUMMARIZING MY UNDERSTANDING

This section gives you an opportunity to show what you know about certain math topics or ideas. Your teacher will give you directions for exactly how to do this. Your teacher may give you a "GO" page to work on. "GO" stands for "Graphic Organizer," a tool you can use to organize your thoughts and communicate your ideas clearly.

Algebra Connections

④ WHAT HAVE I LEARNED?

This section will help you evaluate which types of problems you have seen with which you feel comfortable and those with which you need more help. This section will appear at the end of every chapter to help you check your understanding. Even if your teacher does not assign this section, it is a good idea to try these problems and find out for yourself what you know and what you need to work on.

Solve each problem as completely as you can. The table at the end of this closure section has answers to these problems. It also tells you where you can find additional help and practice on problems like these.

CL 1-70. In (x, y) form, write the coordinates of each point (A through F) circled on the graph at right.

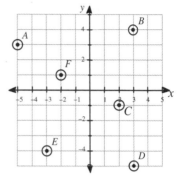

CL 1-71. On graph paper, draw and label x- and y-axes. Find and label the following points:

$G(3, 2)$ $H(1, 4)$ $I(-2, -1)$

$J(4, -2)$ $K(-5, 1)$

CL 1-72. Solve the following problem using Guess and Check. Show your guesses in an organized way.

Alex hangs each pair of pants and each shirt on a separate hanger. He has 51 hangers in his closet all holding clothes. Every time he buys 1 pair of pants he also buys 2 shirts. How many shirts does Alex own?

CL 1-73. On graph paper, draw at least six different-sized rectangles that have an area of 64 square units. Then find the perimeter of each rectangle.

CL 1-74. Copy and complete each of the Diamond Problems below. The pattern used in the Diamond Problems is shown at right.

a.

8

6

b.

−2   6

c.

−28

4

d.

−1

−4

e.

3.25   4

f.

24

−11

CL 1-75. Copy the pattern below onto graph paper. Draw the 1st and 5th figures on your paper.

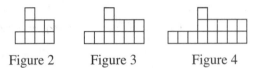

Figure 2   Figure 3   Figure 4

    a.   How many tiles are in each figure?

    b.   Describe how the pattern is changing.

    c.   How many tiles would the 6th figure have? the 10th figure?

CL 1-76. Check your answers using the table at the end of this section. Which problems do you feel confident about? Which problems were hard? Have you worked on problems like these in math classes you have taken before? Use the table to make a list of topics you need help on and a list of topics you need to practice more.

⑤   HOW AM I THINKING?

This course focuses on five different **Ways of Thinking**: reversing thinking, justifying, generalizing, making connections, and applying and extending understanding. These are some of the ways in which you think while trying to make sense of a concept or to solve a problem (even outside of math class). During this chapter, you have probably used each Way of Thinking multiple times without even realizing it!

This closure activity will focus on one of these Ways of Thinking: **making connections**. Read the description of this Way of Thinking at right.

Think about the **connections** that you have made during this chapter. When have you linked one idea with another? What **connections** have you made with ideas that you learned in a previous math class? You may want to flip through the chapter to refresh your memory about the problems that you have worked on. Discuss any of the **connections** you have made with the rest of the class.

Once your discussion is complete, practice thinking this way by making a concept map as described in closure activity #2, *Making Connections*.

Making Connections

You often think this way when you try to show how one idea relates to or links with another idea. For example, when you catch yourself thinking, "*This reminds me of something…*", you are making a connection.

That reminds me of...

Algebra Connections

Answers and Support for Closure Activity #4
What Have I Learned?

Problem	Solution	Need Help?	More Practice
CL 1-70.	a. (−5, 3) b. (3, 4) c. (2, −1) d. (3, −5) e. (−3, −4) f. (−2, 1)	Lesson 1.1.2 Math Notes box	Problems 1-7, 1-14, 1-34, and 1-48
CL 1-71.		Lesson 1.1.2 Math Notes box	Problems 1-7, 1-14, 1-34, and 1-48
CL 1-72.	Alex owns 34 shirts.	Problems 1-41 and 1-42	Problems 1-50, 1-51, 1-54, 1-55, 1-59, 1-60, 1-61, 1-62, 1-63, and 1-65
CL 1-73.	Multiple answers are possible. Rectangles with integer sides have dimensions 1 by 64, 2 by 32, 4 by 16, and 8 by 8. However, to get more than four rectangles with different dimensions, you need to also use non-integer lengths, such as $\frac{1}{2}$ by 128 or $\frac{1}{3}$ by 192.	Lesson 1.1.1 Math Notes box	Problems 1-5, 1-11, 1-23, 1-26, 1-27, and 1-58

Problem	Solution	Need Help?	More Practice
CL 1-74.	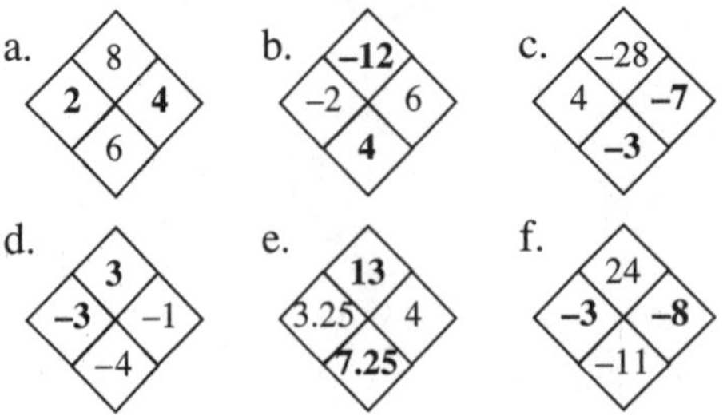 a. (diamond: top 8, left 2, right 4, bottom 6) b. (diamond: top −12, left −2, right 6, bottom 4) c. (diamond: top −28, left 4, right −7, bottom −3) d. (diamond: top 3, left −3, right −1, bottom −4) e. (diamond: top 13, left 3.25, right 4, bottom 7.25) f. (diamond: top 24, left −3, right −8, bottom −11)	Problem 1-4	Problems 1-21, 1-30, 1-36, 1-44, and 1-57

CL 1-74.

a.   b.   c.

d.   e.   f.

CL 1-75.		Lesson 1.1.4	Problems 1-31, 1-32, and 1-67

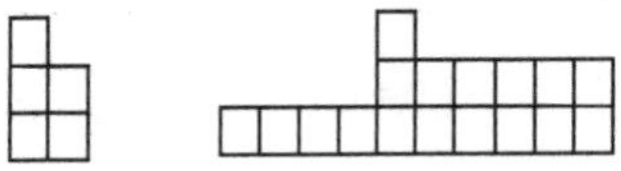

Figure 1   Figure 5

a. 5, 8, 11, 14, 17

b. Each figure has three more tiles than the one before it.

c. The 6th figure would have 20 tiles. The 10th figure would have 32 tiles.

CHAPTER 2   Variables and Proportions

This chapter begins with a focus on the use of variables in algebra (such as x and y). You will use tools called "algebra tiles" to explore how and where to use variables. Since this topic lays the foundation for simplifying expressions and solving equations, it will be revisited and built upon repeatedly throughout the course.

In the second part of this chapter, you will develop methods to solve problems that involve proportional relationships. For example, if you want to know how many people at your school are left-handed, how can you use the information from your class to make a prediction? Questions like these will rely on your intuition about proportions.

In this chapter, you will learn:

> What a variable is.

> How to write and simplify algebraic expressions.

> How to compare two complicated algebraic expressions.

> How to solve for a variable if you know that two expressions are equal.

> How to solve problems involving proportional relationships.

Guiding Questions

Think about these questions throughout this chapter:

What is a variable?

What can I do with a variable?

How can I solve for a variable?

How many different ways can I write an expression?

What's the relationship?

Chapter Outline

Section 2.1   This section introduces algebra tiles to develop the symbolic manipulation skills of combining like terms and solving linear equations. A special focus will be placed on the meaning of "minus" and how to make "zero."

Section 2.2   You will use your intuition about proportional relationships to find new ways to solve proportional problems.

2.1.1 What is a variable?

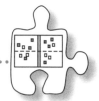

· ·

Exploring Variables and Combining Like Terms

In "The Apartment," problem 1-40, the length and width of each room was unknown. Similarly, the height of the tallest person who could ride the roller coaster safely in "Newton's Revenge," problem 1-15, was unknown. When using Guess and Check, you guessed the value of something that was unknown in order to solve for it.

In Algebra and in future mathematics courses, you will work with unknown quantities that can be represented using **variables**. Today, manipulatives called "algebra tiles" will be introduced to help you and your teammates answer some important questions, such as "What is a variable?" and "How can we use it?"

2-1. Your teacher will distribute a set of algebra tiles for your team to use during this course. As you explore the tiles, address the following questions with your team. Be prepared to share your responses with the class.

- How many different shapes are there? What are all of the different shapes?

- How are the shapes different? How are they the same?

- How are the shapes related? Which fit together and which do not?

2-2. Draw a picture of each size of tile on your paper.

a. The algebra tiles will be referred to by their areas. Since the smallest square has a length of 1 unit, its area is 1 square unit. Thus, the name for this tile is "one" or a "unit tile." Can you use the unit tile to find the other lengths? Why or why not?

b. Name the other tiles using their areas. Be sure to use what you know about the area of a rectangle and the area of a square.

2-3. JUMBLED PILES

Your teacher will show you a jumbled pile of algebra tiles and will challenge you to name all of them. What is the best description for the collection of tiles? Is your description the best possible?

2-4.   Build each collection of tiles represented below. Then name the collection using a
        simpler algebraic expression, if possible. If it is not possible to simplify the
        expression, explain why not.

    a. $3x + 5 + x^2 + y + 3x^2 + 2$ b. $2x^2 + 1 + xy + x^2 + 2xy + 5$

    c. $2 + x^2 + 3x + y^2 + 4y + xy$ d. $3y + 2 + 2xy + 4x + y^2 + 4y + 1$

2-5.   In your Learning Log, explain what a variable is in your own
        words. Describe each type of tile with a diagram that includes
        each dimension and an area label. Explain when tiles can and
        cannot be combined. Be sure to include examples to support your
        statements. Title this entry "Variables" and include today's date.

⊙OOKING DEEPER

Non-Commensurate

MATH NOTES

   Two measurements are called **non-commensurate** if no combination
   of one measurement can equal a combination of the other. For
example, your algebra tiles are called non-commensurate because no
combination of unit squares will ever be exactly equal to a combination of
x-tiles (although at times they may appear close in comparison). In the same
way, in the example below, no combination of x-tiles will ever be exactly
equal to a combination of y-tiles.

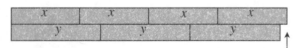

    No matter what number of each size tile,
    these two piles will never exactly match.

2-6.   Suppose you put one of your x-tiles and two unit tiles with another pile of three
        x-tiles and five unit tiles. What is in this new pile? Write it as a sum.

2-7.   Suppose one person in your team has two x^2-tiles, three x-tiles, and one unit tile on his desk and another person has one x^2-tile, five x-tiles, and eight unit tiles on her desk. You decide to put all of the tiles together on one desk. What is the name for this new group of tiles?

2-8.   Copy the following figures onto your paper. Then find the area and perimeter of each shape. Assume that all corners are right angles. Show all work.

a.
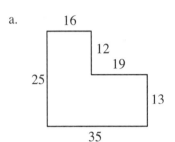

b.
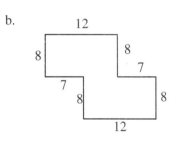

2-9.   Find the perimeter of the entire rectangle shown at right (that is, the outside boundary of the figure). Notice that the areas of two of the parts have been labeled inside the rectangle. Also find the total area. Remember to show all work leading to your solution.

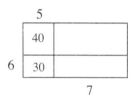

2-10.   One meaning of the word **evaluate** is to find the value of an expression. To evaluate, replace a variable with a number and calculate the result. For example, when you are asked to evaluate the expression $4x - 2$ when $x = -7$, you would put –7 in place of the variable and calculate: $4 \cdot (-7) - 2 = -30$.

Evaluate the expressions below for the given values of x and y.

a. $\frac{6}{x} + 9$ if $x = 3$

b. $8x - 3 + y$ if $x = 2$ and $y = 1$

c. $2xy$ if $x = 5$ and $y = -3$

d. $2x^2 - y$ if $x = 3$ and $y = 8$

2-11.   Use Guess and Check to solve the following problem. Write your solution as a sentence.

A cable 84 meters long is cut into two pieces so that one piece is 18 meters longer than the other. Find the length of each piece of cable.

2.1.2 What's the perimeter?

Simplifying Expressions by Combining Like Terms

While Lesson 2.1.1 focused on the area of algebra tiles, today's lesson will focus on the perimeter. What is perimeter? How can you find it? By the end of this lesson, you will be able to find the perimeter of strange shapes formed by multiple tiles.

Your class will also focus on multiple ways to find perimeter, recognizing that there are different ways to "see," or recognize, perimeter. Sometimes, with complex shapes, a convenient shortcut can help you find the perimeter more quickly. Be sure to share any insight into finding perimeter with your teammates and with the whole class.

While working today, ask yourself and your teammates these focus questions:

How did you see it?

How can you write it?

Is your expression as simplified as possible?

2-12.   Your teacher will provide a set of algebra tiles for your team to use today. Separate one of each shape and review its name (area). Then find the *perimeter* of each tile. Decide with your team how to write a simplified expression that represents the perimeter of each tile. Be prepared to share the perimeters you find with the class.

2-13.   For each of the shapes formed by algebra tiles below:

- Use tiles to build the shape.

- Sketch and label the shape on your paper and write an expression that represents the perimeter.

- Simplify your perimeter expression as much as possible.

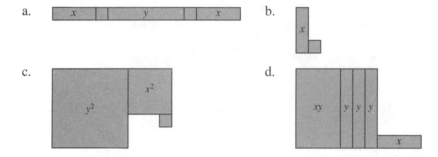

2-14.   Calculate the perimeter of the shapes in problem 2-13 if the length of each *x*-tile is 3 units and the length of each *y*-tile is 8 units. Show all work.

2-15.   EXTENSION

The perimeter of the shape at right is 32 units.
Find possible values for x and y. Is there more
than one possible solution? If so, find another
solution. If not, explain how you know there is
only one solution.

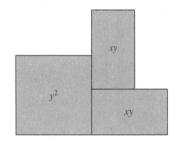

2-16.   In your Learning Log, create your own shape using three different-
shaped tiles. Draw the shape and show how to write a simplified
expression for its perimeter. Label this entry "Finding Perimeter
and Combining Like Terms" and include today's date.

LOOKING DEEPER

Commutative Properties

The **Commutative Property of Addition** states that when *adding* two
or more number or terms together, order is not important. That is:

$$a + b = b + a \qquad \text{For example, } 2 + 7 = 7 + 2$$

The **Commutative Property of Multiplication** states that when *multiplying*
two or more numbers or terms together, order is not important. That is:

$$a \cdot b = b \cdot a \qquad \text{For example, } 3 \cdot 5 = 5 \cdot 3$$

However, *subtraction* and *division* are <u>not</u> commutative, as shown below.

$$7 - 2 \neq 2 - 7 \text{ since } 5 \neq -5$$

$$50 \div 10 \neq 10 \div 50 \text{ since } 5 \neq 0.2$$

2-17.   Simplify each algebraic expression below, if possible. If it is not possible to
simplify the expression, explain why not.

a. $3y + 2y + y^2 + 5 + y$

b. $3y^2 + 2xy + 1 + 3x + y + 2x^2$

c. $3xy + 5x + 2 + 3y + x + 4$

d. $4m + 2mn + m^2 + m + 3m^2$

2-18.   Remember that one meaning of the word "evaluate" is to replace a variable with a number and to calculate the result. For example, when asked to evaluate the expression x^2 when $x = -2$, the solution would be $(-2)^2 = 4$.

Evaluate the expressions below for the given values.

a. $-4d + 3$ if $d = -1$ b. $k - m$ if $k = 4$ and $m = -10$

c. $\frac{t}{w}$ if $t = 6$ and $w = -3$ d. $x^2 + y^2$ if $x = 7$ and $y = 5$

2-19.   The diagram at right is the floor plan of Randy's apartment. All measurements are in feet. Use the diagram to answer the following questions.

a.   What are the dimensions (length and width) of Randy's living room?

b.   Randy's friends are coming to visit him soon. He plans to keep them out of his bedroom. Find the area of each of the other three rooms he will have to clean.

c.   What is the total area of the rooms he will have to clean?

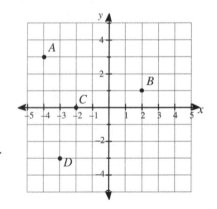

2-20.   Examine the graph at right.

a.   In (x, y) form, name the coordinates of points A, B, C, and D.

b.   On graph paper, draw a set of axes like the ones shown at right. Then plot points $E(5, 2)$, $F(-3, -1)$, $G(0, -4)$, and $H(2, -3)$.

2-21.   If the tiles have the dimensions shown at right, what is the name of the tile collection below? (That is, what is the total area of all of the pieces?) Write the expression algebraically, using x, x^2, y, y^2, and xy.

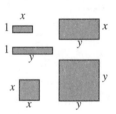

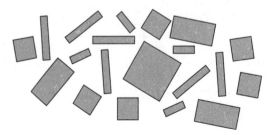

2.1.3 What does "minus" mean?

Writing Algebraic Expressions

In this section, you will look at algebraic expressions and see how they can be interpreted using an expression mat. To achieve this goal, you first need to understand the different meanings of the "minus" symbol, which is found in expressions such as $5-2$, $-x$, and $-(-3)$.

2-22.   What does " $-$ " mean? Find as many ways as you can to describe this symbol and discuss how these descriptions differ from one another. Share your ideas with the class and record the different uses in your Learning Log. Title this entry "Meanings of Minus" and include today's date.

2-23.   USING AN EXPRESSION MAT

Your introduction to algebra tiles in Lessons 2.1.1 and 2.1.2 involved only positive values. Today you will look at how you can use algebra tiles to represent "minus." Below are several tiles with their associated values. Note that the shaded tiles are positive and the unshaded tiles are negative (as shown in the diagram at right, which will appear throughout the text as a reminder).

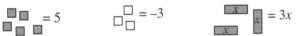

"Minus" can also be represented with a new tool called an **expression mat**, shown at right. An expression mat is an organizing tool that will be used to represent expressions. Notice that there is a positive region at the top and a negative (or "opposite") region at the bottom.

Using the expression mat, the value -3 can be shown in multiple ways, two of which are shown at right.

Note that in these examples, the left-hand diagram uses negative tiles in the "+" region, while the right-hand diagram uses positive tiles in the "−" region.

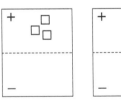

Value: −3   Value: −3

a.   Build two different representations for $-2x$ using an expression mat.

b.   Similarly, build $3x-(-4)$. How many different ways can you build $3x-(-4)$?

2-24.   During your discussion of problem 2-23, did you see all of the different ways to represent "minus"? Discuss how you could use an expression mat to represent the different meanings discussed in class.

2-25.   BUILDING EXPRESSIONS

Use the expression mat to create each of the following expressions with algebra tiles. Find at least two different representations for each expression. Sketch each representation on your paper. Be prepared to share your different representations with the class.

a. $-3x + 4$ b. $-(y - 2)$

c. $-y - 3$ d. $5x - (3 - 2x)$

2-26.   In problem 2-25, you represented algebraic expressions with algebra tiles. In this problem, you will need to **reverse** your thinking in order to write an expression from a diagram of algebra tiles.

Working with a partner, write algebraic expressions for each representation below. Start by building each problem using your algebra tiles.

a.   b.   c.   d.

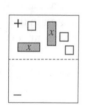   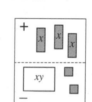   

2-27.   Patti, Emilie, and Carla are debating the answer to part (d) of problem 2-26. Patti wrote $2 - 1 + 2x - 3$. Carla thinks that the answer is $2x + 2 - 4$. Emilie is convinced that the answer is $2x - 2$. Discuss with your team how each person might have arrived at her answer. Who do you think is correct? When you decide, write an explanation on your paper and **justify** your answer.

2-28.   Reflect on what you have learned from today's lesson as you answer the following question in your Learning Log. Title this entry "Representing Expressions on an Expression Mat" and include today's date.

Using an expression mat, find two different ways to represent $x - 1 - (2x - 3)$. Sketch the different representations and write a few sentences to describe the differences in the ways you built each representation.

METHODS AND **M**EANINGS

Evaluating Expressions and the Order of Operations

The word **evaluate** indicates that the value of an expression should be calculated when a variable is replaced by a numerical value.

For example, when you evaluate the expression $xy - 4x + 7$ when $x = 6$ and $y = -5$, the result is:

$$(6)(-5) - 4(6) + 7 \Rightarrow -30 - 24 + 7 \Rightarrow -47$$

When evaluating a complex expression, you must remember to use the **order of operations**. As illustrated in the example below, the order of operations is:

First, evaluate any groups of operations that are defined by **parentheses** or other grouping symbols.

$$15 \div 3 \cdot 4 - (8 - 6)^2 + 6$$

Next, evaluate any **exponents** (such as any numbers that are squared).

$$15 \div 3 \cdot 4 - (2)^2 + 6$$

Then, evaluate any **multiplication** or **division** operations from left to right.

$$15 \div 3 \cdot 4 - 4 + 6$$

Finally, evaluate any **addition** or **subtraction** operations from left to right. In this example, the expression $15 \div 3 \cdot 4 - (8 - 6)^2 + 6$ has the value of 22.

$$20 - 4 + 6$$

$$22$$

Review & Preview

2-29. Copy and simplify the following expressions by combining like terms. Using or drawing sketches of algebra tiles may be helpful.

a. $2x + 3x + 3 + 4x^2 + 10 + x$

b. $4x + 4y^2 + y^2 + 9 + 10 + x + 3x$

c. $2x^2 + 30 + 3x^2 + 4x^2 + 14 + x$

d. $20 + 5xy + 4y^2 + 10 + y^2 + xy$

2-30.   Read the Math Notes box for this lesson. Then evaluate each expression below.

    a.   For $y = 2 + 3x$ when $x = 4$, what does y equal?

    b.   For $a = 4 - 5c$ when $c = -\frac{1}{2}$, what does a equal?

    c.   For $n = 3d^2 - 1$ when $d = -5$, what does n equal?

    d.   For $v = -4(r - 2)$ when $r = -1$, what does v equal?

    e.   For $3 + k = t$ when $t = 14$, what does k equal?

2-31.   Plot the points $A(5, 3)$, $B(-4, 3)$, $C(-4, -6)$, and $D(5, -6)$ on a set of axes. Use a ruler to connect them in order, including D back to A, to form a **quadrilateral** (a shape with four sides).

    a.   What kind of quadrilateral was formed?

    b.   How long is each side of the quadrilateral?

    c.   What is the area of the quadrilateral?

    d.   What is the perimeter of the quadrilateral?

2-32.   Use Guess and Check to solve the following problem. Write your answer in a complete sentence.

Susan is buying three different colors of tiles for her kitchen floor. She is buying 25 more red tiles than beige tiles, and three times as many navy-blue tiles as beige tiles. If Susan buys 435 tiles altogether, how many tiles of each color does she buy?

2-33.   Without a calculator, compute the value of each expression below.

    a. $-14 + (-31)$ b. $-(-8) - (-2)$

    c. $\frac{-16}{-8}$ d. $-11 \cdot 24$

    e. $\frac{1}{2} - \frac{3}{4}$ f. $46 \div (-23)$

2.1.4 What makes zero?

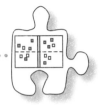

Using Zero to Simplify Algebraic Expressions

Today you will continue your work with rewriting algebraic expressions. As you work with your team, ask yourself and your teammates these focus questions:

How did you see it?

How can you write it?

Is your expression as simplified as possible?

2-34. LIKELY STORY!

Imagine the following situations:

- You baby-sit your neighbor's baby and stuff the $15 you earned into your purse. When you get home, the $15 is nowhere to be found. It must have fallen out of your purse.

- The Burton Pumas football team completes a pass and gains 12 yards. But on the very next play, the quarterback holds onto the ball too long and gets sacked, losing 12 yards.

- You are at the beach. You dig a hole in the sand and place the sand you remove in a pile next to your hole. Someone comes along and pushes the pile back into the hole.

What do each of these situations have in common? Can you represent each of them using symbols? How?

2-35. How can you represent zero with tiles on an expression mat? With your team, try to find at least two different ways to do this (and more if you can). Be ready to share your ideas with the class.

2-36.   Gretchen used seven algebra tiles to build the expression shown below.

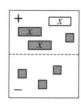

a.   Build this collection of tiles in your own expression mat and write its value.

b.   Represent this same value three different ways, each time using a *different number* of tiles. Be ready to share your representations with the class.

2-37.   Build each expression below so that your representation does not match those of your teammates. Once your team is convinced that together you have found four different, valid representations, sketch your representation on your paper and be ready to share your answer with the class.

a. $-3x + 5 + y$ b. $-(-2y + 1)$ c. $2x - (x - 4)$

2-38.   Write the algebraic expression shown on each expression mat below. Build the model and then simplify the expression by removing as many tiles as you can *without changing the value* of the expression. Finally, write the simplified algebraic expression.

a. 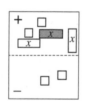   b.

2-39.   Simplify each of the following expressions by building it on your expression mat and removing zeros. Your teacher will give you instructions about how to represent your work on your paper.

a. $3x - (2x + 4)$ b. $7 - (4y - 3) + 2y - 4$

2-40.   In your Learning Log, describe the different ways you can represent zero using your expression mat. Include an example and be sure to draw the tiles. Title this entry "Using Zeros to Simplify" and include today's date.

Algebra Connections

L OOKING DEEPER

Associative and Identity Properties

The **Associative Property of Addition** states that when *adding* three or more number or terms together, grouping is not important. That is:

$$(a+b)+c = a+(b+c)$$ For example, $(5+2)+6 = 5+(2+6)$

The **Associative Property of Multiplication** states that when *multiplying* three or more numbers or terms together, grouping is not important. That is:

$$(a \cdot b) \cdot c = a \cdot (b \cdot c)$$ For example, $(5 \cdot 2) \cdot 6 = 5 \cdot (2 \cdot 6)$

However, *subtraction* and *division* are <u>not</u> associative, as shown below.

$$(5-2)-3 \neq 5-(2-3) \text{ since } 0 \neq 6$$

$$(20 \div 4) \div 2 \neq 20 \div (4 \div 2) \text{ since } 2.5 \neq 10$$

The **Identity Property of Addition** states that adding zero to any expression gives the same expression. That is:

$$a+0 = a$$ For example, $6+0 = 6$

The **Identity Property of Multiplication** states that multiplying any expression by one gives the same expression. That is:

$$1 \cdot a = a$$ For example, $1 \cdot 6 = 6$

Review & Preview

2-41.   Bob, Kris, Janelle, and Pat are in a study team. Bob, Kris, and Janelle have algebra tiles on their desks. Bob has two x^2-tiles, four x-tiles, and seven unit tiles; Kris has one x^2-tile and five unit tiles; and Janelle has ten x-tiles and three unit tiles. Pat's desk is empty. The team decides to put all of the tiles from the three desks onto Pat's desk. Write an algebraic expression for the new collection of tiles on Pat's desk.

2-42. Can zero be represented by any number of tiles? Using only the unit tiles (in other words, only the 1 and –1 tiles), determine if you can represent zero on an expression mat with the number of tiles below. If you can, draw an expression mat demonstrating that it is possible. If it is not possible, explain why not.

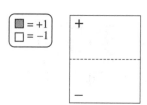

   a. 2 tiles   b. 6 tiles   c. 3 tiles

2-43. Without a calculator, compute the value of each expression below.

   a. $-3+6$ b. $(-2)(-9)$

   c. $-4-9-11$ d. $-12-18$

   e. $\frac{3}{4}(-8)$ f. $(-2)(-2)(2)$

   g. $7+(-19)$ h. $-15 \div 15$

2-44. Write and simplify the algebraic expression shown in each expression mat below.

   a.   b.   c.

 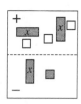 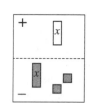

2-45. Write an expression that represents the perimeter of the shape built with algebra tiles at right.

2-46. Copy and complete each of the Diamond Problems below. The pattern used in the Diamond Problems is shown at right.

   a.   b.   c.   d.

2.1.5 How can I simplify the expression?

Using Algebra Tiles to Simplify Algebraic Expressions

Which is greater: 58 or 62? That question might seem easy, because the numbers are ready to be compared. However, if you are asked which is greater, $2x + 8 - x - 3$ or $6 + x + 1$, the answer is not so obvious! In this lesson, you and your teammates will investigate how to compare two algebraic expressions and decide if they are equal.

2-47. For each expression below:

- Use an expression mat to build the expression.

- Find a different way to represent the same expression using tiles.

a. $7x - 3$ b. $-(-2x + 6) + 3x$

2-48. COMPARING EXPRESSIONS

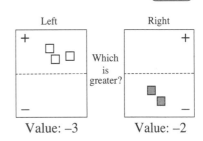

Two expressions can be represented at the same time using an **expression comparison mat**. The expression comparison mat puts two expression mats side-by-side so you can compare them and see which is greater. For example, in the picture at right, the expression on the left represents –3, but the expression on the right represents –2. Since $-2 > -3$, the expression on the right is greater.

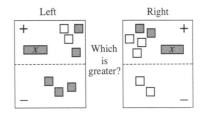

Build the expression comparison mat shown at right. Write an expression representing each side of the expression mat.

a. Can you simplify each of the expressions so that fewer tiles are used? Develop a method to simplify both sides of the expression comparison mats. Why does it work? Be prepared to **justify** your method to the class.

b. Which side of the expression comparison mat do you think is greater (has the largest value)? Agree on an answer as a team. Make sure each person in your team is ready to **justify** your conclusion to the class.

2-49. As Karl simplified some algebraic expressions, he recorded his work on the diagrams below.

- Explain in writing what he did to each expression comparison mat on the left to get the expression comparison mat on the right.

- If necessary, simplify further to determine which expression mat is greater. How can you tell if your final answer is correct?

a.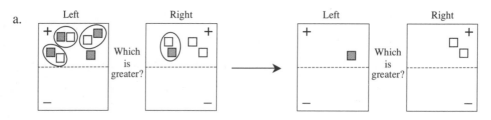

b.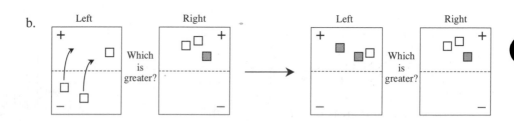

c.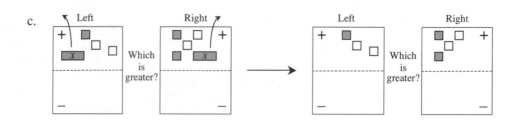

Algebra Connections

2-50.   Use Karl's "legal" simplification moves to determine which side of each expression comparison mat below is greater. Record each of your "legal" moves on the Lesson 2.1.5A Resource Page by drawing on it the way Karl did in problem 2-49. After each expression is simplified, state which side is greater (has the largest value). Be prepared to share your process and reasoning with the class.

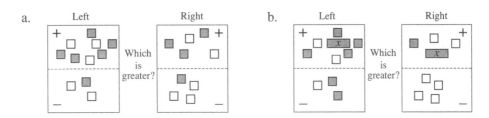

2-51.   In your Learning Log, explain each of the types of "legal" moves that you can use to simplify and compare expressions. For each type of "legal" move, sketch an example. Title this entry "Legal Moves for Simplifying and Comparing Expressions" and include today's date.

METHODS AND MEANINGS

Combining Like Terms

MATH NOTES

Combining tiles that have the same area to write a simpler expression is called **combining like terms**. See the example shown at right.

$$x^2 + 2x + 2$$

When you are not working with actual tiles, it can help to picture the tiles in your mind. You can use these images to combine the terms that are the same. Here are two examples:

Example 1: $2x^2 + xy + y^2 + x + 3 + x^2 + 3xy + 2 \implies 3x^2 + 4xy + y^2 + x + 5$

Example 2: $3x^2 - 2x + 7 - 5x^2 + 3x - 2 \implies -2x^2 + x + 5$

A **term** is an algebraic expression that is a single number, a single variable, or the product of numerals and variables. The simplified algebraic expression in Example 2 above contains three terms. The first term is $-2x^2$, the second term is x, and the third term is 5.

2-52.   Simplify the following expressions by combining like terms, if possible.

a. $x + x - 3 + 4x^2 + 2x - x$

b. $8x^2 + 3x - 13x^2 + 10x^2 - 25x - x$

c. $4x + 3y$

d. $20 + 3xy - 3 + 4y^2 + 10 - 2y^2$

2-53.   Copy and complete each of the Diamond Problems below. The pattern used in the Diamond Problems is shown at right.

a.

b.

c.

d.

2-54.   The two lines at right represent the growing profits of Companies A and B.

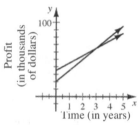

a.   Sketch this graph on your paper. If Company A started out with more profit than Company B, determine which line represents A and which represents B. Label the lines appropriately.

b.   In how many years will both companies have the same profit?

c.   Approximately what will that profit be?

d.   Which company's profits are growing more quickly? How can you tell?

2-55.   Use your mental-math skills to compute the following percentages.

a.   100% of 832

b.   50% of 832

c.   25% of 832

d.   10% of 832

2-56.   Evaluate each expression to find y.

a. $y = 2 + 4.3x$ when $x = -6$

b. $y = (x - 3)^2$ when $x = 9$

c. $y = x - 2$ when $x = 3.5$

d. $y = 5x - 4$ when $x = -2$

2.1.6 Which is greater?

Using Algebra Tiles to Compare Expressions

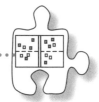

Can you always tell whether one algebraic expression is greater than another? In this lesson, you will compare the values of two expressions, practicing the different simplification strategies you have learned so far.

2-57.   WHICH IS GREATER?

Write an algebraic expression for each side of the expression comparison mats given below. Use the "legal" simplification moves you worked with in Lesson 2.1.5 to determine which expression on the expression comparison mat is greater.

a. 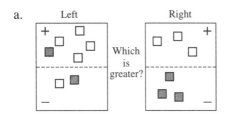   b.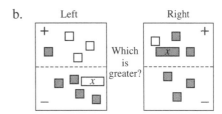

c. 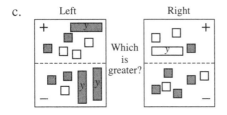   d.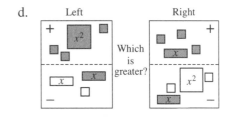

e. 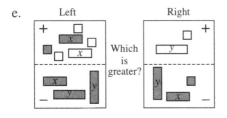   f.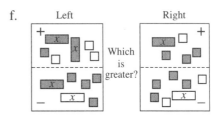

2-58.   Build the expression comparison mat shown below with algebra tiles.

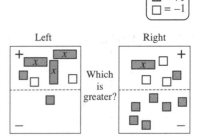

a.   Simplify the expressions using the "legal" moves that you developed in Lesson 2.1.5.

b.   Can you tell which expression is greater? Explain in a few sentences on your paper. Be prepared to share your conclusion with the class.

METHODS AND MEANINGS

Simplifying an Expression

Three common ways to simplify or alter expressions on an expression mat are illustrated below.

- Removing an equal number of opposite tiles that are in the same region. For example, the positive and negative tiles in the same region at right combine to make zero.

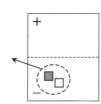

- Flipping a tile to move it out of one region into the opposite region (i.e., finding its opposite). For example, the tiles in the "–" region at right can be flipped into the "+" region.

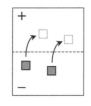

- Removing an equal number of identical tiles from both the "–" and the "+" regions. This strategy can be seen as a combination of the two methods above, since you could first flip the tiles from one region to another and then remove the opposite pairs.

Algebra Connections

2-59.   Find a simplified algebraic expression for each expression mat below.

a.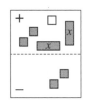

b.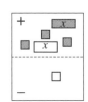

c.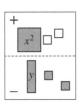

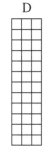

$\boxed{\begin{array}{l}\blacksquare = +1 \\ \square = -1\end{array}}$

2-60.   Cairo wants to create a graph that represents the heights and bases of all rectangles that have an area of 36 square units. He started by drawing the rectangles A, B, C, and D below. Examine the dimensions (length and width) of each rectangle.

D

A

B

C

a.   Copy the graph at right onto graph paper. Then match the letter of each rectangle above with a point on the graph. Which point is not matched?

b.   What are the base, height, and area for the unmatched point?

c.   Why should the unmatched point not be on Cairo's graph?

d.   Find the dimensions of three more rectangles that have areas of 36 square units. At least one of your examples should have dimensions that are not integers. Place a new point on the graph for each new rectangle you find.

e.   Connect all of the points representing an area of 36 square units. Describe the resulting graph.

2-61.   Without a calculator, compute the value of each expression below.

   a. $7 - 2 \cdot (-5)$ b. $6 + 3(7 - 3 \cdot 2)^2$

   c. $5 \cdot (-3)^2$ d. $35 \div (16 - 3^2) \cdot 2$

   e. $-3 \cdot 4 + 5 \cdot (-2)$ f. $7 - 6(10 - 4 \cdot 2) \div 4$

2-62.   One of Teddy's jobs at home is to pump gas for his family's sedan and truck. When
          he fills the truck up with 12 gallons of gas, he notices that it costs him $26.28.

   a.   How much does one gallon of gas cost? Explain how you found your answer.

   b.   How much will it cost him to fill up the sedan if it needs 15 gallons of gas?
        Show your work.

   c.   When Teddy filled up the tank on his moped, it cost $8.76. How much gas did
        his moped need? Explain how you know.

2-63.   Draw a circle on your paper and lightly shade in three-fourths of the circle.

   a.   Divide the entire circle into eight equal parts. How many parts are shaded?

   b.   Using fractions, write and solve a related division problem.

2.1.7 How can I write it?

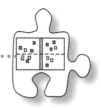

Simplifying and Recording Work

Today you will continue to compare expressions as you strengthen your simplification strategies. At the same time, you will work with your class to find ways to record your work so that another student can follow your strategies.

2-64. Use algebra tiles to build the expressions below on an expression comparison mat. Use "legal" simplification moves to determine which expression is greater, if possible. If it is not possible to tell which expression is greater, explain why.

    a. Which is greater: $3x - (2 - x) + 1$ or $-5 + 4x + 4$?

    b. Which is greater: $2x^2 - 2x + 6 - (-3x)$ or $-(3 - 2x^2) + 5 + 2x$?

    c. Which is greater: $-1 + 6y - 2 + 4x - 2y$ or $x + 5y - (-2 + y) + 3x - 6$?

2-65. RECORDING YOUR WORK

Although using algebra tiles can make some things easier because you can "see" and "touch" the math, it can be difficult to remember what you did to solve a problem unless you take good notes.

Use the simplification strategies you have learned to determine which expression on the expression comparison mat at right is greater. Record each step as instructed by your teacher. Also record the simplified expression that remains after each move. This will be a written record of how you solved this problem. Discuss with your team what the best way is to record your moves.

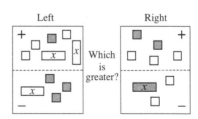

2-66.   While Athena was comparing the
         expressions shown at right, she was
         called out of the classroom. When
         her teammates needed help, they
         looked at her paper and saw the work
         shown below. Unfortunately, she had
         forgotten to explain her simplification
         steps.

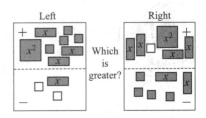

         Can you help them figure out what
         Athena did to get each new set of
         expressions?

Left Expression	Right Expression	Explanation
$3x + 4 - x - (-2) + x^2$	$-1 + x^2 + 4x - (4 + 2x)$	Original expressions
$3x + 4 - x - (-2)$	$-1 + 4x - (4 + 2x)$	
$3x + 4 - x + 2$	$-1 + 4x - 4 - 2x$	
$2x + 6$	$2x - 5$	
6	-5	
Because $6 > -5$, the left side is greater.		

2-67.   For each pair of expressions below, determine which is greater, carefully recording
         your steps as you go. If you cannot tell which expression is greater, state, "Not
         enough information." Make sure that you record your result after each type of
         simplification. For example, if you flip all of the tiles from the "–" region to the "+"
         region, record the resulting expression and indicate what you did using either words
         or symbols. Be ready to share your work with the class.

a. 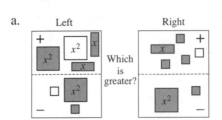   b.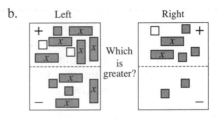

c.   Which is greater: $5 - (2y - 4) - 2$ or $-y - (1 + y) + 4$?

d.   Which is greater: $3xy + 9 - 4x - 7 + x$ or $-2x + 3xy - (x - 2)$?

Algebra Connections

METHODS AND MEANINGS

Solving Problems with Guess and Check

By now you should have seen several ways to organize information as you solve a problem using Guess and Check. One way to organize each guess and its results is using a table. An example of this work is shown below.

Problem: The base of a rectangle is three centimeters more than twice the height. The perimeter is 60 centimeters. Find the base and height of the rectangle.

height

base

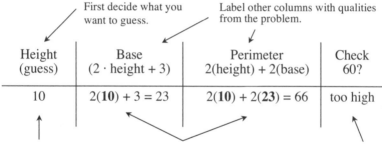

First decide what you want to guess.		Label other columns with qualities from the problem.	
Height (guess)	Base (2 · height + 3)	Perimeter 2(height) + 2(base)	Check 60?
10	2(**10**) + 3 = 23	2(**10**) + 2(**23**) = 66	too high

Make a guess.

Use the relationships stated in the problem to determine the values of the other qualities (such as base and perimeter).

Check to see if your answer is correct. Then revise your guess and try again until you find the correct answer.

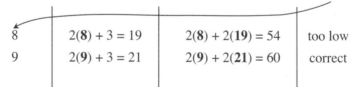

8	2(**8**) + 3 = 19	2(**8**) + 2(**19**) = 54	too low
9	2(**9**) + 3 = 21	2(**9**) + 2(**21**) = 60	correct

2-68.   Solve this problem using Guess and Check. You may want to review the Math Notes box for this lesson. Write your solution in a sentence.

The number of students attending the Fall play was 150 more than the number of adults attending. Student tickets cost $3, and adult tickets cost $5. A total of $4730 was collected. How many students attended the play?

2-69.   Sylvia simplified the expressions on the expression comparison mat shown at right. Some of her work is shown. Are all of her moves "legal"? Explain.

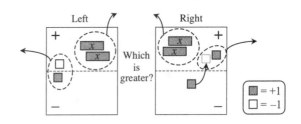

2-70.   Examine the tile pattern at right.

a.   On graph paper, draw Figures 4 and 5.

b.   What would Figure 10 look like? How many tiles would it have? What about Figure 100?

Figure 1   Figure 2   Figure 3

c.   Cami has a different tile pattern. She decided to represent the number of tiles of her pattern in a table, as shown below. Can you use the table to predict how many tiles would be in Figure 5 of her tile pattern? How many tiles would Figure 8 have? Explain how you know.

Figure Number	1	2	3	4
Number of Tiles	5	9	13	17

2-71.   Examine the shape made with algebra tiles at right.

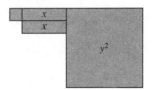

a.   Write an expression that represents the perimeter of the shape. Then evaluate your expression for $x = 6$ and $y = 10$ units.

b.   Write an expression that represents the area of the shape. What is the area if $x = 6$ and $y = 10$ units?

Algebra Connections

2-72.   CALCULATOR CHECK

Use your scientific calculator to compute the value of each expression in the left-hand column below. Match each result to an answer in the right-hand column.

a.	$-3+16-(-5)$	1.	-16
b.	$(3-5)(6+2)$	2.	327
c.	$17(-23)+2$	3.	0.5
d.	$5-(3-17)(-2+25)$	4.	18
e.	$(-4)(-2.25)(-10)$	5.	-90
f.	$-1.5-2.25-(-4.5)$	6.	0.75
g.	$\frac{4-5}{-2}$	7.	-389

2.1.8 What if both sides are equal?

Using Algebra Tiles to Solve for x

Can you always tell whether one algebraic expression is greater than another? In this section, you will continue to practice the different simplification strategies you have learned so far to compare two expressions and see which one is greater. However, sometimes you do not have enough information about the expressions. When both sides of an equation are equal, you can learn even more about x. As you work today, focus on these questions:

How can you simplify?

How can you get x alone?

Is there more than one way to simplify?

Is there always a solution?

2-73.   WHICH IS GREATER?

Build each expression represented below with the tiles provided by your teacher. Use "legal" simplification moves to determine which expression is greater, if possible. If it is not possible to determine which expression is greater, explain why it is impossible. Be sure to record your work on your paper.

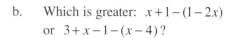

a.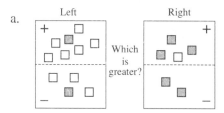

b.   Which is greater: $x+1-(1-2x)$ or $3+x-1-(x-4)$?

2-74. **WHAT IF BOTH SIDES ARE EQUAL?**

If the number 5 is compared to the number 7, then it is clear that 7 is greater. However, what if you compare x with 7? In this case, x could be smaller, larger, *or equal to* 7.

Examine the expression comparison mat below.

a.   If the left expression is smaller than the right expression, what does that tell you about the value of x?

b.   If the left expression is greater than the right expression, what does that tell you about the value of x?

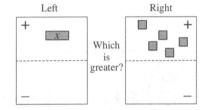

c.   What if the left expression is equal to the right expression? What does x have to be for the two expressions to be equal?

2-75. **SOLVING FOR X**

Later in the course, you will learn more about situations like parts (a) and (b) in the preceding problem, called "inequalities." For now, assume that the left expression and the right expression are equal in order to learn more about x. The two expressions will be brought together on one mat to create an **equation mat**, as shown in the figure below. The double line down the center of an equation mat represents the word "equals." It is a wall that separates the left side of an equation from the right side.

a.   Obtain the "Equation Mat" resource page from your teacher. Build the equation represented by the equation mat at right using algebra tiles. Simplify as much as possible and then solve for x. Be sure to record your work.

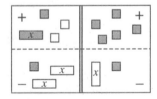

b.   Build the equation $2x - 5 = -1 + 5x + 2$ using your tiles by placing $2x - 5$ on the left side and $-1 + 5x + 2$ on the right side. Then use your simplification skills to simplify this equation as much as possible so that x is alone on one side of the equation. Use the fact that both sides are equal to solve for x. Record your work.

2-76.   Now **apply** this new solving skill by building, simplifying, and solving each equation below for x. Record your work.

    a. $3x - 7 = 2$ b. $1 + 2x - x = x - 5 + x$

    c. $3 - 2x = 2x - 5$ d. $3 + 2x - (x + 1) = 3x - 6$

    e. $-(x + 3 - x) = 2x - 7$ f. $-4 + 2x + 2 = x + 1 + x$

Mᴇᴛʜᴏᴅs ᴀɴᴅ Mᴇᴀɴɪɴɢs

Using an Equation Mat

An **equation mat** can help you visually represent an equation with algebra tiles.

The double line represents the "equals" sign (=).

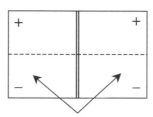

For each side of the equation, there is a positive and a negative region.

For example, the equation $2x - 1 - (-x + 3) = 6 - 2x$ can be represented by the equation mat at right. (Note that there are other possible ways to represent this equation correctly on the equation mat.)

2-77.   WHICH IS GREATER?

For each expression comparison mat below, simplify and determine
which side is greater.

a.
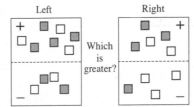

b.
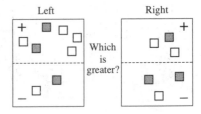

2-78.   Use Guess and Check to solve the problem below. Then state your solution in a
sentence.

Mairé is thinking of two numbers. When she adds them, she gets 40. When she
multiplies them, she gets 351. Help her younger sister, Enya, figure out the
numbers.

2-79.   Simplify each expression below as much as possible.

a. $3y - y + 5x + 3 - 7x$ b. $-1 - (-5x) - 2x + 2x^2 + 7$

c. $6x + 2 - 1 - 4x - 3 - 2x + 2$ d. $\frac{2}{3}x - 3y + \frac{1}{3}x + 2y$

2-80.   Plot the points (0, 0), (3, 2), and (6, 4) on graph paper. Then draw a line through the
points. Name the coordinates of three more points on the same line.

2-81.   Mr. Dexter's teams earned the following scores on a quiz: 15, 20, 19, 20, 16, 20, 14,
18, and 17.

a.   What is the mean (average score)?

b.   What is the median (middle score)?

c.   What is the mode (the score that occurs most often)?

2.1.9 What is x?

More Solving Equations

Today you will explore more equations on the equation mat and will examine all of the tools you have developed so far to solve for x. While you are working on these problems, be prepared to answer the following questions:

How can you simplify?

Can you get the variable alone?

Is there more than one way to simplify?

Is there always a solution?

2-82. On your paper, write the equation represented in each diagram below. For each equation, simplify as much as possible and then solve for x or y. Be sure to record your work on your paper.

a.
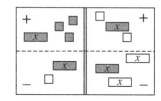

b.
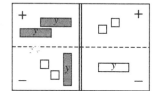

2-83. IS THERE A SOLUTION?

While solving homework last night, Richie came across three homework questions that he thinks have no solution. Build each equation below and determine if it has a solution for x. If it has a solution, find it. If it does not have a solution, explain why not.

a.
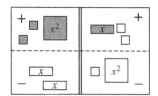

b.
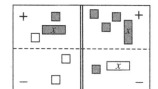

c.
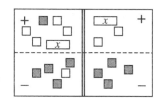

2-84.   Continue to develop your equation-solving strategies by solving each equation below (if possible). Remember to build each equation, simplify as much as possible, and solve for x or y. There are often multiple ways to solve equations, so remember to **justify** that each step is "legal." If you cannot solve for x, explain why not. Be sure to record your work.

a. $-x + 2 = 4$

b. $4x - 2 + x = 2x + 8 + 3x$

c. $4y - 9 + y = 6$

d. $9 - (2 - 3y) = 6 + 2y - (5 + y)$

2-85.   In your Learning Log, explain when you can solve for x in an equation and when you cannot. Be sure to give an example of each situation. Title this entry "Solutions of an Equation" and include today's date.

OOKING DEEPER

Inverse Properties

The **Additive Inverse Property** states that for every number a there is a number $-a$ such that $a + (-a) = 0$. A common name used for the additive inverse is the **opposite**. That is, $-a$ is the opposite of a. For example, $3 + (-3) = 0$ and $-5 + 5 = 0$.

The **Multiplicative Inverse Property** states that for every nonzero number a there is a number $\frac{1}{a}$ such that $a \cdot \frac{1}{a} = 1$. A common name used for the multiplicative inverse is the **reciprocal**. That is, $\frac{1}{a}$ is the reciprocal of a. For example, $6 \cdot \frac{1}{6} = 1$.

2-86.   Translate the equation mat at right into
         an equation. Remember that the double
         line represents "equals."

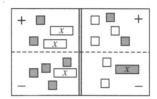

2-87.   Ling wants to save $87 for tickets to a rock concert. If she has $23 now and will
         save $4 per week, how long will it take her to get enough money to buy the tickets?
         Make a Guess and Check table to help you solve this problem.

2-88.   On graph paper, plot the points (0, 0), (–2, 1), and (2, –1). Then draw a line through
         them. Name the coordinates of three more points on the same line that have integer
         coordinates.

2-89.   Copy and complete each of the Diamond Problems below. The
         pattern used in the Diamond Problems is shown at right.

a.   b.   c.   d.

2-90.   Evaluate the expressions below for the given values.

         a. $6m + 2n^2$ for $m = 7$ and $n = 3$ b. $\frac{5x}{3} - 2$ for $x = -18$

         c. $(6x)^2 - \frac{x}{5}$ for $x = 10$ d. $(k-3)(k+2)$ for $k = 1$

2.2.1   How can I solve it?

Solving Problems With Proportional Intuition

In Chapter 1, you looked at ways to organize your algebraic thinking using graphs and tables. In the first part of this chapter, you used algebra tiles to model combining like terms and solving equations. Today you will examine proportional situations. What proportional tools do you already have? What new ways can you and your team find to solve proportional problems?

2-91.   PROPORTIONAL RELATIONSHIPS

Solve the five problems (a) through (e) below. Don't estimate! Instead, use the information to find an answer that is as accurate as possible. There are many different strategies you can use, so be sure to give reasons as you discuss your ideas with your team. To help **justify** your ideas, make sure both to *show* and to *explain* your work. For example:

- Label all numbers with what they represent. For example, don't just write "5"; instead, write "5 pounds."

- Give reasons for each action. For example, if you decided to add 10, say why. (Why did you add? Why 10?)

- Organize your work so that others will understand what you did and why you did it that way.

a.   Mr. Douglas made a copy of the triangle shown at right, but he accidentally enlarged it! The longest side of the new copy had a length of 32 cm. How long are the two shorter legs?

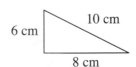

b.   Ferroza's pet ferret eats so much that she has to buy ferret food in bulk. Five pounds cost $17.50. How much would 30 pounds cost? How much would 33 pounds cost?

Problem continues on next page →

2-91.   *Problem continued from previous page.*

c.   Oscar often cleans his teachers' overhead transparencies. He can clean 17 transparencies in 10 minutes. At this rate, how long would it take him to clean 75 transparencies? Now **reverse** the problem: How many transparencies could Oscar clean in one hour?

d.    The Math Club is having a tamale sale! The school has 1600 students, but the club members are not sure how many tamales to make. One day during lunch, the club asked random students if they would buy a tamale. They found that 15 out of 80 students surveyed said they would definitely buy a tamale. How many tamales should the Math Club expect to sell?

e.   When he was little, Miguel could not sleep without his Captain Terrific action figure – it looked so life-like because it was a perfect scale model. The actor who plays Captain Terrific on television is 216 cm tall. Miguel's doll is 10 cm tall.

i.   If the doll's neck is 0.93 cm long, how long is the actor's neck?

ii.   If the actor's head has a circumference of 30 cm, what is the circumference of the doll's head?

2-92.   The five problems above are all examples of situations that involve **proportional relationships**. In your Learning Log, write your observations about what all five of these problems have in common. Title this entry "Proportional Relationships" and label it with today's date.

2-93.   Find the perimeter and area of Jacob's swimming pool shown in the diagram below. Be sure to show all of your work.

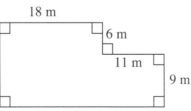

18 m

6 m

11 m

9 m

2-94.   On your paper, write the equation represented in the equation mat at right. Simplify as much as possible and then solve for x.

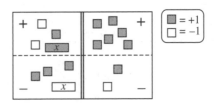

2-95.   For each equation below, draw a picture of the tiles in an equation mat, simplify, and solve for x. Record your work.

a. $2x - 7 = -x + 2$

b. $-2 - 3x = x + 6$

2-96.   Copy and simplify the following expressions by combining like terms.

a. $y + 2x - 3 + 4x^2 + 3x - 5y$

b. $2x - 6x^2 + 9 - 1 - x - 3x$

c. $2y^2 + 30x - 5y^2 + 4x - 4y - y$

d. $-10 + 3xy - 3xy + y^2 + 10 - y^2$

2-97.   Ferroza can buy a 24-ounce bag of ferret food for $1.19, or she can buy a 36-ounce bag for $2.89. Which is the better deal? **Justify** your conclusion.

2-98.   Since the beginning of school, Steven has been saving money to buy a new MP3 player. His bank balance is represented by the graph below.

a.   According to the graph, about how much money had Steven saved after 2 weeks of school?

b.   About how much money did Steven probably have after 4 weeks of school? How can you tell?

c.   If he keeps saving at the same rate, how much will he have saved by Week 7? Explain how you know.

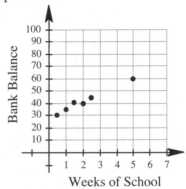

2.2.2 How can I organize my work?

. . . .

Sharing Proportion-Organizing Strategies

In Lesson 2.2.1, you solved problems using proportional reasoning (that is, you used the fact that each situation was proportional to solve the problem). Today you will work with two more proportional situations. This time, your focus will be on how to organize your work and how to explain your reasoning.

2-99. Solve these proportion problems and be ready to present your method. Remember to label all numbers and explain (in words or symbols) the reasons for your work. Be sure to organize your ideas in a way that will help others see what you did.

   a. Toby uses seven tubes of toothpaste every ten months. How many tubes would he use in five years? In two years? How long would it take him to use 100 tubes?

   b. Mr. Douglas is at it again! The little trapezoid below on the left got enlarged in the photocopying machine and turned into the big trapezoid on the right. How long are the missing sides of the shapes (x and y)?

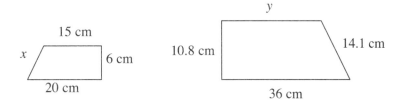

2-100. Look back at the proportion problems you solved today and yesterday. Share your strategies with the class.

   a. Did you always organize your work the same way? What different organizational strategies did you or your classmates use?

   b. What did all of the problems yesterday and today have in common?

2-101. In your Learning Log, show at least two examples of ways to organize your work when solving problems that require proportional reasoning. Title this entry "Solving Proportion Problems" and include today's date.

METHODS AND MEANINGS

Similar Figures

Photocopy-enlargement problems like Mr. Douglas's (see part (a) of problem 2-91 and part (b) of problem 2-99) involve figures that are similar. In plain English, "similar" means "close to the same." But in mathematics, **similar** means that two figures have the same shape but are not necessarily the same size.

Below are examples of some shapes that are similar and other shapes that are not similar.

These pairs of shapes <u>are</u> similar: **These pairs are <u>not</u> similar:**

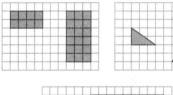      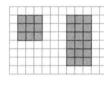   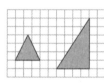

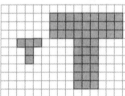   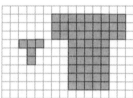

2-102. Use proportional reasoning to solve the following problems.

   a. A typical small bag of colored candies has about 135 candies in it, 27 of which are blue. At this rate, how many blue candies would you expect in a pile of 1000 colored candies?

   b. Ten calculators cost $149.50. How much would 100 cost? 1000? 500?

   c. Tickets to 50 home baseball games would cost $1137.50. How much would it cost to get tickets for all 81 home games? How many games could you go to for $728?

2-103.　At the annual dog show, Chantel noticed that there were three more Schnauzers than Scotties. She also realized that the number of Wirehaired Terriers was three less than twice the number of Schnauzers. If there were 78 dogs in all (counting Schnauzers, Scotties, and Wirehaired Terriers), how many Schnauzers were there?

2-104.　Write the equation represented in the equation mat below.

   a.　Simplify both sides as much as possible, and then solve for x.

   b.　Evaluate both the left side and the right side using your solution from part (a). Remember that if your solution is correct, both sides should have the same value.

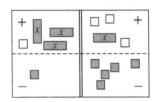

2-105.　For the following equations, draw a picture of the tiles in an equation mat, use "legal" moves to simplify, and then solve for x. Record your work.

   a.　$-3x + 7 = x - 1$　　　　b.　$1 + 2x - 3 = 4x - 2$

2-106.　To bake 100 of his favorite cookies, Mr. Wallis needs 350 grams of sugar.

   a.　How many grams of sugar would he need to bake 10 cookies? What about 20 cookies? Show all work.

   b.　To help him know how much sugar to use when baking cookies, Mr. Wallis started to make a table, as shown at right. Copy and complete his table on your paper.

Cookies	Sugar (g)
100	350
10	
20	
2	
1	
5	
	700
	1400

2-107.　Read the Math Notes box for this lesson, entitled "Similar Figures." Then draw your own example of two figures that are **similar**.

2.2.3 How can I use proportional relationships?

Using Proportional Relationships

How many books in the Library of Congress are science fiction? How many people will vote for your favorite candidate in the next election? How many fish are in the ocean?

To answer questions about huge quantities, it is sometimes best to start by thinking in terms of small quantities. Today you will use proportional relationships to make predictions about large collections of people and things. During today's work, consider:

How are these related?

How can you use this information to make a prediction?

2-108.   COUNTING CANDIES

Can you use the number of candies in a small bag to predict the number of candies in a large bag? To answer this, follow the directions from your teacher and discuss these questions:

- Using the small bag of candy, what could you predict about the large bag?

- Could you also use the large bag of candy to make a prediction about the small bag? Why or why not?

a.   Decide what you will predict about the large bag. For example, you could try to predict the number of red candies in the large bag.

b.   Collect data from the small bag. What should you measure?

c.   Use your data and proportional reasoning to make a prediction about the large bag.

d.   As a class, find a way to determine if your prediction was fairly accurate. If it was not close to being accurate, what do you think happened?

2-109.   Kenny can make seven origami (folded-paper) cranes in ten minutes. He read a
          story about a girl who made 1000 cranes, and was curious about how long it would
          take him to make that many (assuming he worked without stopping).

    a.   Instead of solving this problem using tables, Kenny represented it using similar
          triangles. He drew the diagram below. What do the corresponding parts of his
          two triangles represent?

    b.   Use the diagram in part (a) to finish Kenny's geometric solution. How long
          would it take him to make 1000 cranes?

    c.   Next, Kenny drew the two similar
          triangles at right for a related
          problem. What question do you think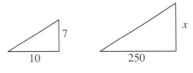
          he is trying to answer? In other
          words, what do you think x would
          represent? Find x.

2-110.   How many people are in your math class? How many of those people are left-
          handed? Use this information to make predictions about other groups of people.

    a.   How many students are in your grade? About how many of those students
          would you expect to be left-handed?

    b.   How many students are in your entire school? About how many of those
          students would you expect to be left-handed?

    c.   Now **reverse** the process: The Kennedy Middle School Left-Handers' Club has
          counted 270 left-handed students in their school. About how many students do
          you think there are at Kennedy Middle School?

    d.   Across town, Grand Prairie High has 1060 *right*-handed students. About how
          many students would you expect there to be at Grand Prairie High?

2-111.   Where else does the idea of a proportional relationship between part and whole
          appear? Read the Math Notes box following this problem and explain how one part
          of the Sierpinski Triangle is similar to the whole triangle.

ⓛOOKING DEEPER

Fractals

Fractals are geometric structures developed by repeating a process over and over. A famous example of a fractal is the **Sierpinski Triangle**, shown below. To create this design, make three copies of a triangle and place them into a larger triangle, as shown in Figure 1. Then repeat the process by taking the large triangle of Figure 1 and copying it in the same arrangement, shown in Figure 2. If this process is continued infinitely, the result is the Sierpinski Triangle.

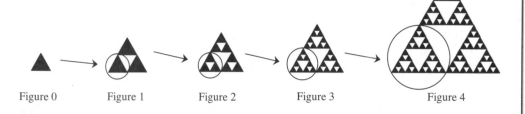

Figure 0   Figure 1   Figure 2   Figure 3   Figure 4

Review & Preview

2-112.   When baking cookies for his class of 21 students, Sammy needed two eggs. Now he wants to bake cookies for the upcoming science fair. If he expects 336 people to attend the science fair, how many eggs will he need?

2-113.   The graph below shows distances traveled by Car A and Car B. Car A is represented by the line containing point A, and Car B is represented by the line containing point B. Use the graph to answer the following questions.

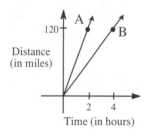

a.   Which car is traveling faster? How can you tell?

b.   Find the coordinates of point A and point B.

c.   How fast did Car A travel (in miles per hour)? How fast did Car B travel?

Algebra Connections

2-114. Solve the equations below for x and check your solutions.

a. $-3 + x = -2x + 6$
b. $5 - x = 3x + 1$

c. $-4x = 2x + 9$
d. $-(x - 3) = -4x$

2-115. Simplify the following expressions.

a. $x + 3x - 3 + 2x^2 + 8x - 5$
b. $3y + 14y^2 - 6y^2 - 9y + 1 - y - 3y$

c. $2y^2 + 30xy - 2y^2 + 4y - 4x$
d. $x - 0.2x$

2-116. Mr. Wallis has done it again! He has started to create more tables to help him figure out things like how many gallons of gas it takes to travel a certain number of miles or how many minutes it takes to walk a certain number of blocks. Use proportional reasoning to complete his tables below.

a.

# of Books	Days
2	10
10	50
	60
3	
1	
$\frac{1}{5}$	
	365

b.

Minutes	Blocks
10	25
5	12.5
1	
20	
30	
	0
	35

c.

Miles	Gallons
280	14
140	7
	21
20	
100	
1000	
	17.5

Chapter 2 Closure   What have I learned?

Reflection and Synthesis

The activities below offer you a chance to reflect on what you have learned during this chapter. As you work, look for concepts that you feel very comfortable with, ideas that you would like to learn more about, and topics you need more help with. Look for **connections** between ideas as well as **connections** with material you learned previously.

①   TEAM BRAINSTORM

With your team, brainstorm a list for each of the following three topics. Be as detailed as you can. How long can you make your list? Challenge yourselves. Be prepared to share your team's ideas with the class.

Topics: What have you studied in this chapter? What ideas and words were important in what you learned? Remember to be as detailed as you can.

Problem Solving: What did you do to solve problems? What different strategies did you use?

Connections: What topics, ideas, and words that you learned *before* this chapter are **connected** to the new ideas in this chapter? Again, make your list as long as you can.

The following is a list of the vocabulary used in this chapter. The words that appear in bold are new to this chapter. Make sure that you are familiar with all of these words and know what they mean. Refer to the glossary or index for any words that you do not yet understand.

algebra tiles	area	**combining like terms**
equal	**equation**	**equation mat**
equivalent	**evaluate**	**expression**
expression comparison mat	**expression mat**	**greater**
minus	**negative**	**opposite**
order of operations	**proportional**	**simplify**
solution	**solve**	sum
term	**variable**	**zero**

Make a concept map showing all of the **connections** you can find among the key words and ideas listed above. To show a **connection** between two words, draw a line between them and explain the **connection**, as shown in the example below. A word can be **connected** to any other word as long as there is a **justified connection**. For each key word or idea, provide a sketch of an example.

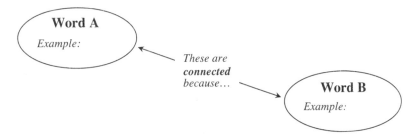

Your teacher may provide you with vocabulary cards to help you get started. If you use the cards to plan your concept map, be sure either to re-draw your concept map on your paper or to glue the vocabulary cards to a poster with all of the **connections** explained for others to see and understand.

While you are making your map, your team may think of related words or ideas that are not listed above. Be sure to include these ideas on your concept map.

③　　SUMMARIZING MY UNDERSTANDING

This section gives you an opportunity to show what you know about certain math topics or ideas. Your teacher will give you directions for exactly how to do this. Your teacher may give you a "GO" page to work on. "GO" stands for "Graphic Organizer," a tool you can use to organize your thoughts and communicate your ideas clearly.

④　　WHAT HAVE I LEARNED?

This section will help you evaluate which types of problems you have seen with which you feel comfortable and those with which you need more help. This section appears at the end of every chapter to help you check your understanding. Even if your teacher does not assign this section, it is a good idea to try the problems and find out for yourself what you know and what you need to work on.

Solve each problem as completely as you can. The table at the end of this closure section has answers to these problems. It also tells you where you can find additional help and practice on problems like these.

CL 2-117. Examine the expression mat at right.

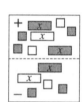

a.　　Copy the expression mat onto your paper.

b.　　Write an expression for the tiles as they appear.

c.　　On your drawing, circle all of the zeros that you can find to simplify the expression.

d.　　Write the completely simplified expression.

CL 2-118. Zeke lives 30 miles from his aunt, Zelda, and is riding his bike home from her house. Interpret the graph to tell a story about what could have happened on his ride home.

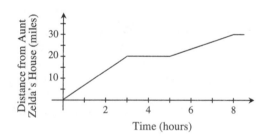

CL 2-119. Write expressions for each side of the expression comparison mat. Use "legal" moves to simplify and determine which is greater.

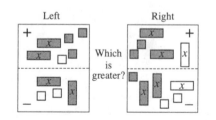

CL 2-120. Solve the following problem using Guess and Check. Show your guesses in an organized way.

Ralph and Alphonse are shooting marbles. Ralph has five more marbles than Alphonse, and they have a total of 73 marbles. How many marbles does each of them have?

CL 2-121. Simplify each expression with or without algebra tiles. Record your steps.

a. $3 + 7x - (2 + 9x)$

b. $6 - (3x - 4) + 7x - 11$

CL 2-122. Copy the pattern below onto graph paper. Draw Figures 1 and 5 on your paper.

a. How many tiles are in each figure?

b. How is the pattern changing?

c. How many tiles would Figure 6 have?

Figure 2   Figure 3   Figure 4

CL 2-123. Silvia has a picture from her trip to the Grand Canyon. The photo is 4 inches tall by 6 inches wide.

a. She would like to make a larger photo for her wall that is as big as possible. The widest the enlarged photo can be is 48 inches. How tall will the enlarged photo be?

b. Silvia also wants a wallet-sized photo to carry around and show her friends that is 1.5 inches tall. How wide will the wallet-sized photo be?

CL 2-124. Evaluate $6x - (3y + 7) - xy$ when $x = 5$ and $y = 3$.

CL 2-125. Simplify the expression below by combining like terms:

$$3x^2 + 10 - y^2 + 4x - 8x^2 - 5y - 8 + y^2 + 3$$

CL 2-126. Solve this equation to find x: $2 - (3x - 4) = 2x - 9$.

CL 2-127. Check your answers using the table at the end of the closure section. Which problems do you feel confident about? Which problems were hard? Use the table to make a list of topics you need help on and a list of topics you need to practice more.

HOW AM I THINKING?

This course focuses on five different **Ways of Thinking**: reversing thinking, justifying, generalizing, making connections, and applying and extending understanding. These are some of the ways in which you think while trying to make sense of a concept or to solve a problem (even outside of math class). During this chapter, you have probably used each Way of Thinking multiple times without even realizing it!

This closure activity will focus on one of these Ways of Thinking: **justifying**. Read the description of this Way of Thinking at right.

Think about the topics that you have learned during this chapter. When did you need to convince someone that your thinking was correct? What types of **justification** did you need to use? You may want to flip through the chapter to refresh your memory about the problems that you have worked on. Discuss any ideas you have with the rest of the class.

Once your discussion is complete, analyze how **justifications** work below.

Justifying

You often think this way when you try to convince yourself or someone else that an idea or solution is correct. Often, a justification is the answer to the questions "Why?" or "How do you know for sure?" When you catch yourself thinking, "*I think this is true because…*", you are justifying.

This is true because...

a.   While simplifying the expressions shown in the expression comparison mat at right, the four members of a study team made the following statements. Which students **justified** their statements? And were the **justifications** convincing? Explain why or why not.

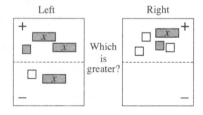

Rosalita: "I think we can take the positive unit tile and negative unit tile away from the left side because they make zero."

Anthony: "I think we can take an *x*-tile away from both sides."

Barry: "I don't think we can tell which side is greater because there are more *x*-tiles on the left side than on the right."

Deshawn: "I think we can remove a positive and negative unit tile from the "+" region on the right side because they are opposites, so they make zero."

Continues on next page →

Algebra Connections

Continued from previous page.

    b.   Your teammate needs help understanding why $-(-2x-3) = 2x+3$. She thinks that $-(-2x-3) = 2x-3$. **Justify** why $-(-2x-3) = 2x+3$ so that she is convinced.

    c.   Examine the tile pattern below. What do you think Figure 0 must look like? **Justify** why your Figure 0 fits the pattern.

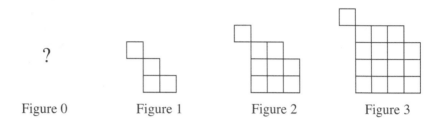

Figure 0   Figure 1   Figure 2   Figure 3

Answers and Support for Closure Activity #4
What Have I Learned?

Problem	Solution	Need Help?	More Practice
CL 2-117.	b. $2x - x + 3 - 2 - (x - x + 2 - 1)$ c. one possible answer: d. x	Problem 2-23, Lesson 2.1.6 Math Notes box	Problems 2-26, 2-36, 2-38, 2-39, 2-42, 2-44, and 2-59
CL 2-118.	There are many possible stories for this graph. Make sure your story explains the changes in speed and the stops and starts in the graph. Zeke travels 20 miles during the first 3 hours and then rests for 2 hours. Then he travels 10 miles in the next 3 hours and reaches his house after 8 hours.	Lesson 1.1.3	Problems 2-98 and 2-113 (also problems 1-6, 1-9, 1-20, 1-47, 1-48, and 1-68)
CL 2-119.	Left: $-1 + 2x + 3 - (2x - 2) = 4$ Right: $2x + 2 - x - (2x - x - 2 + 1) = 3$ The left expression is greater than the right expression.	Problem 2-48, Lesson 2.1.6 Math Notes box	Problems 2-49, 2-50, 2-57, 2-58, 2-65, 2-66, 2-67, 2-69, 2-73, and 2-77

Problem	Solution	Need Help?	More Practice
CL 2-120.	Ralph has 39 marbles, and Alphonse has 34 marbles.	Lesson 2.1.7 Math Notes box	Problems 2-11, 2-32, 2-68, 2-78, 2-87, and 2-103
CL 2-121.	a. $-2x+1$ b. $4x-1$	Lesson 2.1.4, Lesson 2.1.6 Math Notes box	Problems 2-38, 2-39, 2-44, and 2-59
CL 2-122.	a. 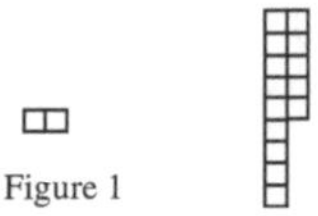 Figure 1 Figure 5 b. Each figure has three more tiles than the one before it. c. Figure 6 would have 17 tiles.	Lesson 1.1.4	Problem 2-70 (also problems 1-31, 1-32, and 1-67)
CL 2-123.	a. The picture would be 32 inches tall. b. The picture would be 2.25 inches wide.	Lessons 2.2.1 and 2.2.3	Problems 2-91, 2-99, 2-102, 2-106, 2-108, 2-109, 2-110, 2-112, and 2-116
CL 2-124.	$6 \cdot 5 - (3 \cdot 3 + 7) - 5 \cdot 3 = -1$	Lesson 2.1.3 Math Notes box	Problems 2-10, 2-18, 2-30, 2-56, and 2-90
CL 2-125.	$-5x^2 + 4x - 5y + 5$	Lesson 2.1.1, Lesson 2.1.5 Math Notes box	Problems 2-4, 2-17, 2-29, 2-52, 2-79, 2-96, and 2-115
CL 2-126.	$x = 3$	Problems 2-74 and 2-75, Lesson 2.1.8 Math Notes box	Problems 2-76, 2-82, 2-83, 2-84, 2-95, 2-105, and 2-114

3

Graphs and Equations

CHAPTER 3

Graphs and Equations

In this chapter you will **extend** your understanding of the use of variables in algebra (such as x and y). You will learn about tools (such as graphing calculators) that will help you explore how variables affect tile patterns, tables, and graphs. You will also continue to develop your ability to solve equations, started in Chapter 2, and will begin a study of the multiple representations of data. You will study the **connections** between graphing and solving equations in Chapter 4.

In this chapter, you will learn:

➢ How to find a rule from a table.

➢ How to represent a situation using a table, a rule, and a graph.

➢ How to graph linear and parabolic rules using an appropriate scale.

➢ What it means for something to be the solution to an equation and also what it means for an equation to have no solution.

➢ How to determine the number of solutions to an equation.

Guiding Questions

Think about these questions throughout this chapter:

What is a variable?

What is the pattern?

How many different ways can I represent it?

How can I solve it?

How can I check my answer?

Chapter Outline

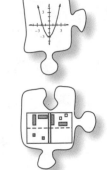

Section 3.1 In this section, you will learn the graphing mechanics that you will need throughout the rest of this course. You will also learn how to create tables, write rules, and draw graphs to represent situations and patterns.

Section 3.2 Section 3.2 will **extend** the work you did in Section 2.2. You will learn how to solve linear equations without using algebra tiles and will learn the significance of solutions.

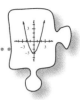

3.1.1 What is the rule?

Extending Patterns and Finding Rules

You have been learning how to work with variables and how to find values for variables in equations. In this section, you will learn how to **extend** patterns and how to **generalize** your pattern with a rule. As you work with your team, use these questions to focus your ideas:

How is the pattern growing?

What is the rule?

Is there another way to see it?

How can you tell if your rule is correct?

3-1. Some people describe mathematics as "the study of patterns." For each tile pattern below, draw Figure 1 and Figure 5 on graph paper. First try it individually, and then consult with your team. What does Figure 100 look like? Explain how you know.

a.

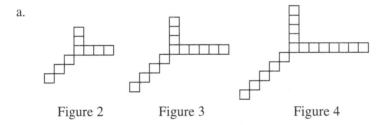

Figure 2   Figure 3   Figure 4

b.

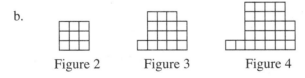

Figure 2   Figure 3   Figure 4

3-2.   FINDING RULES FROM TABLES

How can you describe the rule that governs a pattern or table? Obtain the Lesson
3.1.1A Resource Page from your teacher and find the tables below. Then, as a class,
find the pattern, fill in the missing parts, and **extend** each table with at least two
more $x \rightarrow y$ pairs that fit the pattern. Then **generalize** the pattern's rule in words.

a.

IN (x)	OUT (y)
	C
L	N
	F
Q	
W	Y

Rule:

b.

IN (x)	OUT (y)
easy	
	light
hot	cold
up	down
left	

Rule:

c.

IN (x)	OUT (y)
△	⬠
⬠	
	⬡
⬡	⬡
⬣	

Rule:

d.

IN (x)	OUT (y)
8	17
−2	
	9
12	25
10	21

Rule:

e.

IN (x)	OUT (y)
100	51
4	
6	4
30	16
	31

Rule:

f.

IN (x)	OUT (y)
4	16
−1	1
	9
12	
−6	

Rule:

3-3.   Obtain the Lesson 3.1.1B Resource Page from your teacher. For each $x \rightarrow y$ table
given, find the pattern and fill in the missing entries. Then write the rule for the
pattern in words. Be sure to share your thinking with your teammates.

a.

IN (x)	OUT (y)
	8
0	−2
−4	−10
10	18
−2	
	198
0.5	

Rule:

b.

IN (x)	OUT (y)
3	−9
10	
−1	3
	6
0	
	−36
−5	15

Rule:

c.

IN (x)	OUT (y)
0.5	
	37
2	5
−10	101
−5	
0	1
	50

Rule:

Problem continues on next page →

3-3.   *Problem continued from previous page.*

d.

IN (x)	OUT (y)
6	
11	5
	−4
23	17
−7	
	40
−4	−10

Rule:

e.

IN (x)	OUT (y)
2	6
4	20
10	110
−3	
	30
7	56
1	

Rule:

f.

IN (x)	OUT (y)
−8	
10	53
3	18
0	
	8
19	
4	23

Rule:

(L)OOKING DEEPER

Patterns in Nature

Patterns are everywhere, especially in nature. One famous pattern that appears often is called the Fibonacci Sequence, a sequence of numbers that starts 1, 1, 2, 3, 5, 8, 13, 21, …

The Fibonacci numbers appear in many different contexts in nature. For example, the number of petals on a flower is often a Fibonacci number, and the number of seeds on a spiral from the center of a sunflower is, too.

To learn more about Fibonacci numbers, search the Internet or check out a book from your local library. The next time you look at a flower, look for Fibonacci numbers!

Review & Preview

3-4.   WHICH IS GREATER?

Write the algebraic expressions shown below. Use "legal" simplification moves to determine which expression in the expression comparison mat is greater.

■ = +1
□ = −1

a.

b.

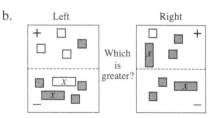

3-5.   Evaluate the expressions below for the given values.

   a. $3(2x+1)$ for $x = -8$ b. $\frac{x-6}{4} - 1$ for $x = -14$

   c. $-2m^2 + 10$ for $m = -6$ d. $k \cdot k \div k \cdot k \div k$ for $k = 9$

3-6.   At the fair, Kate found a strange machine with a
         sign on it labeled, "Enter a number." When she
         pushed the number 15, the machine displayed 9.
         When she entered 23, the machine displayed 17.
         Perplexed, she tried 100, and the machine
         displayed 94.

   a.   What is the machine doing?

   b.   What would the machine display if she
         entered 77?

3-7.   Ms. Nguyen needs to separate $385 into three parts to pay some debts. The second
         part must be five times as large as the first part. The third part must be $35 more
         than the first part. How much money must be in each part?

3-8.   GO GOLDEN GOPHERS!

         The graph below describes the
         distance two cars have traveled after
         leaving a football game at the
         University of Minnesota.

   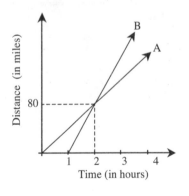

   a.   Which car was traveling faster? How
         can you tell?

   b.   The lines cross at (2, 80). What does
         this point represent?

   c.   Assuming that Car A continued to travel
         at a constant rate, how far did Car A
         travel in the first 4 hours?

3.1.2 How can I make a prediction?

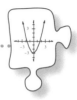

Using Tables, Graphs, and Rules to Make Predictions

In Lesson 3.1.1, you wrote rules for patterns found in $x \rightarrow y$ tables. In this lesson, you will focus on using variables to write algebraic rules for patterns and contextual situations. You will use a graph to help predict the output for fractional x-values and will then use a rule to predict the output when the input is too large and does not appear on the graph.

While working today, focus on these questions:

How can you write the rule without words?

What does x represent?

How can you make a prediction?

3-9.   SILENT BOARD GAME

During Lesson 3.1.1, you created written rules for patterns that had no tiles or numbers. You will now write algebraic rules using a table of jumbled in/out numbers. Focus on finding patterns and writing rules as you play the Silent Board Game. Your teacher will put an incomplete $x \rightarrow y$ table on the overhead or board. Study the input and output values and look for a pattern. Then write the rule in words and symbols that finds each y-value from its x-value.

3-10.   JOHN'S GIANT REDWOOD, Part One

John found the data in the table below about his
favorite redwood tree. He wondered if he could use it
to predict the height of the tree at other points of time.
Consider this as you analyze the data and answer the
questions below. Be ready to share (and **justify**) your
answers with the class.

Number of Years after Planting	3	4	5
Height of Tree (in feet)	17	21	25

a.   How tall was the tree 2 years after it was
planted? What about 7 years after it was
planted? How do you know?

b.   How tall was the tree the year it was planted?

c.   Estimate the height of the tree 50 years after it was planted. How did you
make your prediction?

3-11.   John decided to find out more about his favorite redwood tree by graphing the data.

a.   On the Lesson 3.1.2B Resource Page provided by your teacher, plot the points
that represent the height of the tree over time. What does the graph look like?

b.   Does it make sense to connect the points? Explain your thinking.

c.   According to the graph, what was the height of the tree 1.5 years after it was
planted?

d.   Can you use your graph to predict the height of the redwood tree 20 years after
it was planted? Why or why not?

3-12.   John is still not satisfied. He wants to be able to predict
the height of the tree at any time after it was planted.

a.   Find John's table on your resource page and
extend it to include the height of the tree in the
0th year, 1st year, 2nd year, and 6th year.

b.   If you have not already, use the ideas from the Silent Board Game to write an
algebraic rule for the data in your table. Be sure to work with your team and
check that the rule works for all of the data.

c.   Use your rule to check your prediction in part (c) of problem 3-10 for how tall
the tree will be in its 50th year. How close was your prediction?

Algebra Connections

3-13. Write the equation represented in each diagram below on your paper. For each part, simplify as much as possible and then solve for x. Be sure to record your work on your paper.

a.

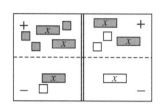

b.

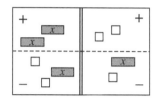

3-14. Evaluate the following expressions given the values below.

  a. $ab + bc + ac$ for $a = 2$, $b = 5$, and $c = 3$

  b. $\frac{20 - x^2}{y - x}$ for $x = -2$ and $y = 6$

3-15. Copy and simplify the following expressions by combining like terms.

  a. $x + 3x - 3 + 2x^2 + 8 - 5x$ b. $2x + 4y^2 - 6y^2 - 9 + 1 - x + 3x$

  c. $2x^2 + 30y - 3y^2 + 4xy - 14 - x$ d. $20 + 3xy - 3xy + y^2 + 10 - y^2$

3-16. Use the order of operations to simplify the following expressions.

  a. $5 - 2 \cdot 3^2$ b. $(-2)^2$

  c. $18 \div 3 \cdot 6$ d. -2^2

  e. $(5 - 3)(5 + 3)$ f. $24 \cdot \frac{1}{4} \div -2$

  g.   Why are your answers for parts (b) and (d) different?

3-17. Mrs. Swanson gives out only one type of candy for Halloween. The local discount store sells six pounds of butterscotch candies for $7.50. Use proportional reasoning to determine the information below. Be sure to explain your answer and organize your reasoning.

  a.   What is the cost of 18 pounds of butterscotch candies?

  b.   What is the cost of 10 pounds of butterscotch candies?

3.1.3 What is a graph and how is it useful?

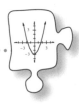

Using the Graphing Calculator and Identifying Solutions

In the last two lessons, you examined several patterns and learned how to represent the patterns in a table and with a rule. For the next few days, you will learn a powerful new way to represent a pattern and make predictions.

As you work with your team today, use these focus questions to help direct your discussion:

What is the rule?

How can you represent the pattern?

3-18.   Find the "Big Cs" pattern shown at right on the Lesson 3.1.3 Resource Page provided by your teacher.

Figure 1   Figure 2   Figure 3

a.   Draw Figure 0 and Figure 4 on the grid provided on the resource page.

b.   On the resource page, represent the number of tiles in each figure with:

- An $x \rightarrow y$ table.

- An algebraic rule.

- A graph.

c.   How many tiles will be in Figure 5? **Justify** your answer in at least two different ways.

d.   What will Figure 100 look like? How many tiles will it have? How can you be sure?

3-19.   Use the graphing technology provided by your teacher to analyze the pattern further and make predictions.

a.   Enter the information from your $x \rightarrow y$ table for problem 3-18 into your grapher. Then plot the points using a window of your choice. What do you notice?

b.   Find another $x \rightarrow y$ pair that you think belongs in your table. Use your grapher to plot the point. Does it look correct? How can you tell?

c.   Imagine that you made up 20 new $x \rightarrow y$ pairs. Where do you think their points would lie if you added them to the graph?

Algebra Connections

3-20.   In the same window that contains the data points, graph the algebraic equation for the pattern from problem 3-18.

   a.   What do you notice? Why did that happen?

   b.   Charles wonders about connecting the points of the "Big Cs" data. When the points are connected with an unbroken line or curve, the graph is called **continuous**. If the graph of the tile pattern is continuous, what does that suggest about the tile pattern? Explain.

   c.   Jessica prefers to keep the graph of the tile-pattern data as separate points. This is called a **discrete** graph. Why might a discrete graph be appropriate for this data?

3-21.   If necessary, re-enter your data from the "Big Cs" pattern into your grapher. Re-enter the rule you found in problem 3-18 and graph the data and rule in the same window.

   For the following problems, **justify** your conclusions with the *graph*, the *rule*, and the *figure* (whenever practical). Your teacher may ask your team to present your solution to one of these problems. Be sure to justify your ideas using all three representations.

   a.   Frangelica thinks that Figure 6 in the "Big Cs" pattern has 40 tiles. Decide with your team whether she is correct and **justify** your answer by using the rule, drawing Figure 6, and adding the point to your graph of the data. Be prepared to show these three different ways to **justify** your conclusion.

   b.   Giovanni thinks that the point (16, 99) belongs in the table for the "Big Cs" pattern. Decide with your team whether he is correct and **justify** your conclusion by examining the graph and the rule.

   c.   Jeremiah is excited because he has found another rule for the "Big Cs" pattern! He thinks that $y = x + 8$ also works. Prove or disprove Jeremiah's claim. Be prepared to convince the class that your conclusion is correct.

   d.   LaTanya has been thinking hard and has found another rule for the same pattern! She is sure that $y = 3(2x + 1)$ is also correct. Prove or disprove LaTanya's position in as many ways as you can.

3-22.   Look back at the prediction you made in problem 3-18 for Figure 100 in the "Big Cs" pattern. Decide now if your prediction was correct and be ready to defend your position with all of the math tools you have.

METHODS AND MEANINGS

Discrete and Continuous Relationships

When a graph of data is limited to a set of separate, non-connected points, that relationship is called **discrete**. For example, consider the relationship between the number of bicycles parked at your school and the number of bicycle wheels. If there is one bicycle, it has two wheels. Two bicycles have four wheels, while three bicycles have six wheels. However, there cannot be 1.3 or 2.9 bicycles. Therefore, this data is limited because the number of bicycles must be a whole number, such as 0, 1, 2, 3, and so on.

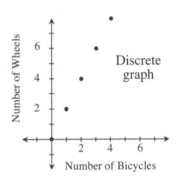

When graphed, a discrete relationship looks like a collection of unconnected points. See the example of a discrete graph above.

When a set of data is not confined to separate points and instead consists of connected points, the data is called **continuous**. "John's Giant Redwood," problem 3-10, is an example of a continuous situation because even though the table focused on integer values of years (1, 2, 3, etc.), the tree still grows between these values of time. Therefore, the tree has a height at any non-negative value of time (such as 1.1 years after it is planted).

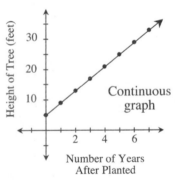

When the data for a continuous relationship is graphed, its points are connected to show that the relationship also holds true for all of the points between the table values. See the example of a continuous graph above.

Note: In this course, tile patterns will represent elements of continuous relationships and will be graphed with a continuous line or curve.

3-23.   On your paper, write the equation represented at right. Simplify as much as possible and then solve for x.

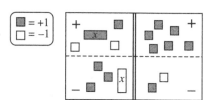

3-24.   Find the value of x that makes each equation below true.

a. $x + 7 = 2$

b. $-5 = \frac{1}{2}x$

c. $3x = -45$

d. $2 = -x$

e. $-5 = \frac{x}{2}$

f. $x^2 = 9$ (*all* possible values for x)

3-25.   For the following equations, draw a picture of the tiles on an equation mat, simplify, and solve for the variable. Record your work.

a. $3c - 7 = -c + 1$

b. $-2 + 3x = 2x + 6 + x$

3-26.   Solve this problem using Guess and Check. Write your solution in a sentence.

West High School's population is 250 students fewer than twice the population of East High School. The two schools have a total of 2858 students. How many students attend East High School?

3-27.   Solve the following problems using the order of operations. Show your steps. Verify your answers with your calculator.

a. $(-4)(-2) - 6(2 - 5)$

b. $23 - (17 - 3 \cdot 4)^2 + 6$

c. $14(2 + 3 - 2 \cdot 2) \div (4^2 - 3^2)$

d. $12.7 - 18.5 + 15 + 6.3 - 1 + 28.5$

3-28.   Copy the table below onto your paper and use your pattern skills to complete it.

IN (x)	2	10	0	7	–3		–10	100	x
OUT (y)	–6	–30	0			15			

a.   Explain in words what is done to the input value, x, to produce the output value, y.

b.   Write the process you described in part (a) in algebraic symbols.

3-29.   Write the equation represented in the equation mat at right.

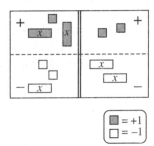

a.   Simplify as much as possible and solve for x.

b.   Evaluate both the left side and the right side using your solution from part (a). Remember that if your solution is correct, both sides should have the same value.

3-30.   For the following equations, draw a picture of the tiles in an equation mat, use "legal" moves to simplify, and solve for the variable. Record your work.

a. $-3x + 7 = -x - 1$ b. $1 - 2p + 5 = 4p + 6$

3-31.   Combine like terms in each part below.

a.   Liha has three x^2-tiles, two x-tiles, and eight unit tiles, while Makulata has five x^2-tiles and two unit tiles. At the end of class, they put their pieces together to give to Ms. Singh. Write an algebraic expression for each student's tiles and find the sum of their pieces.

b.   Simplify the expression $4x + 6x^2 - 11x + 2 + x^2 - 19$.

c.   Write the length of the line below as a sum. Then combine like terms.

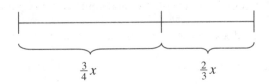

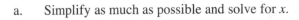

3.1.4 How should I graph?

Completing Tables and Drawing Graphs

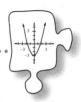

In Lesson 3.1.3, you used a graphing tool to represent all of the $x \rightarrow y$ pairs that follow a particular rule. Today you will learn how to make your own graphs for rules and how to recognize patterns that occur in graphs.

3-32.   CLASS GRAPH

Your teacher will give your team some x-values. For each x-value, calculate the corresponding y-value that fits the rule $y = -5x + 12$. Then mark the point you have calculated on the class graph.

3-33.   Use the rule $y = 2x + 1$ to complete parts (a) through (c) below.

a.   Make a table like the one below and use the rule provided above to complete it.

IN (x)	−4	−3	−2	−1	0	1	2	3	4
OUT (y)									

b.   Examine the numbers in the table. What are the greatest x- and y-values in the table? What are the smallest x- and y-values? Use this information to set up x- and y-axes that are scaled appropriately.

c.   Plot and connect the points on a graph. Be sure to label your axes and write numbers to indicate scale.

3-34.   Calculate the y-values for the rule $y = -3x + 1$ and complete the table below.

IN (x)	−4	−3	−2	−1	0	1	2	3	4
OUT (y)									

a.   Examine the x- and y-values in the table. Is it possible to use the same set of axes as problem 3-33? If so, graph and connect these points on the axes from problem 3-33. If not, plot and connect the points on a new set of axes.

b.   What does your graph look like? Describe the result.

c.   How is this graph similar to the graph in problem 3-33? How is it different?

3-35.   Calculate the y-values for the rule $y = x^2$ and complete the table below.

IN (x)	-4	-3	-2	-1	$-\frac{1}{2}$	0	$\frac{1}{2}$	1	2	3	4
OUT (y)											

a.   Examine the x- and y-values in the table. Use this information to set up a new set of x- and y-axes that are scaled appropriately. Plot and connect the points on your graph, and then label your graph with its rule.

b.   This graph is an example of a **parabola**. Read about parabolas in the Math Notes box below. Where is the vertex of the parabola you graphed in part (a)?

METHODS AND MEANINGS

MATH NOTES

Parabolas

One kind of graph you will study in this class is called a **parabola**. Two examples of parabolas are graphed at right. Note that parabolas are smooth "U" shapes, not pointy "V" shapes.

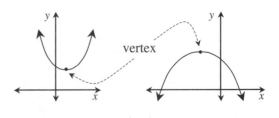
vertex

The point where a parabola turns (the highest or lowest point) is called the **vertex**.

Review & Preview

3-36.   Complete a table like the one provided in problem 3-33 for the rule $y = x + 2$. Plot and connect the points on graph paper. Be sure to label the axes and include the scale.

3-37.   Use your pattern skills to copy and complete the table below.

IN (x)	2	10	6	7	-3		-10	100	x
OUT (y)	5	21	13			-15			

a.   Explain in words what is being done to the input value, x, to produce the output value, y.

b.   Write the process you described in part (a) in algebraic symbols.

3-38.   For the following equations, draw a picture of the tiles in an equation mat like the one shown at right. Then use "legal" moves to simplify and solve for the variable. Record your work.

a. $-2 + x = -x + 2$

b. $2 + 3x = x + 7$

3-39.   Evaluate each expression below.

a.   For $y = 5 + 8x$ when $x = 4$, what does y equal?

b.   For $a = 3 - 5c$ when $c = -0.5$, what does a equal?

c.   For $n = 2d^2 - 5$ when $d = -2$, what does n equal?

d.   For $v = -3(r - 3)$ when $r = -1$, what does v equal?

3-40.   Peggy Sue decided to enter her famous "5-Alarm Chili" at her local chili-cooking contest. Normally, she needs five tomatoes to make enough chili for her family of seven.

a.   How many tomatoes should she expect to use to make her famous recipe for 100 people?

b.   When she gets to the contest, she realizes that she only packed 58 tomatoes. How many people can she expect to feed?

3.1.5 How can I graph it?

Graphs, Tables, and Rules

In Lesson 3.1.4, you practiced setting up the correct axes to graph data from a table. Today you will graph a rule by first making a table, and then by plotting the points from your table on a graph. You will also continue to find patterns in tables and graphs.

3-41. SILENT BOARD GAME

Your teacher will put an incomplete $x \rightarrow y$ table on the board or overhead. Try to find the pattern (rule) that gets each y-value from its x-value. Find and write the rule for the pattern you find.

3-42. GOOD TIPPER

Mr. Wallis needs your help. He is planning on taking his new girlfriend out to dinner and wants to be prepared to give a tip at the end of the meal. He knows that with any miscalculation, he may leave too little or too much, which might change her view of him and jeopardize their relationship. Therefore, he would like to create a "tip table" that would help him quickly determine how much tip to leave.

a. Create a table like the one shown below. What are reasonable values of x? Mr. Wallis needs a tip table that will help him quickly determine a tip for a bill that may occur after a nice dinner for two. Discuss this with your team and then choose eight values for x.

Dinner Bill (in dollars)								
Amount of Tip (in dollars)								

b. Mr. Wallis is planning to leave a 15% tip. That means that for a bill of $10, he would leave a $1.50 tip. Determine the tip for all of the values in your table from part (a). This is Mr. Wallis's tip table.

c. Use the tip table to estimate the tip quickly if the bill is $36. What if the bill is $52.48?

Problem continues on next page →

Algebra Connections

3-42.   *Problem continued from previous page.*

d.   Mr. Wallis is worried that he may not be able to quickly estimate using his table for unusual amounts, such as $52.48. He would like a graph to help him determine a 15% tip for *all possible* dollar amounts between $10 and $100. With your team, determine how to set up axes and then graph the points from the tip table. Use the questions below to help guide your discussion.

- Should the tip be graphed on the *x*-axis or the *y*-axis? Read the Math Notes box for this lesson about **dependent** and **independent variables** to help you decide.

- Which quadrants are useful for this graph? Why?

- What are the greatest and smallest values of *x* and *y* that must fit on the graph? How can you scale your axes to create the most effective graph for Mr. Wallis?

e.   Use your tip graph from part (d) to test your estimations in part (c). Which representation (table or graph) helped to find the most accurate tip? Which was easiest to use? Explain.

3-43.   ONE OF THESE POINTS IS NOT LIKE THE OTHERS

a.   Plot and connect the points in the table below.

IN (*x*)	–2	4	1	6	–5	0
OUT (*y*)	–6	–2	–3	2	–9	–4

b.   Identify the point that does not appear to fit the pattern.

c.   Correct the point found in part (b) above so it fits the pattern.

3-44.   Copy and complete the table below for the rule $y = \frac{1}{2}x + 6$.

IN (*x*)	–4	–3	–2	–1	0	1	2	3	4
OUT (*y*)									

a.   Graph and connect the points from your table on graph paper. Remember to label the graph with its rule.

b.   Does the point (10, 12) lie on this graph? How can you tell?

METHODS AND MEANINGS

Independent and Dependent Variables

MATH NOTES

When one quantity (such as the height of a redwood tree) depends on another (such as the number of years after the tree was planted), it is called a **dependent variable**. That means its value is determined by the value of another variable. The dependent variable is usually graphed on the *y*-axis.

If a quantity, such as time, does not depend on another variable, it is referred to as the **independent variable**, which is graphed on the *x*-axis.

For example, in problem 3-42, you compared the amount of a dinner bill with the amount of a tip. In this case, the tip depends on the amount of the dinner bill. Therefore, the tip is the dependent variable, while the dinner bill is the independent variable.

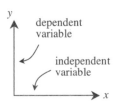

3-45. Create an $x \rightarrow y$ table using at least eight points from the graph at right. Write the rule for the pattern in the table.

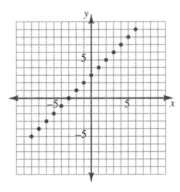

3-46. For each rule below, make a table of *x*- and *y*-values. Then graph and connect the points from your table on graph paper using an appropriate scale. Label each graph with its equation.

a. $y = -2x + 7$

b. $y = 11x$

Algebra Connections

3-47.   On graph paper, draw Figure 0 and Figure 4 for
         the pattern at right.

    a.   Represent the number of tiles in each
          figure in an $x \rightarrow y$ table. Let x be the
          figure number and y be the total
          number of tiles.

    b.   Use the table to graph the pattern.

    c.   Without drawing Figure 5, predict
          where its point would lie on the graph.
          Justify your prediction.

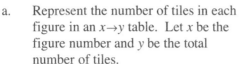

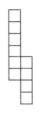

Figure 1   Figure 2   Figure 3

3-48.   Use your pattern skills to copy and complete the table below.

IN (x)	2	10	6	7	–3		–10	100	x
OUT (y)	2	6	4			15			

    a.   Explain in words what is done to the input value, x, to produce the output
          value, y.

    b.   Write the process you described in part (a) in algebraic symbols.

3-49.   For the following equations, simplify and solve for the variable. Record your work.

    a. $2x - 7 = -2x + 1$ b. $-2x - 5 = -4x + 2$

3.1.6 What makes a complete graph?

Complete Graphs

Over the past several days you have learned to make graphs from tables, then graphs from rules. Today you will continue to study graphs by deciding what needs to go into a graph to make it complete.

3-50. SILENT BOARD GAME

Your teacher will put an incomplete $x \rightarrow y$ table on the board or overhead. Try to find the pattern (rule) that gets each y-value from its x-value. Find and write the rule for the pattern you find.

3-51. Examine the following graphs and answer the question associated with each one. What do you notice?

Note: This stoplight icon will appear periodically throughout the text. Problems with this icon display common errors that can be made. Be sure not to make the same mistakes yourself!

a. What are the coordinates of point A?

b. Where will the line be when $x = 5$?

c. What is t when $k = 1$?

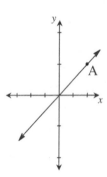

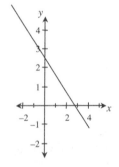

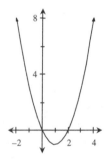

3-52. On your own graph paper, graph $y = -3x + 2$. Then, as a class, decide what needs to be included to make a graph complete. Copy the qualities of a complete graph as a Learning Log entry. Title this entry "Qualities of a Complete Graph" and include today's date.

Algebra Connections

3-53.   Make your own complete graph for each of the following rules:

a. $y = -x + 1$ b. $y = 0.5x + 2$ c. $y = x^2 - 4$

3-54.   Examine the graphs from problem 3-53.

a.   How are they different? Be as specific as you can.

b.   Label the (x, y) coordinates on each of your graphs for the point where each graph crosses the y-axis. These points are called **y-intercepts**.

c.   Label the (x, y) coordinates on each of your graphs for the point or points where each graph crosses the x-axis. These points are called **x-intercepts**.

Review & Preview

3-55.   Complete a table for the rule $y = x^2 + 2$. Then plot and connect the points on a graph. Be sure to label the axes and include the scale. Use negative, positive, and zero values for x.

3-56.   Complete a table for the rule $y = -x + 3$. Then plot and connect the points on a graph. Be sure to label the axes and include the scale. Use negative, positive, and zero values for x.

3-57.   On graph paper, draw Figure 0 and Figure 4 for the pattern below. Describe Figure 100 in detail.

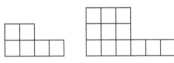
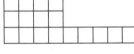

Figure 1   Figure 2   Figure 3

3-58.   Write an expression that represents the perimeter of the shape built with algebra tiles at right. Then find the perimeter if $x = 3$ units and $y = 7$ units.

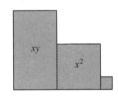

3-59.   For the following equations, draw a picture of the tiles on an equation mat, use "legal" moves to simplify, and then solve for the variable. Record your work.

a. $3x - 7 + 3 + 2x = -x + 2$ b. $-2k + 5 + (-k) + 1 = 0$

3.1.7 What is wrong with this graph?

Identifying Common Graphing Errors

In this chapter you have used rules to find *y*-values to go with *x*-values in tables. Then you graphed the *x*→*y* pairs you found. Today you will be examining how rules, tables, and graphs can be used to represent new situations. You will also learn how to avoid common graphing errors. As you work, revisit the following questions:

What *x*-values should go in my table?

How can I correct this error?

How should I scale my graph?

3-60. Ms. Cai's class is studying the "dented square" shape shown at right. This shape is formed by removing a square with side length 1 from a larger square. Her students decided to let *x* represent the side length of the large square and *y* represent the perimeter of the entire shape.

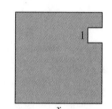

a. What is the perimeter of the "dented square?" That is, what rule could help you find the perimeter for any value of *x*?

b. Make a table for the rule Ms. Cai's class found. Make sure the *x*-values you use are appropriate for this situation. What are the possible *x*-values?

c. Make a graph from your *x*→*y* table.

d. Do you think the points on your graph should be connected? **Justify** your answer.

Algebra Connections

3-61.   GOOFY GRAPHING

Now Ms. Cai's class is studying a tile pattern. Her students
decided to represent the pattern with the $x \to y$ table at right.

x	y
2	8
3	17
5	35
6	44

a.   Ms. Cai wants her class to graph the data in this table.
Write (*x*, *y*) coordinates for each point that needs to be
plotted.

b.   When Ms. Cai's students started to graph this data, they made mistakes right
from the beginning. The diagrams below show how some of Ms. Cai's
students set up their axes. Your teacher will assign your team one of these
diagrams.

Your Task: Find all of the mistakes the students made in
setting up the graph your teacher assigns you. (There may be
more than one mistake in each graph!) Explain why this is an
incorrect way to set up a graph, or why this is not the best way
to set up the graph for this problem. Be ready to present your
team's ideas to the class.

i.

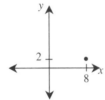

ii.

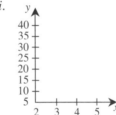

iii.

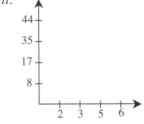

iv.

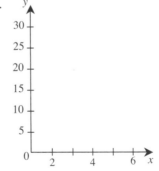

3-62.   Sheila is in Ms. Cai's class. She noticed that the
graph of the perimeter for the "dented square" in
problem 3-60 was a line. "I wonder what the graph
of its area looks like," she said to her teammates.

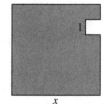

1

a.   Write an equation for the area of the "dented
square" if x represents the length of the large
square and y represents the area of the square.

x

b.   On graph paper, graph the rule you found for the area in part (a). Why does a
1st-quadrant graph make sense for this situation?

c.   Explain to Sheila what the graph of the area looks like.

d.   Use the graph to approximate x when the area of the shape is 20 square units.

3-63.   Looking back at the mistakes Ms. Cai's students made, write a
Learning Log entry that includes a checklist of errors you should
make sure to avoid when setting up a graph. Title this entry
"Graphing Errors" and label it with today's date.

Review & Preview

3-64.   Pat delivers newspapers every morning.
On average, she can deliver newspapers
to 17 homes in 12 minutes.

a.   If her normal route has 119 homes,
how long does it take her to deliver
the mail on average?

b.   When another deliverer is sick, Pat's
route expands to a total of 155 homes.
How long does this route take her?

Algebra Connections

3-65.   ONE OF THESE POINTS IS NOT LIKE THE OTHERS, Part Two

a.   Plot and connect the points listed in the table below.

IN (x)	−2	4	1	−4	0	3	−3	2
OUT (y)	0	12	−3	12	−4	5	−2	0

b.   Identify the point that does not fit the pattern.

c.   What shape does the graph appear to make?

d.   Correct the point identified in part (b) so it fits the pattern. Write the points in (x, y) notation.

3-66.   For each rule below, make a table of x- and y-values and then graph the rule on graph paper. Label each graph with its equation.

a. $y = x^2$ b. $y = -x^2$

c.   Compare the graphs. What do you notice?

d.   For the graph of $y = x^2$, estimate the x-values corresponding to $y = 5$.

e.   For the graph of $y = -x^2$, estimate the x-values corresponding to $y = -10$.

3-67.   Paris is trying to solve the equation $3x^2 - (2x - 4) = 3 + 3x^2 + 1$. Her work is partially recorded below. Copy her table and fill in her missing work to solve for x.

Left Expression	Right Expression	Explanation
$3x^2 - (2x - 4)$	$3 + 3x^2 + 1$	Starting expressions.
$3x^2 - 2x + 4$	$3 + 3x^2 + 1$	
		Remove $3x^2$ from both sides.
$-2x$	0	
		Divide both sides by −2.

3-68.   Copy and complete each of the Diamond Problems below. The pattern used in the Diamond Problems is shown at right.

a.   b.   c.   d.

3.2.1 How can I check my answer?

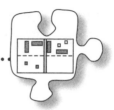

Solving Equations and Testing the Solution

In Section 2.2, you learned to solve equations on an equation mat. In this section, you will practice your equation-solving skills while adding a new element: You will check your answer to make sure it is correct.

While solving equations in this lesson, keep these focus questions in mind:

What is your goal?

How can you start?

How can you simplify?

Can you get x alone?

3-69.　For this activity, share algebra tiles and an equation mat with your partner.

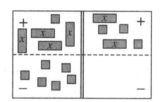

a.　Start by setting up your equation mat as shown at right. Write the equation on your paper.

b.　Next, solve the equation on your equation mat one step at a time. Every time you make a step, record your work in two ways:

- Record the step that was taken to get from the old equation to the new equation.

- Write a new equation that represents the tiles in the equation mat.

c.　With your partner, find a way to check if your solution is correct.

3-70.　WHAT IS A SOLUTION?

In this lesson you have found solutions to several algebraic equations. But what exactly is a solution? Answer each of these questions with your study team, but *do not use algebra tiles*. Be prepared to **justify** your answers!

a.　Preston solved the equation $3x - 2 = 8$ and got the solution $x = 100$. Is he correct? How do you know?

b.　Edwin solved the equation $2x + 3 - x = 3x - 5$ and got the solution $x = 4$. Is he correct? How do you know?

c.　With your partner, discuss what you think a solution to an equation is. Write down a description of what you and your partner agree on.

Algebra Connections

3-71.   Work with your partner to solve these equations, being careful to record your work. After solving each equation, be sure to check your solution, if possible.

a. $3x + 4 = x + 8$

b. $4 - 2y = y + 10$

c. $5x + 4 - 2x = -(x + 8)$

d. $-2 - 3k - 2 = -2k + 8 - k$

3-72.   IS THERE ANOTHER WAY?

Compare your solution to part (c) of problem 3-71 with the solution that another pair of students got. Did both solutions involve the same steps? Were the steps used in the same order? If not, copy the other pair's solution onto your paper. If both pairs used the same steps in the same order to solve the equation, come up with a different way to solve the problem and record it on your paper.

MATH NOTES

METHODS AND **M**EANINGS

Complete Graph

A complete graph has the following components:

- x-axis and y-axis labeled, clearly showing the scale.
- Equation of the graph near the line or curve.
- Line or curve extended as far as possible on the graph.
- Coordinates of special points stated in (x, y) format.

x	–1	0	1	2	3
y	6	4	2	0	–2

Tables can be formatted horizontally, like the one above, or vertically, as shown below.

x	y
–1	6
0	4
1	2
2	0
3	–2
4	–4

Throughout this course, you will continue to graph lines and other curves. Be sure to label your graphs appropriately.

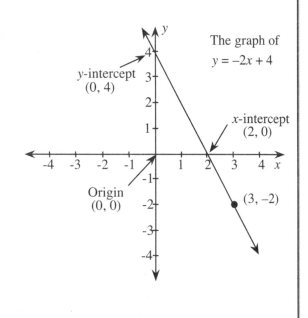

3-73.   For the following equations, solve for x. Be sure to check your answer, if possible. Show all work.

a. $3x + 7 = -x - 1$ b. $1 - 2x - 5 = 4x + 2$

c. $-3x = x - (6 - 2x)$ d. $2x + 3 = -2x + 5$

3-74.   For the rule $y = -2x + 1$, calculate the y-values that complete the table below.

IN (x)	−4	−3	−2	−1	0	1	2	3	4
OUT (y)									

a.   Graph your rule on a set of axes. Be sure to create a <u>complete</u> graph. If necessary, see the Math Notes box for this lesson to review what makes a graph complete.

b.   Describe your resulting graph. What does your graph look like?

3-75.   Simplify each expression below.

a. $4x + 7 + 3y - (1 + 3y + 2x)$ b. $16x^2 - 4x + 5 - (16x^2 - 8x) + 1$

c. $(32x - 7y) - (28x - 11y)$ d. $y + 2 + 2y + 2 + 2y - 2x + y$

3-76.   Burgers-o-rama is the best hamburger place in town. The owner, Ms. Hamm, buys two 5-pound packages of meat for $27.50. Use proportional reasoning to determine the information below. Be sure to explain your answer and organize your reasoning.

a.   What should Ms. Hamm pay for 25 pounds of meat?

b.   How many pounds can Ms. Hamm buy for $55.00?

3-77.   I'm thinking of a number. When I double my number, subtract five, and then add my original number, I get one. What's my number?

3.2.2 How many solutions are there?

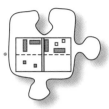

Determining the Number of Solutions

In Lesson 3.2.1, you reviewed your equation-solving skills to remember how to find a solution to an equation. But do all equations have a solution? And how can you tell if an equation does not have a solution?

Today you will continue to practice solving equations and will continue to investigate the meaning of a solution.

3-78.   GUESS MY NUMBER

Today you will play the "Guess My Number" game. You will need a pencil and a piece of paper. Your teacher will think of a number and tell you some information about that number. You will try to figure out what your teacher's number is. (You can use your paper if it helps.) When you think you know what the mystery number is, sit silently and do not tell anyone else. This will give others a chance to think about it.

3-79.   Use the process your teacher illustrated to analyze Game #3 of "Guess My Number" algebraically.

    a.   Start by writing an equation that expresses the information in the game.

    b.   Solve your equation, writing down each step as you go. When you reach a conclusion, discuss how it agrees with the answer for Game #3 you found as a class.

    c.   Repeat this process to analyze Game #4 algebraically.

3-80.   How many solutions does each equation below have? To answer this question, solve these equations, recording all of your steps as you go along. Check your solution, if possible.

    a. $4x - 5 = x - 5 + 3x$ b. $-x - 4x - 7 = -2x + 5$

    c. $3 + 5x - 4 - 7x = 2x - 4x + 1$ d. $4x - (-3x + 2) = 7x - 2$

    e. $x + 3 + x + 3 = -(x + 4) + (3x - 2)$ f. $x - 5 - (2 - x) = -3$

3-81.   In your Learning Log, explain how to find the number of
         solutions to an equation. How do you know when an equation
         has no solution? How do you know when an equation has an
         infinite number of solutions? Give examples of each kind of
         equation, as well as an equation with exactly one solution. Title
         your entry "How Many Solutions?" and label it with today's
         date.

3-82.   Create your own "Guess My Number" game like the ones you worked with in class
         today. Start it with, "I'm thinking of a number that…" Make sure it is a game you
         know the answer to! Write the equation and solve it.

3-83.   Draw Figure 0 and Figure 4 for the pattern below on graph paper.

         a.   Represent the number of tiles in
               each figure with:

               • An $x \rightarrow y$ table.

               • An algebraic rule.

               • A graph.

Figure 1   Figure 2   Figure 3

         b.   Without drawing Figure 5, predict where its point would lie on the graph.
               Justify your prediction.

3-84.   For the following equations, simplify and solve for the variable. Show all work and
         check your solution, if possible.

         a. $-2 + x = -x + 2$ b. $-(x - 1) = -4x - 2$

         c. $2 + 3x = 3x + 2$ d. $-(-x + 6) = -3x$

3-85.   For each equation, a possible solution is given. Check to see if the
         given solution is correct.

         a. $3x + 7 = x - 1$, solution $x = -4$?

         b. $-2x - 4 = -4x + 3$, solution $x = 3$?

         c. $-3x + 5 + 5x - 1 = 0$, solution $x = 2$?

         d. $-(x - 1) = 4x - 5 - 3x$, solution $x = 3$?

3-86.   Examine the graph at right.

a.   Use the graph to complete the table:

IN (x)					
OUT (y)					

b.   Use the graph to find the rule:

y = _____

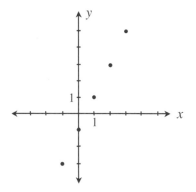

3.2.3 How can I use my equation-solving skills?

Solving Equations to Solve Problems

In the last two lessons you have practiced solving equations. In this lesson you will **apply** your equation-solving skills to the patterns you found at the beginning of this chapter. As you solve these problems, keep these questions in mind:

How can you simplify?

Is there more than one way to solve?

Can you get x alone?

How can you check your solution?

3-87.   In Lesson 3.1.3, you investigated the "Big Cs" pattern of tiles, shown at right. The rule you found for this pattern was $y = 6x + 3$, where x represented the figure number and y represented the number of tiles in the figure.

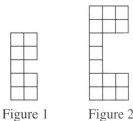 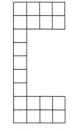

Figure 1   Figure 2   Figure 3

Penelope wants to know how many tiles will be in Figure 50. How can you determine this? Write out in words what you would need to do with your rule to answer her question. Then answer Penelope's question: How many tiles will be in Figure 50?

3-88. Lew wants to **reverse** the process: He says he has a "Big Cs" figure made up of 45 tiles. He wants to know which figure number this pattern is.

    a. In the rule $y = 6x + 3$, which variable must equal 45 to solve Lew's problem?

    b. Write an equation you could use to solve Lew's problem. Then solve your equation, recording all of your steps. Which "Big Cs" figure is made up of 45 tiles?

    c. How can you check your answer to be sure it is correct? Check your solution.

3-89. Norm says he has a "Big Cs" pattern made up of 84 tiles. He wants to know which figure number this pattern is. Write and solve an equation as you did in problem 3-88. Does your solution make sense? Why or why not?

3-90. For the following equations, solve for x. Record your work and check your solution.

    a. $\frac{1}{2}x - 2 = x - 4$ b. $8 - 0.25x = 0.5x + 2$

    c. $x + 2 - 0.5x = 1 + 0.5x + 1$ d. $7x - 0.15 = 2x + 0.6$

3-91. Can an equation be solved using a graph? Consider this as you answer the questions below.

    a. Solve the equation $5 = 1.6x + 1$. Check your solution.

    b. Complete a table for the rule $y = 1.6x + 1$. Then, on graph paper, graph the line.

    c. Use the graph from part (b) to find x when $y = 5$. Did you get the same result as in part (a)?

3-92.   Evaluate the expressions below for the given values.

a. $30 - 2x$ for $x = -6$

b. $x^2 + 2x$ for $x = -3$

c. $-\frac{1}{2}x + 9$ for $x = -6$

d. $\sqrt{k}$ for $k = 9$

3-93.   For the following equations, solve for x. Check your solution, if possible. Record your work.

a. $3x - 7 = 3x + 1$

b. $-2x - 5 = -4x + 2$

c. $2 + 3x = x + 2 + 2x$

d. $-(x - 2) = x + 2$

3-94.   The length of a rectangle is three centimeters more than twice the width. The perimeter is 78 centimeters. Use Guess and Check to find out how long and how wide the rectangle is.

3-95.   Use a diagram of the equation mat or some other method to explain why $-(x - 3) = -x + 3$.

3-96.   For the rule $y = 4 - x^2$, calculate the y-values that complete the table below. The first value is given for you.

IN (x)	−3	−2	−1	0	1	2	3
OUT (y)	−5						

a.   Create an x-axis and a y-axis and label your units. Plot and connect the points on your graph, and then label your graph with its rule.

b.   What does your graph look like?

3.2.4 How can I use my equation-solving skills?

More Solving Equations to Solve Problems

3-97.   JOHN'S GIANT REDWOOD, Part Two

In Lesson 3.1.2, you looked at how a tree increases in height as it gets older. Review the data below and, if possible, find your work from problem 3-10.

Number of Years after Planting	3	4	5
Height of Tree (in feet)	17	21	25

a.   Assuming the tree continues to grow at a constant rate, find a rule for the height of the tree using x and y.

b.   In your rule, what real-world quantity does x stand for? What real-world quantity does y stand for?

c.   John wants to know how tall the tree will be when it is 20 years after planting. Use your rule to answer his question.

d.   The tallest tree in the world, in Montgomery Woods State Reserve in California, is 367 feet high. John wants to know how long it would take for his tree to get that tall if it keeps growing at the same rate. Write and solve an equation you could use to answer John's question. Be sure to check your solution.

e.   Did you use algebra tiles to solve the equation in part (d)? Would it be easy to use algebra tiles to do so? Why or why not?

3-98.   For the following equations, solve for the given variable. Record your work and check the solution, if possible.

a. $75c - 300 = 25c + 200$ b. $26y - 4 - 11y = 15y + 6$

c. $-\frac{1}{2}x = 6$ d. $0.8 - 2t = 1 - 3t$

3-99.   MR. WALLIS IS BACK!

After much consideration, Mr. Wallis decided to use the tip table below to help him estimate what a 15% tip would be for various costs of dinner.

Cost of Dinner	$10	$20	$30	$35	$40	$45	$50	$100
Amount of Tip	$1.50	$3	$4.50	$5.25	$6	$6.75	$7.50	$15

a.   Find a rule for his table. That is, find a rule that calculates the amount of tip (y) based on the cost of the dinner (x). How did you find your rule?

b.   During the date, Mr. Wallis was so distracted that he forgot to write down the cost of the meal in his checkbook. All he remembers is that he left a $9 tip. What was the original cost of the meal before he paid the tip? Use your equation from part (a) to answer this question. Show all work.

c.   What was the total cost of the meal?

METHODS AND MEANINGS

Solutions to an Equation with One Variable

MATH NOTES

A **solution** to an equation gives a value of the variable that makes the equation true. For example, when 5 is substituted for x in the equation at right, both sides of the equation are equal. So $x = 5$ is a solution to this equation.

$$4x - 2 = 3x + 3$$
$$4(5) - 2 = 3(5) + 3$$
$$18 = 18$$

An equation can have more than one solution, or it may have no solution. Consider the examples at right.

Equation with no solution:
$$x + 2 = x + 6$$

Notice that no matter what the value of x is, the left side of the first equation will never equal the right side. Therefore, we say that $x + 2 = x + 6$ has **no solution**.

Equation with infinite solutions:
$$x - 3 = x - 3$$

However, in the equation $x - 3 = x - 3$, no matter what value x has, the equation will always be true. So all numbers can make $x - 3 = x - 3$ true. Therefore, we say the solution for the equation $x - 3 = x - 3$ is **all numbers**.

3-100. Copy and complete each of the Diamond Problems below. The pattern used in the Diamond Problems is shown at right.

a.

b.

c.

d.

3-101. The science club is selling homemade cookies to raise money for a field trip. They know that 12 dozen cookies uses 3 pounds of flour. Use proportional reasoning to determine the information below. Be sure to explain your answer and organize your reasoning.

    a. How much flour is needed for 18 dozen cookies?

    b. How many cookies can be made with 10 pounds of flour?

3-102. Simplify each of the following equations and solve for the variable. Show all work and check your solution, if possible.

    a. $3x - 7 + 9 - 2x = x + 2$ b. $-2m + 8 + m + 1 = 0$

    c. $2 = x + 6 - 2x$ d. $0.5p = p + 5$

3-103. Use your pattern-finding skills to copy and complete the table below.

IN (x)	1	2	3		5	6	8	12	24	x
OUT (y)	24	12		6	4.8	4		2		

    a. Explain the pattern you found in your table. How are x and y related?

    b. Write the rule you described in part (a) in algebraic symbols.

    c. Use the points in your table to graph this rule on graph paper. Describe the resulting shape.

3-104. Translate each algebraic expression into ordinary words.

    a. $5x - 3$ b. $2(x + y)$ c. $3 - (x + 5)$

Chapter 3 Closure   What have I learned?

Reflection and Synthesis

The activities below offer you a chance to reflect on what you have learned during this chapter. As you work, look for concepts that you feel very comfortable with, ideas that you would like to learn more about, and topics you need more help with. Look for **connections** between ideas as well as **connections** with material you learned previously.

①   TEAM BRAINSTORM

With your team, brainstorm a list for each of the following topics. Be as detailed as you can. How long can you make your list? Challenge yourselves. Be prepared to share your team's ideas with the class.

Topics: What have you studied in this chapter? What ideas and words were important in what you learned? Remember to be as detailed as you can.

Connections: What topics, ideas, and words that you learned *before* this chapter are **connected** to the new ideas in this chapter? Again, make your list as long as you can.

MAKING CONNECTIONS

The following is a list of the vocabulary used in this chapter. The words that appear in bold are new to this chapter. Make sure that you are familiar with all of these words and know what they mean. Refer to the glossary or index for any words that you do not yet understand.

area	**continuous**	coordinates
dependent variable	**discrete**	equation
equation mat	evaluate	**figure number**
graph	**independent variable**	**input value (x)**
output value (y)	**parabola**	pattern
prediction	quadrant	**rule**
scale on axes	simplify	solution
variable	$x \rightarrow y$ **table**	**x- and y-intercept**

Make a concept map showing all of the **connections** you can find among the key words and ideas listed above. To show a **connection** between two words, draw a line between them and explain the **connection**, as shown in the example below. A word can be **connected** to any other word as long as there is a **justified connection**. For each key word or idea, provide a sketch that illustrates the idea (see the example below).

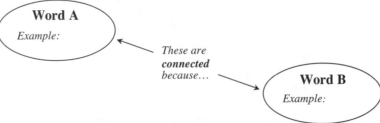

Your teacher may provide you with vocabulary cards to help you get started. If you use the cards to plan your concept map, be sure either to re-draw your concept map on your paper or to glue the vocabulary cards to a poster with all of the **connections** explained for others to see and understand.

While you are making your map, your team may think of related words or ideas that are not listed above. Be sure to include these ideas on your concept map.

③   SUMMARIZING MY UNDERSTANDING

This section gives you an opportunity to show what you know about certain math topics or ideas. Your teacher will give you directions for exactly how to do this. Your teacher may give you a "GO" page to work on. The "GO" stands for "Graphic Organizer," a tool you can use to organize your thoughts and communicate your ideas clearly.

WHAT HAVE I LEARNED?

This section will help you evaluate which types of problems you have seen with which you feel comfortable and those with which you need more help. This section appears at the end of every chapter to help you check your understanding. Even if your teacher does not assign this section, it is a good idea to try the problems and find out for yourself what you know and what you need to work on.

Solve each problem as completely as you can. The table at the end of the closure section has answers to these problems. It also tells you where you can find additional help and practice on problems like these.

CL 3-105. For the $x \rightarrow y$ table below, fill in the missing values and find the rule. Then find the zero of the rule (the input that makes the output zero).

IN (x)	−10	0	5	1	25	−6	8	−1.5	6	10
OUT (y)		3		5	53	−9				23

CL 3-106. One year ago, Josie moved into a new house and noticed a beautiful vine growing on the back fence. She recorded the data in the table below.

Weeks Since Josie Moved In	4	5	6
Height of Vine (in inches)	16	19	22

Assuming that the vine continues to grow at a constant rate:

a. How tall was the vine 7 weeks after Josie moved in?

b. How tall was the vine 3 weeks after Josie moved in?

c. How tall was the vine when Josie moved in? How do you know?

d. Predict how tall the vine was 19 weeks after Josie moved into her house. **Justify** your answer.

e. Predict when the vine reached the top of the garage (94 inches tall). How did you find your answer?

CL 3-107. Examine the tile pattern at right.

a. Draw Figure 1 and Figure 5.

Figure 2   Figure 3   Figure 4

b. Make an $x \rightarrow y$ table for the pattern.

c. Make a complete graph. Include points for Figures 0 through 5.

CL 3-108. Clifford is making a cake for his sister's birthday. The recipe calls for twice as much flour as sugar. It also calls for 20 ounces of ingredients other than flour and sugar. All the ingredients together total 80 ounces. How much flour does Clifford need?

CL 3-109. Simplify the expression $3x^2 - 5x - 4 + xy - (2xy + 2x^2)$. Then evaluate the result if $x = -1$ and $y = 6$.

CL 3-110. Follow the order of operations to simplify.

   a. $6^2 - (5 - 4) + 2(8 - 2^2) \div 8$ b. $\dfrac{2(9-6)^2}{18}$

CL 3-111. Raphael had 5 hits in 7 at bats. If he continues this pattern, how many hits will he have in 210 at bats?

CL 3-112. Solve $6 - x - 3 = 4x - 12$ for x, recording your steps as you work.

CL 3-113. Make an $x \rightarrow y$ table from the points on the graph at right. Then write a rule for the table.

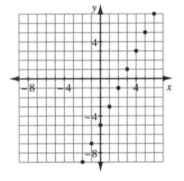

CL 3-114. Make an $x \rightarrow y$ table and complete graph for the equation $y = -2x + 5$.

CL 3-115. Jessica was solving an equation. After she finished simplifying, her result was $0 = 2$. This result confused her. Explain to Jessica what her result means. Explain your reasoning thoroughly.

CL 3-116. Check your answers using the table at the end of the closure section. Which problems do you feel confident about? Which problems were hard? Use the table to make a list of topics you need help on and a list of topics you need to practice more.

HOW AM I THINKING?

This course focuses on five different **Ways of Thinking**: reversing thinking, justifying, generalizing, making connections, and applying and extending understanding. These are some of the ways in which you think while trying to make sense of a concept or to solve a problem (even outside of math class). During this chapter, you have probably used each Way of Thinking multiple times without even realizing it!

This closure activity will focus on one of these Ways of Thinking: **generalizing**. Read the description of this Way of Thinking at right.

Think about the topics that you have learned during this chapter. When did you need to describe patterns? When did you draw a conclusion or make a **general** statement? You may want to flip through the chapter to refresh your memory about the problems that you have worked on. Discuss any ideas you have with the rest of the class.

Once your discussion is complete, examine some of the ways you have **generalized** as you answer the questions below.

Generalizing

To generalize means to make a general statement or conclusion about something from partial evidence. You think this way when you describe patterns, because you are looking for a general statement that describes each term in the pattern. Often, a generalization is the answer to the question, "What is in common?" When you catch yourself thinking, "*I think this is always true...*", you are generalizing.

a.   Examine the tile pattern below.

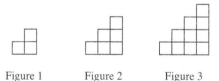

Figure 1   Figure 2   Figure 3

   i.   Draw Figure 4 and Figure 5 on graph paper.

   ii.   How do the figures appear to be growing? Make a **general** statement describing how all of the figures change to become the next figure in the pattern.

   iii.   Sketch and describe Figure 100.

   iv.   In **general**, what does each figure look like? That is, describe Figure *n*.

Continues on next page →

Continued from previous page.

b. During Section 3.2, you probably **generalized** about how to solve equations. For example, in Chapter 2, you solved equations with algebra tiles, such as those shown on the equation mat at right. However, during this chapter, you have solved some equations that cannot easily be expressed using algebra tiles. How? Because you **generalized** the process to include any type of linear equation, such as $8 - 0.25x = 0.5x + 2$ from problem 3-90. Consider this as you answer the questions below.

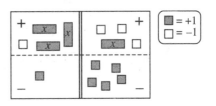

  i. In **general**, what are some strategies you can use no matter how many x-tiles and unit tiles are placed on both sides of the equation?

  ii. Use the general strategies you described in (*i*) above to solve the equation below. Show all work and check your solution.

$$\tfrac{1}{4}x - (3 - \tfrac{3}{4}x) = \tfrac{1}{2}x - 7$$

  iii. Some equations have no solution. In **general**, describe how you know if an equation has no solution. Because you do not have a specific equation to solve, this description must help to describe all situations in which an equation has no solution. This is another example of a **generalization**.

c. Examine the data in the table below. Find a rule that describes how all of the x-values and y-values are related. Since this rule describes a **general** property that all of these points share, it is also an example of a **generalization**.

IN (x)	−10	0	5	1	25	−6	8	−1	6	10
OUT (y)	−26	4	19	7	79	−14	28	1	22	34

Answers and Support for Closure Activity #4
What Have I Learned?

Problem	Solution	Need Help?	More Practice
CL 3-105.	The missing *y*-values, in order, are: $-17, 13, 19, 1, 15$. The rule is $y = 2x + 3$.	Lesson 3.1.1	Problems 3-2, 3-3, 3-28, 3-37, 3-48, and 3-103
CL 3-106.	a. 25 inches b. 13 inches c. 4 inches d. 61 inches e. 30 weeks after Josie moved in	Lesson 3.1.2	Problems 3-10 and 3-97
CL 3-107.	a. 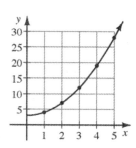 Figure 1 Figure 5	Section 3.1	Problems 3-1, 3-18, 3-47, 3-57, and 3-83

b.

x	1	2	3	4	5
y	4	7	12	19	28

c.

Note: In this course, tile patterns will represent elements of continuous relationships and will be graphed with a continuous line or curve.

Problem	Solution	Need Help?	More Practice
CL 3-108.	40 ounces	Lesson 2.1.7 Math Notes box	Problems 3-7, 3-26, 3-77, and 3-94
CL 3-109.	$x^2 - xy - 5x - 4$ $= (-1)^2 - (-1)(6) - 5(-1) - 4$ $= 8$	Lessons 2.1.1, 2.1.3, 2.1.5, and 2.1.6 Math Notes boxes	Problems 3-5, 3-14, 3-15, 3-31, 3-39, 3-75, and 3-92
CL 3-110.	a. 36 b. 1	Lesson 2.1.3 Math Notes box	Problems 3-16 and 3-27
CL 3-111.	150 hits	Lessons 2.2.1 and 2.2.3	Problems 3-17, 3-40, 3-64, 3-76, and 3-101
CL 3-112.	$x = 3$	Lesson 2.1.8 Math Notes box	Problems 3-24, 3-25, 3-30, 3-38, 3-49, 3-59, 3-73, 3-84, and 3-90
CL 3-113.	$\begin{array}{c\|ccccccccc} x & -2 & -1 & 0 & 1 & 2 & 3 & 4 & 5 & 6 \\ \hline y & -9 & -7 & -5 & -3 & -1 & 1 & 3 & 5 & 7 \end{array}$ $y = 2x - 5$	Lesson 3.1.4	Problems 3-45 and 3-86
CL 3-114.	$\begin{array}{c\|cccccccc} x & -3 & -2 & -1 & 0 & 1 & 2 & 3 & 4 \\ \hline y & 11 & 9 & 7 & 5 & 3 & 1 & -1 & -3 \end{array}$ 	Lesson 3.1.4, Lesson 3.2.1 Math Notes box	Problems 3-46, 3-55, 3-56, 3-66, 3-74, and 3-96
CL 3-115.	There is no solution for x in this equation.	Lesson 3.2.1, Lesson 3.2.4 Math Notes box	Problems 3-71, 3-80, and 3-93

CHAPTER 4   Multiple Representations

This chapter builds on the work you did in Chapters 2 and 3. The primary focus of Chapter 4 is to investigate the **connections** between the four representations of data: graphs, tables, patterns, and equations (also referred to as "rules"). You will also explore situations that can be represented by a line and study what it means when two lines intersect (cross each other). By the end of this chapter, you will know how to use graphs, tables, patterns, and rules to solve almost any problem involving lines.

In this chapter, you will learn:

➢ How to change any representation of data (such as a graph, pattern, rule, or table) to any of the other representations.

➢ How to write an equation from a word problem.

➢ How to find the point where two lines intersect.

➢ How to use the connections between graphs, tables, rules, and patterns to solve problems.

Guiding Questions

Think about these questions throughout this chapter:

What is the connection?

Is there a pattern?

How many different ways can it be represented?

How does the pattern show up in the rule, table, and graph?

How does the pattern grow?

Chapter Outline

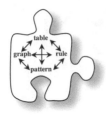

Section 4.1   In this section, you will shift between different representations of linear patterns by using the web shown at left. By finding connections between each representation, you and your team will find ways to change from one representation to each of the other three representations.

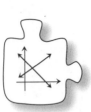

Section 4.2   Section 4.2 will start by examining word problems in which two amounts are compared. You will use your knowledge of graphs and rules to write equations for word problems. Then, using the equation mat, you will solve a linear equation to determine where two lines cross. A final challenge will bring together word problems and the representations in the web.

4.1.1 What's the connection?

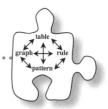

Finding Connections Between Representations

In Chapter 3 you studied different ways to represent patterns. You organized information into tables, graphed information about patterns, and learned how to find the rules that govern specific patterns.

Starting today and continuing throughout this chapter, you will find **connections** between different representations of the same pattern, explore each representation more deeply, and learn shorter ways to go from one representation to another. By the end of this chapter, you will have a deeper understanding of many of the most powerful tools of algebra.

4-1.   TILE PATTERN TEAM CHALLENGE

Your teacher will assign your team a tile pattern (one of the patterns labeled (a) through (e) on the next page). Your team's task is to create a poster showing every way you can represent your pattern and highlighting all of the connections between the representations that you can find. For this activity, **finding and showing the connections are the most important parts.** Clearly presenting the connections between representations on your poster will help you convince your classmates that your description of the pattern makes sense.

Pattern Analysis:

- **Extend** the pattern: Draw Figures 0, 4, and 5. Then describe Figure 100. Give as much information as you can. What will it look like? How will the tiles be arranged? How many tiles will it have?

- **Generalize** the pattern by writing a rule that will give the number of tiles in any figure in the pattern. Show how you got your answer.

- Find the number of tiles in each figure. Record your data in a table and on a graph.

- Demonstrate how the pattern grows using color, arrows, labels, and other math tools to help you show and explain. Show growth in each representation.

- What **connections** do you see between the different representations (graph, figures, and $x \rightarrow y$ table)? How can you show these **connections**?

Problem continues on next page →

4-1.   *Problem continued from previous page.*

Presenting the Connections:

As a team, organize your work into a large poster that clearly shows each representation of your pattern, as well as a description of Figure 100. When your team presents your poster to the class, you will need to support each statement with a reason from your observations. Each team member must explain something mathematical as part of your presentation.

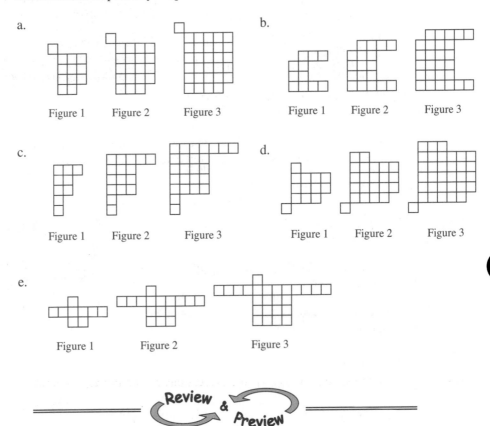

a.

Figure 1   Figure 2   Figure 3

b.

Figure 1   Figure 2   Figure 3

c.

Figure 1   Figure 2   Figure 3

d.

Figure 1   Figure 2   Figure 3

e.

Figure 1   Figure 2   Figure 3

——————— Review & Preview ———————

4-2.   For each tile pattern in problem 4-1, draw Figures 0, 4, and 5 on graph paper. If it helps, copy Figures 1, 2, and 3 onto your paper.

4-3.   Make an $x \rightarrow y$ table for the rule $y = x^2 - 2x$.

a.   Plot and connect the points on a complete graph.

b.   Does your graph look like a full parabola? If not, add more points to your table and graph to complete the picture.

4-4.   THE GAME SHOW

Susan had an incredible streak of good
fortune as a guest on the exciting game
show, "The Math Is Right." She
amassed winnings of $12,500, a sports
car, two round-trip airline tickets, and
five pieces of furniture.

In an amazing finish, Susan then
landed on a "Double Your Prize"
square and answered the
corresponding math question correctly!
She instantly became the show's
biggest winner ever, earning twice the
amounts of all her previous prizes.

A week later, $25,000, a sports car, four round-trip airline tickets, and five pieces of
furniture arrived at her house. Susan felt cheated. What was wrong?

4-5.   Write the equation represented by the
diagram at right.

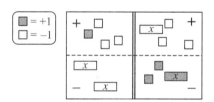

a.   Simplify as much as possible and
then solve for x.

b.   Check your solution.

4-6.   Copy and simplify the following expressions by combining like terms.

a. $y + 3x - 3 + 2x^2 + 8x - 5y$ b. $2x + 4x^2 - 6x^2 - 9 + 1 - x - 3x$

c. $2y^2 + 30y - 3y^2 + 4y - 14 - y$ d. $-10 + 3xy - 3xy + y^2 + 10 - y^2$

4-7.   Use your pattern-finding techniques to fill in the missing entries for the table below.
Then find a rule for the pattern.

IN (x)	4	8	3	–2	–6	0	5	7
OUT (y)	17	65	10	5		1	26	

4.1.2 How does it grow?

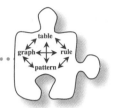

Seeing Growth in Different Representations

In Lesson 4.1.1, you looked at four different ways of representing patterns and began to find **connections** between them.

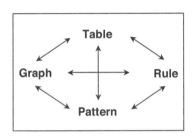

Throughout this chapter you will explore **connections** and find shortcuts between the representations. Today, you will look for specific connections between geometric patterns and equations. As you work today, keep these questions in mind:

How can you see growth in the rule?

How do you know your rule is correct?

What does the representation tell you?

What are the connections between the representations?

At the end of this lesson, put your work from today in a safe place, because you will need to use it during Lesson 4.1.3!

4-8.   **Tile Pattern #1:**

Examine the tile pattern at right.

a.   What do you notice? After everyone has had a moment on his or her own to examine the figures, discuss what you see with your team.

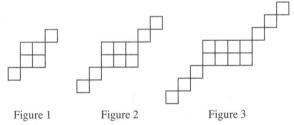

Figure 1   Figure 2   Figure 3

b.   Sketch the next figure in the sequence (Figure 4) on your resource page. Sketch the figure that comes before Figure 1 (Figure 0).

c.   How is the tile pattern growing? Where are the tiles being added with each new figure? Color in the new tiles in each figure with a marker or colored pencil on your resource page.

d.   What would Figure 100 look like? Describe it in words. How many tiles would be in the 100th figure? Find as many ways as you can to **justify** your conclusion. Be prepared to report back to the class with your team's findings and methods.

Algebra Connections

4-9.   Answer questions (a) through (d) from problem 4-8 for each of the patterns below. Use color to shade in the new tiles on each pattern on your resource page. Choose one color for the new tiles in part (a) and a different color for the new tiles in part (b).

a.   **Tile Pattern #2:**

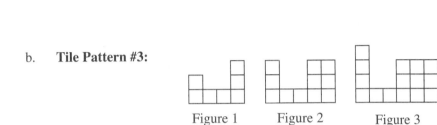

Figure 1   Figure 2   Figure 3

b.   **Tile Pattern #3:**

Figure 1   Figure 2   Figure 3

4-10.   PUTTING IT TOGETHER

Look back at the three different tile patterns in problems 4-8 and 4-9 to answer these questions.

a.   What is the same and what is different between these three patterns? Explain in a few sentences.

b.   Write an equation (rule) for the number of tiles in each pattern.

c.   What connections do you see between your equations and the tile pattern? Show and explain these connections.

d.   Imagine that the team next to you created a new tile pattern that grows in the same way as the ones you have just worked with, but they refused to show it to you. What other information would you need in order to predict the number of tiles in Figure 100? Explain your reasoning.

4-11.   Consider **Tile Pattern #4**, shown below.

a.   Draw Figures 0 and 4 on the
resource page.

Figure 1   Figure 2   Figure 3

b.   Write an equation (rule) for
the number of tiles in this
pattern. Use a new color to
show where the numbers in
your rule appear in the tile
pattern.

c.   What is the same about this pattern and Tile Pattern #3? What is different?
What do those similarities and differences look like in the tile pattern? In the
equation?

d.   How is the growth represented in each equation?

*Don't forget to put your work from today in a safe place, because you will need to use it during
the next lesson.*

4-12.   For today's Learning Log entry, draw a web of the different
representations, starting with the diagram below. Draw lines and/or
arrows to show which representations you have connected so far.
Explain the connections you learned today. Be sure to include
anything you figured out about how the numbers in equations (rules)
relate to tile patterns. Title this entry "Starting the Web" and label it
with today's date.

```
              Table



Graph                      Rule



          Pattern
```

Algebra Connections

4-13. Write the equation represented in the equation mat at right.

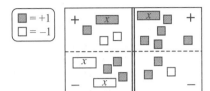

a. Simplify as much as possible and then solve for x.

b. Check your solution.

4-14. Simplify each of the following equations and solve for x. Show all work and check your solution.

a. $7 - 3x = -x + 1$

b. $-2 + 3x = -(x + 6)$

4-15. Leala can write a 500-word essay in an hour. If she writes an essay in 10 minutes, approximately how many words do you think the essay contains?

4-16. Copy and complete the table below.

IN (x)	2	10	6	7	−3		−10	1000	x
OUT (y)	9	25	17			15			

a. Explain in words what is done to the input value (x) to produce the output value (y).

b. Write the rule you described in part (a) with algebraic symbols.

4-17. When Susan's brother went to college, she and her two sisters evenly divided his belongings. Among his possessions were 3 posters, 216 books, and 24 CDs. How were these items divided?

4.1.3 How does it grow?

· ·

Connecting Linear Rules and Graphs

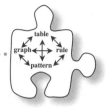

You have been looking at geometric patterns and ways that those patterns can be represented with equations, graphs, and $x \rightarrow y$ tables. In Lesson 4.1.2 you worked with four different tile patterns and looked for **connections** between the geometric shapes and the numbers in the equations. Today you will go back to those four equations and look for **connections** to other representations.

By the end of this lesson, you should be able to answer the following target questions:

How is growth shown in a rule?

How is growth shown in a graph?

How can you determine the number of tiles in Figure 0 from a graph?

How can you determine which tile pattern grows faster from a graph?

4-18.   Examine your Lesson 4.1.2 Resource Page ("Pattern Analysis").

   a.   Make sure you have a rule for each tile pattern.

   b.   Draw a graph. Put all patterns on the same set of axes. Use different colors for each, matching the color you used on the resource page.

   c.   Explain how the growth appears in the pattern, in the rule, and in the graph.

   d.   What **connections** do you see between these representations? Describe any **connections** you see.

4-19.   The graph at right is also on the Lesson
         4.1.3 Resource Page provided by your
         teacher. It gives information about three
         new tile patterns. **Note:** In this course, tile
         patterns will be considered to be elements
         of continuous relationships and thus will be
         graphed with a continuous line or curve.

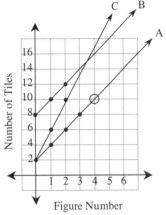

         Answer the following questions as a team.

         a.   What information does the circled point
               (○) on the graph tell you about tile
               pattern A?

         b.   Find the growth of each tile pattern. For
               example, how much does tile pattern A
               increase from one figure to the next? Explain how you know.

         c.   Look at the lines for tile patterns A and B. What is the same about the two
               lines? What conclusion can you make about these tile patterns? What is
               different about the lines? What does this tell you about the tile patterns?
               Justify your answers, based on the graph.

         d.   Look at lines A and C on the graph. What do these two lines have in common?
               In what ways are the lines different? What does this tell you about the tile
               patterns? Explain completely.

4-20.   In your Learning Log, answer the target questions for this lesson,
         reprinted below:

                     How is growth shown in a rule?

                     How is growth shown in a graph?

              How can you determine the number of tiles in Figure 0 from a graph?

              How can you determine which tile pattern grows faster from a graph?

         Be sure to include at least one example. Title this entry "Connecting Linear Rules
         and Graphs" and label it with today's date.

4-21.   Two of the connections in your representations web are pattern → table and
          pattern → rule. Practice these connections as you answer the questions below.

          a.   On graph paper, draw Figure 0
               and Figure 4 for the pattern at
               right.

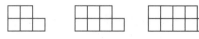

          Figure 1   Figure 2   Figure 3

          b.   Represent the number of tiles in
               each figure with a table.

          c.   Represent the number of tiles in each figure with an algebraic rule.

4-22.   For the rule $y = x^2 - 4$, calculate the y-values that complete the table below. Plot
          the points and connect them on a complete graph on graph paper. What does your
          graph look like?

IN (x)	−3	−2	−1	0	1	2	3
OUT (y)							

4-23.   For each of the equations below, solve for x. Show all work and check your
          solution.

          a. $-2 + 2x = -x + 2 + x$ b. $2 - 3x = x + 2$

4-24.   The length of a rectangle is five centimeters more than twice its width. The
          perimeter is 100 centimeters. Use Guess and Check to find out how long and how
          wide the rectangle is.

4-25.   Another one of the connections in your
          representations web is graph → table. In
          Chapters 1 through 3, you developed tools to
          find a table from a graph. Consider this
          connection as you complete the table below
          based on the graph at right.

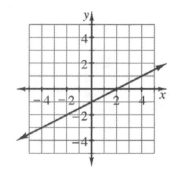

IN (x)	−3	−2	−1	0	1	2	3
OUT (y)							

4.1.4 What's the rule? How can I use it?

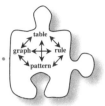

$y = mx + b$

In Lessons 4.1.2 and 4.1.3, you investigated connections between tile patterns, $x \rightarrow y$ tables, graphs, and rules (equations). Today you will use your observations about growth and Figure 0 to write rules for linear patterns and to create new tile patterns for given rules.

4-26.   UNDERSTANDING $y = mx + b$

With your team, list some of the equations you have been working with in the past two lessons.

a.   What do all of these rules have in common?

Rules for linear patterns can all be written in the form $y = mx + b$, where x and y represent variables, but m and b represent **constants** (numbers that stay the same in the equation after they are chosen). Discuss these questions with your team:

b.   What does m tell you about the pattern?

c.   What does b tell you about the pattern?

4-27.   GRAPH $\rightarrow$ RULE

Allysha claims she can find the equation of a line by its graph without a table. How is that possible? Discuss this idea with your team and then try to find the equation of the line at right without first making a table. Be ready to share with the class how you found the rule.

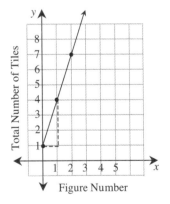

4-28.   TABLE → RULE

Allysha wonders if she can use the idea of m and b to find the equation of a line from its table.

a.   For example, if she knows the information about a linear pattern given in the table below, how can she find the equation of the line? Work with your team to complete the table and find the rule.

IN (x)	0	1	2	3	4	5	6
OUT (y)	−2						

+5   +5   +5   +5   +5   +5

b.   Use this same idea to find the rule of the linear tile patterns represented by the tables below.

i.

IN (x)	−1	0	1	2	3	4	5
OUT (y)	3	5	7	9	11	13	15

ii.

IN (x)	0	1	2	3	4	5	6
OUT (y)	7	4	1	−2	−5	−8	−11

c.   Write a summary statement explaining how you used your knowledge about m and b to quickly write a rule.

4-29.   RULE → PATTERN

In each problem below, invent your own pattern that meets the stated conditions. Draw Figures 0, 1, 2, and 3 and write the rule (equation) for your pattern.

a.   A tile pattern that has $y = 4x + 3$ as a rule.

b.   A tile pattern that decreases by 2 tiles and Figure 2 has 8 tiles.

4-30.   Invent two different tile patterns that grow by 4 every time but have different $x \rightarrow y$ tables. Draw Figures 0, 1, 2, and 3 and find rules for each of your patterns. What is different about your rules? What is the same?

4-31.   The linear equations you have been working with can be written in the general form:

$$y = mx + b$$

In your Learning Log, summarize what you know about m and b so far. What does the m tell you about a pattern? What does the b tell you about a pattern? Where can you see m and b in each representation? Sketch examples if it helps. Title this entry "$y = mx + b$" and label it with today's date.

4-32.   For each equation below, solve for x. Check your solution, if possible, and show all work.

a. $3x - 6 + 1 = -2x - 5 + 5x$

b. $-2x - 5 = 2 - 4x - (x - 1)$

4-33.   I am thinking of a number. When I double my number and then subtract the result from five, I get negative one. What is my number? Write and solve an equation.

4-34.   Copy this table and use your pattern skills to complete it.

IN (x)	2	10				−3			x
OUT (y)	4	28	13	−17	10		2.5	148	$3x-2$

a.   Explain in words what is done to the input value, x, to produce the output value, y.

b.   Explain the process you used to find the missing input values.

4-35.   Examine the $x \rightarrow y$ table at right.

a.   Invent a tile pattern that fits this data.

b.   What is the pattern's growth factor? Show where the growth factor appears in the $x \rightarrow y$ table and the tile pattern.

Figure Number	Number of Tiles
0	5
1	9
2	13
3	17

4-36.

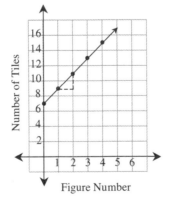

Figure Number

Look at the graph at left. What statements can you make about the tile pattern the graph represents? How many tiles are in Figure 0? Figure 1? What is the growth factor?

4.1.5 What are the connections?

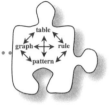

Checking the Connections

In the last several lessons you have been finding **connections** and relationships between different representations of patterns. You have worked backward and forward and have used information about Figure 0 (or the starting point) and the growth factor in order to write rules. In today's activity, you will check your **connections** by using pieces of information from different parts of the web to generate a complete pattern.

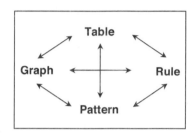

4-37.   CHECKING THE CONNECTIONS: TEAM CHALLENGE

Today you are going to **apply** what you know about the starting point (Figure 0), growth factor, and the **connections** between representations to answer some challenging questions. The information in each question, parts (a) through (d), describes a different pattern. The graph of each pattern is a line. From this information, generate the rule, $x \rightarrow y$ table, graph, and tile pattern (Figures 0 through 3) that follow the pattern. You may answer these questions in any order, but make sure you answer each one completely before starting another problem.

Work together as a team. The more you listen to how other people see the **connections** and the more you share your own ideas, the more you will know at the end of the lesson. Stick together and be sure to talk through every idea.

Each person will turn in his or her own paper at the end of this activity, showing four complete representations for each pattern. Your work does not need to be identical to your teammates' work, but you should have talked and agreed that all explanations are correct.

a.

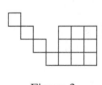

Figure 3

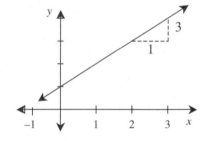

Problem continues on next page →

4-37.   *Problem continued from previous page.*

b.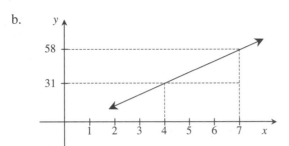

c.

Figure Number	Number of Tiles
0	
1	
2	
3	12

Figure 8

d. $y = -3x + 7$

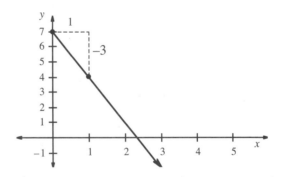

4-38.   REPRESENTATIONS WEB

Update your representations web from problem 4-12 with any new **connections** you have found. Pay attention to which direction(s) the arrow points.

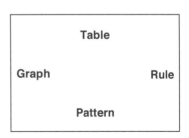

4-39.   For each equation below, solve for x. Check your solutions, if possible, and show all work.

   a. $-3 + x = -x + 5$

   b. $-(x - 3) = 2x - 4 - 3x$

   c. $2 + 4k = 2k + 9$

   d. $-(-t + 4) = -3t$

4-40.   Copy and complete each of the Diamond Problems below. The pattern used in the Diamond Problems is shown at right.

   a.   b.   c.   d.

4-41.   Complete a table for the rule $y = 3x - 2$.

   a.   Draw a complete graph for this rule.

   b.   Is $(-50, -152)$ a point on the graph? Explain how you know.

4-42.   Write down everything you know about the tile pattern represented by the $x \rightarrow y$ table at right. Be as specific as possible.

x	y
3	25
5	39
6	46
1	11

4-43.   Simplify each of the expressions below. You may use an equation mat and tiles.

   a. $-(5x + 1)$

   b. $6x - (-5x + 1)$

   c. $-(1 - 5x)$

   d. $-5x + (x - 1)$

4-44.   Invent a tile pattern that grows by 4 each time. Draw Figures 0, 1, 2, and 3. Use color or shading to show the growth.

4-45.   For each equation below, solve for x. Check your solutions, if possible, and show all work.

   a. $3p - 7 + 9 - 2p = p + 2$ b. $-2x + 5 + (-x) - 5 = 0$

   c. $12 = r + 6 - 2r$ d. $-(y^2 - 2) = y^2 - 5 - 2y^2$

4-46.   Sketch a graph to match each story below using axes labeled as shown at right.

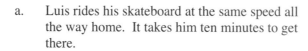

   a.   Luis rides his skateboard at the same speed all the way home. It takes him ten minutes to get there.

   b.   Corinna jogs along at the same speed until she reaches a hill, and then she slows down until she finally stops to rest.

   c.   Sergei is talking with his friends at the donut shop when he realizes that it's almost time for math class! He runs toward school, but slows to a walk when he hears the bell ring and realizes that he is already late. He sits down in class four minutes after he left the donut shop.

4-47.   Complete a table for the rule $y = 3 - x$.

   a.   Draw a complete graph for this rule.

   b.   Is $(32, -29)$ a point on this graph? Explain why or why not.

4-48.   Mr. Wallis decided to create another table to figure out how much it costs to send a certain number of regular letters through the mail. Use proportional reasoning to complete his table at right.

Number of Letters	Cost of Stamps
10	$3.40
2	$0.68
	$5.10
7	
1	
500	
	$14.28

4.1.6 How can I use growth?

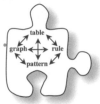

Graphing a Line Without an $x \rightarrow y$ Table

You have now used your knowledge of growth factors and Figure 0 to create tile patterns and $x \rightarrow y$ tables directly from rules. You have also looked at graphs to determine the equation or rule for the pattern. Today you will reverse that process and use an equation to create a graph without the intermediate step of creating an $x \rightarrow y$ table.

4-49.   For each of the graphs below:

- Write a rule.

- Describe how the pattern changes and how many tiles are in Figure 0.

a.

b.

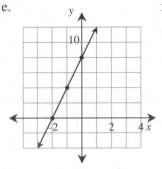

c.

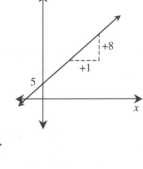

d.

e.

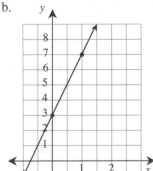

f.

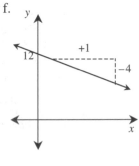

Algebra Connections

4-50.   Now **reverse** the process. Graph the following rules without first making a table. Parts (a) and (b) can go on the same set of axes, as can parts (c) and (d). Label each line with its equation, **y-intercept** (where it crosses the y-axis), and a growth triangle.

a. $y = 4x + 3$ b. $y = 3x$

c. $y = -3x + 8$ d. $y = x - 1$

4-51.   Sketch a graph that fits each description below and then label each line with its equation. You can put all of the graphs on one set of axes if you label the lines clearly. Use what you know about growth factor and Figure 0 to help you.

a.   A pattern that has three tiles in Figure 0 and adds four tiles in each new figure.

b.   A pattern that shrinks by three tiles between figures and starts with five tiles in Figure 0.

c.   A pattern that has two tiles in all figures.

4-52.   Now **reverse** your process to describe the pattern represented by the rule $y = -2x + 13$. Be as detailed as you can.

4-53.   CONSOLIDATING YOUR LEARNING

a.   Find the web that you updated at the end of Lesson 4.1.5. On it, add arrows for any new connections that you have made.

b.   In your Learning Log, write a step-by-step process for **graphing directly from a rule**. A student who has not taken algebra yet should be able to read your process and understand how to create a graph. It may help you to think about these questions as you write:

What information do you get from your rule?

How does that information show up on the graph?

Where does your graph start?

How do you figure out the next point?

What should you label to make it a complete graph?

Title this entry "Graphing Without an $x \rightarrow y$ Table," and label it with today's date.

4-54. Use what you know about m and b to graph each rule below without making a table. Draw a growth triangle for each line.

a. $y = 2x - 3$ b. $y = -2x + 5$

c. $y = 3x$ d. $y = \frac{1}{2}x + 1$

4-55. Examine the graph at right showing three tile patterns.

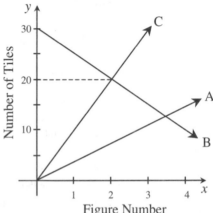

a. What do you know about Figure 0 for each of the three patterns?

b. Which pattern changes most quickly? How quickly does it change? Show how you know.

c. Which figure number has the same number of tiles in patterns B and C? Explain how you know.

d. Write a rule for pattern B.

4-56. Translate these algebraic statements into words: $y = 2x + 5$ and $y = 6x + 5$.

a. What do you know about Figure 0 for each pattern?

b. Which pattern grows most quickly? How do you know?

4-57. Evaluate each expression below when $x = -3$.

a. $4x + 16$ b. $3x^2 - 2x + 1$

4-58. Ms. B is making snickerdoodle cookies. Her recipe uses one-and-a-half teaspoons of cinnamon to make two-dozen cookies. If she needs to make thirteen-dozen cookies in order to give one cookie to each of her students, how much cinnamon will she need?

4.1.7 What are the connections?

Completing the Web

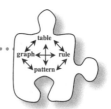

After all of the work you have done with equations in $y = mx + b$ form, you know a lot about starting with one representation of a pattern and moving to different representations. Today you will work with your team to make sure you are confident moving around the representations web.

Answer problems 4-59 and 4-60 on graph paper. Discuss each problem with your team to get as much as you can out of these problems.

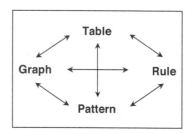

4-59.   GRAPH → PATTERN and TABLE → PATTERN

On graph paper, draw tile patterns (Figures 0, 1, and 2) that could represent the data shown below. Be creative, but make sure that the growth of each pattern makes sense to your teammates.

a.

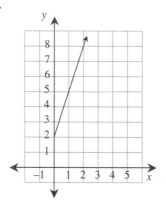

b.

x	y
0	14
1	11
2	8
3	5
4	2

4-60.   REVISITING "GROWING, GROWING, GROWING"

Problem 1-32 from Chapter 1 asked you to determine which figure in the pattern shown below would have 79 tiles. Now that you know more about graphs, $x \rightarrow y$ tables, rules, and tile patterns themselves, you can show the answer to this question in multiple ways.

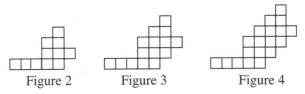

Figure 2   Figure 3   Figure 4

Your Task: Solve this problem by completing the following tasks. Use a graphing calculator or other graphing technology to help you find a graph and a table. Be sure to record your work and **justify** your thinking.

- Copy the three figures above onto a piece of graph paper. Extend the pattern on graph paper to include Figures 1 and 5.

- Find a rule, table, and graph for this pattern.

- Which figure will have 79 tiles? Use as many representations as you can to justify your answer.

4-61.   EXTENSION

Invent an equation to fit these clues: The x-intercept is 2, and the pattern grows by 4. Show and explain your reasoning.

MⒺTHODS AND MEANINGS

Multiple Representations

Consider the areas of the figures in the **tile pattern** below. The number of tiles in each figure can also be represented in an $x \rightarrow y$ **table**, on a **graph**, or with a **rule** (equation).

Remember that in this course, tile patterns will be considered to be elements of continuous relationships and thus will be graphed with a continuous line or curve.

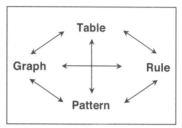

| Figure 0 | Figure 1 | Figure 2 |

Tile Pattern

Graph

$$y = 2x + 3$$

Rule (Equation)

Figure Number (x)	0	1	2
Number of Tiles (y)	3	5	7

$x \rightarrow y$ **Table**

Review & Preview

4-62.   Use what you know about m and b to graph each equation below without making a table. Show a growth triangle on each graph and label the x- and y-intercepts.

a. $y = 3 - 2x$

b. $y = 2x$

c. $y = 3$

d. $y = -\frac{1}{2}x + 3$

4-63. Copy and complete each $x \rightarrow y$ table below on your paper. Using what you know about m and b, write an equation that represents the data in the table.

a.

x	y
0	5
1	7
2	9
3	11
4	13
30	
200	
	505
x	

b.

x	y
0	4
1	2
2	0
3	-2
4	-4
30	
150	
300	
x	

c.

x	y
-2	7
-1	4
0	1
1	-2
2	-5
3	
100	
	70
x	

4-64. Solve each of the following equations and check your answers.

a. $2x - 3 = 7$

b. $3x + 5 - x = x - 3$

c. $5x - (x + 1) = 6 - 2x$

d. $0.5x - 5 = x + 4$

4-65. For a tile pattern with the rule $y = 6x + 4$ (where x represents the figure number and y represents the number of tiles), which figure number has 40 tiles in it? How do you know?

4-66. Josie and Jules are building a model car. They find that the real car is 54 inches tall and 180 inches long. They decide to make their model 3 inches tall, but now they are having a disagreement. Josie thinks that their model should be 10 inches long and Jules thinks it should be 129 inches long. Help them settle their argument by deciding if either of them is correct. Explain how you know exactly how long their model should be.

4.2.1 When are they the same?

Introduction to Systems of Equations

In Section 4.1, you graphed lines and curves that represented tile patterns. But what happens when you graph two lines at the same time? What can you learn? Today you will use data, graphs, and rules to examine what happens when two lines (or curves) intersect.

4-67.   The Iditarod Trail Sled Dog Race is famous for its incredible length and its use of dogs. In 2003, the sled drivers, known as mushers, started their dog sleds at Fairbanks, Alaska and rode through the snow for many days until they reached Nome, Alaska. Along the route there were stations where the competitors checked in, so data was kept on the progress of each team.

Joyla and her team of dogs made it through the first five checkpoints. At the same time, her buddy Evie left Nome (the finish line) on the day the race started in an effort to meet Joyla and offer encouragement. Evie traveled along the route toward the racers on her snowmobile. The progress of each person is shown on the graph below.

Your Task: With your team, analyze the data in the graph. Consider the questions below as you work. Be prepared to defend your results.

- Which data represents Evie? Which represents Joyla? How can you tell?

- When did Evie meet Joyla?

- How long was the race? How can you tell?

- Who traveled faster? Explain how you know.

- Approximately how long did it take Joyla to finish the race? How did you find your answer?

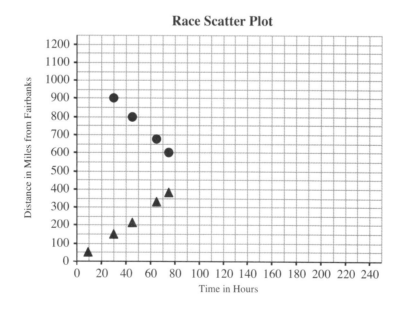

4-68.   The point where two lines (or curves) cross is called a **point of intersection**. Two or more lines (or curves) are called a **system of equations**. When you work with data, points of intersection can be meaningful, as you saw in the last problem.

   a.   On graph paper, graph $y = 3x - 4$ and $y = -2x + 6$ on the same set of axes.

   b.   Find the point of intersection of these two lines and label the point with its coordinates; that is, write it in the form (x, y).

4-69.   The meaning of a point of intersection depends on what the graph is describing. For example, in problem 4-67, the point where Joyla's and Evie's lines cross represents when they met during the race.

   Examine each of the graphs below and write a brief story that describes the information in the graph. Include a sentence explaining what the point of intersection represents.

a.
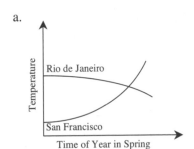

b.
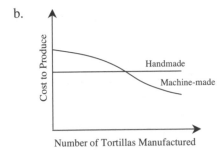

c.
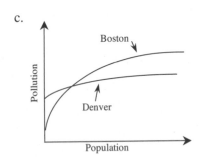

d.
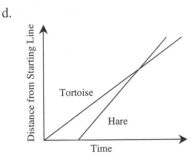

4-70.   In your Learning Log, write your own situation like the ones in problem 4-69 and make a graph. Have at least two lines or curves intersect. Explain what the intersection represents in your situation. Title this entry "Points of Intersection" and label it with today's date.

Algebra Connections

METHODS AND MEANINGS

Systems of Equations Vocabulary

The point where two lines (or curves) intersect is called a **point of intersection**. This point's significance depends on the context of the problem.

Two or more lines or curves used to find a point of intersection are called a **system of equations**. A system of equations can represent a variety of contexts and can be used to compare how two or more things are related. For example, the system of equations graphed at right compares the temperature in two different cities over time.

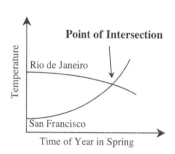

Point of Intersection

Rio de Janeiro

San Francisco

Time of Year in Spring

Review & Preview

4-71.   To ride to school, Elaine takes 15 minutes to ride 8 blocks. Assuming she rides at a constant speed, how long should it take her to go 20 blocks? Justify your answer.

4-72.   Find the area of the entire rectangle in each diagram below. Show all work.

a.

48
102

b.
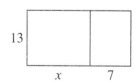
13
x 7

c.

20
32   13

d.
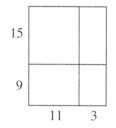
15
9
11   3

4-73. Gale and Leslie are engaged in a friendly 60-mile bike race that started at noon. The graph at right represents their progress so far.

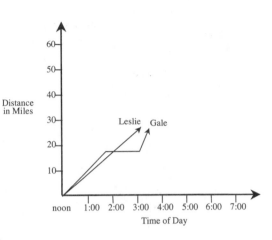

Distance in Miles

Time of Day

a. What does the intersection of the two lines represent?

b. At what time (approximately) did Leslie pass Gale?

c. About how far had Leslie traveled when she passed Gale?

d. What do you think happened to Gale between 1:30 and 3:00?

e. If Leslie continues at a steady pace, when will she complete the race?

4-74. Write an equation (rule) for each of the $x \rightarrow y$ tables below. Then, on one set of axes, use each rule to graph.

a.

x	y
8	23
2	5
-3	-10
9	26
x	

b.

x	y
6	32
-2	-8
0	2
10	52
x	

4-75. Translate each part below from symbols into words or from words into symbols.

a. $-y + 8$

b. $2x - 48$

c. $(x + 3)^2$

d. The opposite of six times the square of a number.

e. A number multiplied by itself, then added to five.

4.2.2 When are they the same?

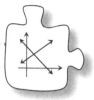

Writing Rules from Word Problems

In Lesson 4.2.1, you discovered that the point of intersection of two lines or curves can have an important meaning. Finding points of intersection is another strategy you can use to solve problems, especially those with two quantities being compared.

Analyze the following situations using the multiple tools you have studied so far.

4-76.   BUYING BICYCLES

Latanya and George are saving up money because they both want to buy new bicycles. Latanya opened a savings account with $50. She just got a job and is determined to save an additional $30 a week. George started a savings account with $75. He is able to save $25 a week.

Your Task: Use at least **two different ways** to find the time (in weeks) when Latanya and George will have the same amount of money in their savings accounts. Be prepared to share your methods with the class.

4-77.   Did you graph the scenario in problem 4-76? If not, graph a line for Latanya and another line for George on the same set of axes. Confirm your answer to problem 4-76 on the graph. Consider the questions below to help you decide how to set up the graph.

- What should the *x*-axis represent? What should the *y*-axis represent?

- How should the axes be scaled?

- Should the amounts in the savings accounts be graphed on the same set of axes or graphed separately? Why?

4-78.   If you have not done so already, consider how to use rules to confirm the point of intersection for Latanya's and George's lines.

a.   Write a rule for Latanya's savings account.

b.   Write a rule for George's savings account.

c.   Use the rules to check your solution to problem 4-76.

4-79.   Gerardo decided to use tables to find the point of intersection of the lines $y = 4x - 6$ and $y = -2x + 3$. His tables are shown below.

$y = 4x - 6$

IN (x)	−3	−2	−1	0	1	2	3
OUT (y)	−18	−14	−10	−6	−2	2	6

$y = -2x + 3$

IN (x)	−3	−2	−1	0	1	2	3
OUT (y)	9	7	5	3	1	−1	−3

a.   Examine his tables. Is there a common point that makes both rules true? If not, can you describe where the point of intersection is?

b.   Now graph the rules on the same set of axes. Where do the lines intersect?

c.   Use the rules to confirm your answer to part (b).

4-80.   It's the end of the semester, and the clubs at school are recording their profits. The Science Club started out with $20 and has increased its balance by an average of $10 per week. The Math Club saved $5 per week and started out with $50 at the beginning of the semester.

a.   Create an equation for each club. Let x represent the number of weeks and y represent the balance of the club's account.

b.   Graph both lines on one set of axes. When do the clubs have the same balance?

c.   What is the balance at that point?

4-81.   Examine the rectangle formed with algebra tiles at right.

a.   Find the area of the entire rectangle. That is, what is the sum of the areas of the algebra tiles?

b.   Find the perimeter of the entire rectangle. Show all work.

4-82.   On graph paper, plot the points (−3, 7) and (2, −3) and draw a line through them. Then name the x- and y-intercepts of the line.

Algebra Connections

4-83.   Use the rectangle at right to answer the following questions.

   a.   Find the area of the entire rectangle. Explain how you
        found your solution.

   b.   Calculate the perimeter of the figure.

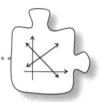

4-84.   In Spring, the daily high temperature in Boulder, Colorado rises about $\frac{1}{3}$ degree per
          day. On Friday, May 2, the temperature reached 74°. Predict when the temperature
          will reach 90°.

4.2.3 When are they the same?

Solving Systems Algebraically

So far in Section 4.2, you have solved systems of equations by graphing two lines and finding
where they intersect. However, it is not always convenient (nor accurate) to solve by graphing.

Today you will explore a new way to approach solving a system of equations. Questions to ask
your teammates today include:

> How can you find a rule?
>
> How can you compare two rules?
>
> How can you use what you know about solving?

4-85.   CHUBBY BUNNY

   Use tables, rules, and a graph to find
   and check the solution for the problem
   below.

   Barbara has a bunny that weighs 5
   pounds and gains 3 pounds per
   year. Her cat weighs 19 pounds
   and gains 1 pound per year. When
   will the bunny and the cat weigh
   the same amount?

4-86.   SOLVING SYSTEMS OF EQUATIONS ALGEBRAICALLY

In problem 4-85, you found rules like those shown below to represent the weights of Barbara's cat and bunny. For these rules, x represents the number of years and y represents the weight of the animal.

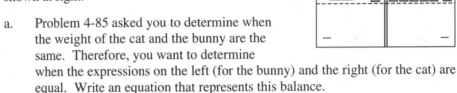

$$y = \underbrace{5 + 3x}_{\substack{\text{weight of} \\ \text{bunny}}} \quad \text{and} \quad y = \underbrace{19 + x}_{\substack{\text{weight of} \\ \text{cat}}}$$

Since you want to know when the weights of the cat and bunny are the same, you can use an equation mat to represent this relationship, as shown at right.

a.   Problem 4-85 asked you to determine when the weight of the cat and the bunny are the same. Therefore, you want to determine when the expressions on the left (for the bunny) and the right (for the cat) are equal. Write an equation that represents this balance.

b.   Solve your equation for x, which represents years. According to your solution, how many years will it take for the bunny and the cat to weigh the same number of pounds? Does this answer match your answer from the graph of problem 4-85?

c.   How much do the cat and bunny weigh at this time?

4-87.   CHANGING POPULATIONS

Post Falls High School in Idaho has 1160 students and is growing by 22 students per year. Richmond High School in Indiana has 1900 students and is shrinking by 15 students per year.

a.   Without graphing, write a rule that represents the population at Richmond High School and another rule that represents the population at Post Falls High School. Let x represent years and y represent population.

b.   Graphing the rules for part (a) is challenging because of the large numbers involved. Using a table could take a long time. Therefore, this problem is a good one to solve algebraically, the way you solved problem 4-86.

    Use the rules together to write an equation that represents when these high schools will have the same population. Then solve your equation to find out when the schools' populations will be the same.

c.   What will the population be at that time?

Algebra Connections

4-88.   PUTTING IT ALL TOGETHER

Find the solution to the problem below by **graphing** and also by **solving an equation**. The solutions using both methods should match, so be sure to review your work carefully if the results disagree.

Your school planted two trees when it was first opened. One tree, a ficus, was 6 feet tall when it was planted and has grown 1.5 feet per year. The other tree, an oak, was grown from an acorn (on the ground) and has grown 2 feet per year. When will the trees be the same height? How tall will the trees be when they are the same height?

4-89.   Ms. Harlow calls the method you have been using today to solve equations the **Equal Values Method**. Explain why this name makes sense.

METHODS AND MEANINGS

Solving a Linear Equation

When solving an equation like the one shown below, several important strategies are involved.

- **Simplify.** Combine like terms and "make zeros" on each side of the equation whenever possible.

- **Keep equations balanced.** The "equals" sign in an equation indicates that the expressions on the left and right are balanced. Anything done to the equation must keep that balance.

$$3x - 2 + 4 = x - 6 \quad \text{combine like terms}$$
$$3x + 2 = x - 6$$
$$\underline{-x \qquad = -x} \quad \text{subtract } x \text{ on both sides}$$
$$2x + 2 = -6$$
$$\underline{-2 = -2} \quad \text{subtract 2 on both sides}$$
$$\frac{2x}{2} = \frac{-8}{2} \quad \text{divide both sides by 2}$$
$$x = -4$$

- **Get x alone.** Isolate the variable on one side of the equation and the constants on the other.

- **Undo operations.** Use the fact that addition is the opposite of subtraction and that multiplication is the opposite of division to solve for x. For example, in the equation $2x = -8$, since the 2 and x are multiplied, dividing both sides by 2 will get x alone.

4-90. A local restaurant offers a Dim Sum lunch special that includes two dumplings, three egg rolls, a sweet bun, and a drink. Susan and her friends ordered four Dim Sum lunch specials.

How many of each item should they receive?

4-91. Kenneth claims that (2, 0) is the point of intersection of the lines $y = -2x + 4$ and $y = x - 2$. Is he correct? How do you know?

4-92. Graph the lines $y = 2x - 3$ and $y = -x + 3$.

a. Where do they intersect? Label the point on the graph.

b. Find the point of intersection using the Equal Values Method. That is, start by combining both equations into one equation that you can solve for x.

c. Which method is easier, graphing or using algebra to solve?

4-93. Determine the coordinates of each point of intersection without graphing.

a. $y = 2x - 3$
    $y = 4x + 1$

b. $y = 2x - 5$
    $y = -4x - 2$

4-94. MORE OR LESS

Judy has $20 and is saving at a rate of $6 per week. Ida has $172 and is spending at a rate of $4 per week. After how many weeks will each have the same amount of money?

a. Write an equation using x and y for Judy and Ida. What does x represent? What does y represent?

b. Solve this problem using any method you choose.

4.2.4 How can I use $y = mx + b$?

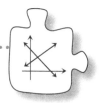

Extending the Web to Other Linear Situations

Today you will take what you have learned in this chapter and **apply** it to linear situations that are not tile patterns.

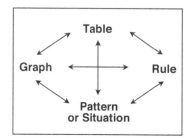

4-95.   EXTENDING THE WEB TO NEW
          SITUATIONS: TEAM CHALLENGE

Today you are going to **apply** what you
know about the starting point (Figure 0),
growth factor, and the **connections** between
representations to answer some challenging questions in real-life situations. The
information in each question, parts (a) through (e) below, describes a different
situation. All of the situations are **linear** (when graphed, they are lines).

Based on the given information, answer the questions in each problem. Show your
answers completely and explain your strategies for answering the questions. You
may answer these problems in any order, but make sure you answer each one
completely before moving to another problem.

Work together as a team. The more you listen to how other people see the
connections and share your own ideas, the more you will know at the end of this
challenge. Stick together and be sure to talk through every idea.

Each person will turn in his or her own paper at the end of activity, showing
solutions and explanations to each problem. Your work does *not* need to be identical
to your teammates' work, but you should have talked and agreed that all
explanations are correct.

a.   SAVING MONEY

Julia has $325 in her savings account. She just got a
new job and will be saving money every month. If she
always deposits the same amount, how much money
will be in her account after she has been saving for a
year? (Assume she never spends money from this
account.)

Number of Months	Money in Account
...	...
7	$780
8	$845
9	$910
...	...

Problem continues on next page →

4-95. *Problem continued from previous page.*

b.   POPULATION GROWTH

The $x \rightarrow y$ table, graph, rule, and words below each describe a different town. Based on the information you are given about each town's population, decide which town is growing the fastest. Explain how you know.

Population of Town A

Year	Number of People
1975	32,000
1979	50,000
1980	54,500

Population of Town B

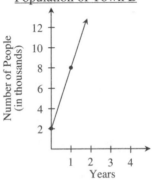

Population of Town C

If x = year and y = number of people, then:

$$y = 46000 - 5200x$$

Population of Town D

Town D is growing. Oddly, the same number of people moves to the town each year. Two years ago, the town had 9100 people. Now the town has 15,500 people.

c.   FUNDRAISING

The graph at right describes the money two clubs are earning from fundraising. In how many weeks will the two clubs have the same amount of money? Explain your thinking completely.

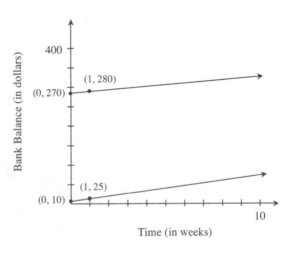

Problem continues on next page →

4-95.   *Problem continued from previous page.*

d.   STORY TIME

The graph and $x \to y$ tables below describe a situation. Write a story that fits the given information. Show the **connections** between the information you are given and the information in your story. Your story must give meaning to the point of intersection.

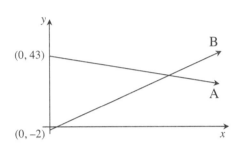

Line A			Line B	
x	*y*		*x*	*y*
⋮	⋮		⋮	⋮
8	11		4	22
9	7		5	28
10	3		⋮	⋮
⋮	⋮			

e.   VIDEO RENTAL

Gina has a prepaid video rental card. She currently has a credit of $84 on the card.

The graph at right describes the amount of money there was on the card recently. Use this information to determine:

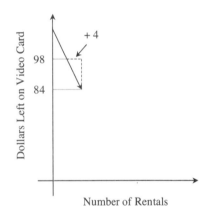

- How much one video rental costs.

- How many more videos can Gina rent before the card is used up.

METHODS AND MEANINGS

MATH NOTES

The Equal Values Method

The **Equal Values Method** is a non-graphing method to find the point of intersection or solution to a system of equations.

Start with two equations in $y = mx + b$ form, such as $y = -2x + 5$ and $y = x - 1$. Take the two expressions that equal y and set them equal to each other. Then solve this new equation to find x. See the example at right.

$$-2x + 5 = x - 1$$
$$-3x = -6$$
$$x = 2$$

Once you know the x-coordinate of the point of intersection, substitute your solution for x into *either* original equation to find y. In this example, the first equation is used.

$$y = -2x + 5$$
$$y = -2(2) + 5$$
$$y = 1$$

A good way to check your solution is to substitute your solution for x into *both* equations to verify that you get equal y-values.

$$y = x - 1$$
$$y = (2) - 1$$
$$y = 1$$

Write the solution as an ordered pair to represent the point on the graph where the equations intersect.

$$(2, 1)$$

Review & Preview

4-96.   Ariyonne claims that (3, 6) is the point of intersection of the lines $y = 4x - 2$ and $y = \frac{1}{2}x + 5$. Is she correct? How do you know?

4-97.   Determine the coordinates of each point of intersection without graphing.

a. $y = -x + 8$
       $y = x - 2$

b. $y = -3x$
       $y = -4x + 2$

4-98.   Graph the lines $y = 2x - 3$ and $y = 2x + 1$.

  a.   Where do they intersect?

  b.   Solve this system using the Equal Values Method.

  c.   Explain how your graph and algebraic solution relate to each other.

4-99.   CHANGING POPULATIONS

  Highland has a population of 12,200. Its population has been increasing at a rate of 300 people per year. Lowville has a population of 21,000 but is declining by 250 people per year. Assuming these rates do not change, in how many years will the populations be equal?

  a.   Write an equation that represents each city's population over time. What do your variables represent?

  b.   Solve the problem. Show your work.

4-100.   The table below shows the amount of money Francis had in his bank account each day since he started his new job.

Days at New Job	Money in Account
0	$27
1	$70
2	$113
3	$156

  a.   Write a rule for the amount of money in Francis's account. Let x represent the number of days and y represent the number of dollars in the account.

  b.   When will Francis have more than $1000 in his account?

4-101.   Kathy is thinking of a number. When she triples her number, adds eighteen, and then subtracts her original number from the sum, she gets four. What is Kathy's original number?

4-102. Graph the equation $y = -2x^2 - 4x$. Start by making an $x \rightarrow y$ table. Be sure to include negative values for x.

4-103. Solve this problem using Guess and Check. Write your solution in a sentence.

The number of students attending the Fall play was 150 fewer than three times the number of adults. Together, students and adults purchased 1778 tickets. How many students attended the Fall play?

4-104. Predict where each rule will cross the y-axis.

a. $y = 17x + 3$ b. $y = \frac{16}{3}x - \frac{5}{12}$ c. $y = 12 - 4x$

4-105. When Ellen started with Regina's favorite number and tripled it, the result was twelve more than twice the favorite number. Define a variable, write an equation, and then use the equation to find Regina's favorite number.

4-106. Graph the lines $y = -4x - 3$ and $y = -4x + 1$ on graph paper.

a.   Where do they intersect?

b.   Solve this system using the Equal Values Method.

c.   Explain how your graph and algebraic solution relate to each other.

Algebra Connections

Chapter 4 Closure   What have I learned?

Reflection and Synthesis

The activities below offer you a chance to reflect on what you have learned during this chapter. As you work, look for concepts that you feel very comfortable with, ideas that you would like to learn more about, and topics you need more help with. Look for **connections** between ideas as well as **connections** with material you learned previously.

①   TEAM BRAINSTORM

With your team, brainstorm a list for each of the following topics. Be as detailed as you can. How long can you make your list? Challenge yourselves. Be prepared to share your team's ideas with the class.

Topics: What have you studied in this chapter? What ideas and words were important in what you learned? Remember to be as detailed as you can.

Connections: What topics, ideas, and words that you learned *before* this chapter are **connected** to the new ideas in this chapter? Again, make your list as long as you can.

MAKING CONNECTIONS

The following is a list of the vocabulary used in this chapter. The words that appear in bold are new to this chapter. Make sure that you are familiar with all of these words and know what they mean. Refer to the glossary or index for any words that you do not yet understand.

b	continuous	coordinates
dependent variable	discrete	**Equal Values Method**
equation	**Figure 0**	graph
growth	independent variable	*m*
pattern	**point of intersection**	**representation**
rule	solution	starting value
system of equations	**web**	$x \rightarrow y$ table
x- and *y*-intercepts	$y = mx + b$	

Make a concept map showing all of the **connections** you can find among the key words and ideas listed above. To show a **connection** between two words, draw a line between them and explain the **connection**, as shown in the example below. A word can be **connected** to any other word as long as there is a **justified connection**. For each key word or idea, provide a sketch that illustrates the idea (see the example below).

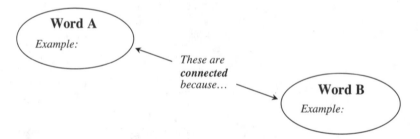

Your teacher may provide you with vocabulary cards to help you get started. If you use the cards to plan your concept map, be sure either to re-draw your concept map on your paper or to glue the vocabulary cards to a poster with all of the **connections** explained for others to see and understand.

While you are making your map, your team may think of related words or ideas that are not listed above. Be sure to include these ideas on your concept map.

③　　　SUMMARIZING MY UNDERSTANDING

This section gives you an opportunity to show what you know about certain math topics or ideas. Your teacher will give you directions for exactly how to do this.

④　　　WHAT HAVE I LEARNED?

This section will help you evaluate which types of problems you have seen with which you feel comfortable and those with which you need more help. This section appears at the end of every chapter to help you check your understanding. Even if your teacher does not assign this section, it is a good idea to try the problems and find out for yourself what you know and what you need to work on.

Solve each problem as completely as you can. The table at the end of the closure section has answers to these problems. It also tells you where you can find additional help and practice on problems like these.

CL 4-107. Examine the pattern below.

Figure 1

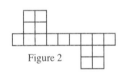
Figure 2

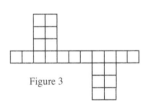
Figure 3

a.　On graph paper, sketch Figure 0 and Figure 4.

b.　Make a table showing Figure 0 through Figure 4.

c.　Write a rule to represent the pattern.

d.　On graph paper, create a graph of the number of tiles in each figure.

e.　What is the growth for the pattern?

f.　Predict how many tiles Figure 100 will have.

CL 4-108. Are the two expressions below equal? Show how you know.

$$4x^2 + 2x - 5 - 3x \quad \text{and} \quad 6x^2 - x + 3 - 2x^2 - 8$$

CL 4-109. Priscilla and Ursula went fishing. Priscilla brought a full box of 32 worms and used one worm every minute. Ursula brought a box with five worms and decided to dig for more before she began fishing. Ursula dug up two worms per minute. When did Priscilla and Ursula have the same number of worms? Show how you know.

CL 4-110. Examine the graph at right.

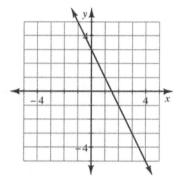

a. Give two ways you can tell that the rule $y = 2x - 3$ does not match the graph.

b. Make a graph that matches the rule $y = 2x - 3$.

c. Find a rule that represents the graph at right.

CL 4-111. Consider the rule $y = 5x + 7$.

a. How many tiles are in Figure 0?

b. Which figure has 37 tiles?

c. In the equation $y = mx + b$, what do the letters m and b represent?

CL 4-112. For each pair of lines below, solve the system by **graphing** and solve it **algebraically** using the Equal Values Method. Explain how the graph confirms the algebraic result.

a. $y = 7x - 5$ and $y = -2x + 13$

b. $y = 3x - 1$ and $y = 3x + 2$

CL 4-113. To rent a jet ski at Sam's costs $25 plus $3 per hour. At Claire's, it costs $5 plus $8 per hour. At how many hours will the rental cost at both shops be equal?

a. Write an equation that represents each shop's charges. What do your variables represent?

b. Solve the problem. Show your work.

Algebra Connections

CL 4-114. Simplify the following expressions, if possible.

a. $x + 4x - 3 + 3x^2 - 2x$

b. $2x + 4y^2 - 6y^2 - 9 - x + 3x$

c. $3x^2 + 10y - 2y^2 + 4x - 14$

d. $20 + 3xy - 4xy + y^2 + 10 - y^2$

e. Evaluate the expressions in parts (a) and (b) above when $x = 5$ and $y = -2$.

CL 4-115. Copy and complete the table for the linear pattern below.

IN (x)	−4	−3	−2	−1	0	1	2	3	4
OUT (y)					−2	3	8		

a. What is the y-intercept? What is the growth factor?

b. Find the rule for this line.

c. If the output number (y) is –52, what was the input number (x)?

CL 4-116. Use Guess and Check to solve the problem below.

For the school play, the advance tickets cost $3 and tickets at the door cost $5. Thirty more tickets were sold at door than in advance, and $2630 was collected. How many tickets were sold at the door? Write your answer in a sentence.

CL 4-117. Check your answers using the table at the end of the closure section. Which problems do you feel confident about? Which problems were hard? Use the table to make a list of topics you need help on and a list of topics you need to practice more.

⑤   HOW AM I THINKING?

This course focuses on five different **Ways of Thinking**: reversing thinking, justifying, generalizing, making connections, and applying and extending understanding. These are some of the ways in which you think while trying to make sense of a concept or to solve a problem (even outside of math class). During this chapter, you have probably used each Way of Thinking multiple times without even realizing it!

This closure activity will focus on one of these Ways of Thinking: **reversing thinking**. Read the description of this Way of Thinking at right.

Think about the topics that you have learned during this chapter. When did you undo a process? When did you try to go backward in your problem-solving process? You may want to

Reversing Thinking

To reverse your thinking can be described as "thinking backward." You think this way when you want to understand a concept in a new direction. Often, it requires you to try to undo a process. When you catch yourself thinking, *"What if I try to go backwards?"*, you are reversing your thinking.

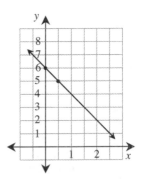

What if I go backwards?

flip through the chapter to refresh your memory about the problems that you have worked on. Discuss any ideas you have with the rest of the class. Once your discussion is complete, examine some of the ways you have **reversed your thinking** as you answer the questions below.

a. If you know how to go from one representation to another, then there is a way to **reverse the process**. Consider the web connection graph ↔ rule.

   i.   Find the equation of the line graphed at right.

   ii. Now **reverse the process**. On graph paper, graph the rule $y = 2x - 3$.

   iii. Explore another connection on the web where you **reversed your thinking**. Find or create a problem that represents one direction of solving. Then write and solve another problem that requires you to reverse the process.

Continues on next page →

Algebra Connections

⑤ *Continued from previous page.*

b. Usually, if you change an expression into an equivalent expression, there is a way to **reverse the process** to return to the original expression. Consider this as you answer the questions below.

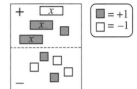

i.   On your paper, write and simplify the expression represented on the expression mat at right.

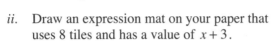

ii. Draw an expression mat on your paper that uses 8 tiles and has a value of $x + 3$.

iii. Explain how you **reversed your thinking** from part (*i*) to solve part (*ii*) above.

c. Now consider how you can **reverse your thinking** when solving a problem with proportional relationships.

i.   For example, if Mr. Wallis pays $25 for 10 gallons of gasoline, how much would he pay to fill his scooter (which uses 3 gallons of gasoline)?

ii. Now write a question about Mr. Wallis's gasoline use that would require you to **reverse your thinking** from part (a) to solve. Explain why and how it requires you to **reverse your thinking**.

Answers and Support for Closure Activity #4
What Have I Learned?

Problem	Solution	Need Help?	More Practice
CL 4-107.	a.	Sections 3.1 and 4.1, Lesson 4.1.7 Math Notes box	Problems 4-8, 4-9, 4-11, 4-21, 4-35, 4-36, 4-37, 4-49, 4-59, and 4-60

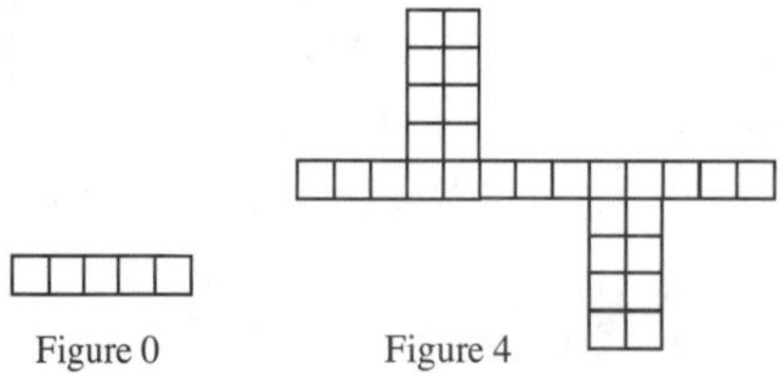

a.

Figure 0   Figure 4

b.

Figure Number	0	1	2	3	4
Number of Tiles	5	11	17	23	29

c. $y = 6x + 5$

d.

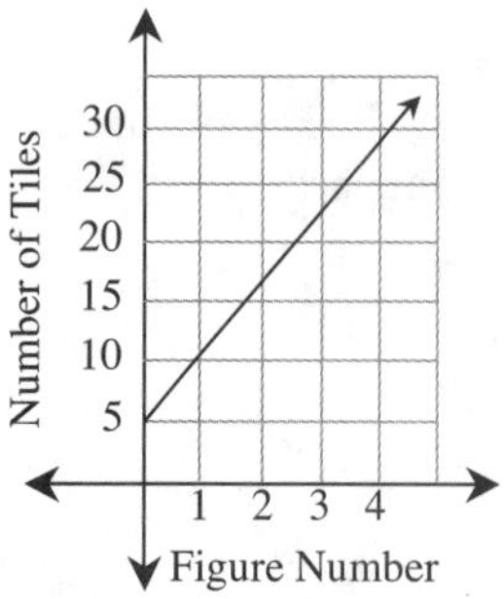

Number of Tiles

30
25
20
15
10
5

1 2 3 4
Figure Number

e. Each figure has 6 more tiles than the previous figure.

f. Figure 100 will have 605 tiles.

CL 4-108. yes; $4x^2 - x - 5 = 4x^2 - x - 5$

Lesson 2.1.5 Math Notes box

Problem 4-6

CL 4-109. They will have the same number of worms after 9 minutes.

Lesson 4.2.1 Math Notes box, Lesson 4.2.2

Problems 4-80, 4-85, 4-87, 4-88, 4-94, and 4-99

Problem	Solution	Need Help?	More Practice
CL 4-110.	a. The line goes down as x increases. The y-intercept is at +3. b. See graph at right. c. $y = -2x + 3$ 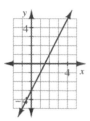	Lessons 4.1.3, 4.1.4, and 4.1.6; Lesson 4.1.7 Math Notes box	Problems 4-19, 4-27, 4-36, 4-49, 4-50, 4-51, 4-54, and 4-55
CL 4-111.	a. There are 7 tiles in figure 0. b. Figure 6 has 37 tiles. c. m represents the growth factor, and b represents the number of tiles in Figure 0.	Lessons 4.1.2 and 4.1.4, Lesson 4.1.7 Math Notes box	Problems 4-10, 4-11, 4-26, 4-29, 4-52, 4-54, 4-56, and 4-62
CL 4-112.	a. The two lines intersect at the point (2, 9). 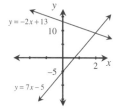 b. There is no solution to the system of equations, because the lines are parallel. 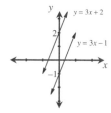	Lesson 4.2.1 Math Notes box, Lesson 4.2.3, problem 4-86, Lesson 4.2.4 Math Notes box	Problems 4-68, 4-88, 4-92, 4-96, 4-97, 4-98, and 4-106
CL 4-113.	a. $y = 25 + 3x$ and $y = 5 + 8x$; x represents the number of hours rental, and y represents the cost. b. After 4 hours of ski rental, the cost at both shops will be equal.	Lesson 4.2.1 Math Notes box, Lesson 4.2.2	Problems 4-80, 4-85, 4-87, 4-88, 4-94, and 4-99

Problem	Solution	Need Help?	More Practice
CL 4-114.	a. $3x^2 + 3x - 3$ b. $-2y^2 + 4x - 9$ c. It cannot be simplified any further. d. $-xy + 30$ e. (a) 87; (b) 3	Lesson 2.1.3 Math Notes box, Lesson 2.1.5 Math Notes box	Problems 4-6 and 4-57

CL 4-115.

IN (x)	−4	−3	−2	−1	0
OUT (y)	−22	−17	−12	−7	−2

table continued:

1	2	3	4
3	8	13	18

a. The starting value is −2. The growth factor is 5.

b. $y = 5x - 2$

c. −10

Need Help? Lesson 4.1.4, Lesson 4.1.7 Math Notes box

More Practice: Problems 4-7, 4-28, 4-34, 4-35, 4-63, 4-74, and 4-100

CL 4-116.	340 tickets were sold at the door.	Problems 1-41 and 1-42, Lesson 2.1.7 Math Notes box	Problems 4-24 and 4-103

MULTIPLICATION AND PROPORTIONS

5

CHAPTER 5   Multiplication and Proportions

In Chapter 2, you focused on simplifying expressions by adding and subtracting like terms. In Section 5.1, you will focus on multiplying expressions. You will also solve equations that contain products. While these new ideas will be introduced using algebra tiles, you will also develop a method to multiply expressions without using tiles.

Then in Section 5.2, you will continue your study of proportional situations started in Section 2.2. By the end of this chapter, you will develop an algebraic method to solve problems involving proportional relationships.

In this chapter, you will learn:

➢ How to distribute an expression with and without algebra tiles.

➢ How to multiply binomials and trinomials using algebra tiles and a generic rectangle.

➢ How to use the Distributive Property to rewrite expressions and solve equations.

➢ How to solve multi-variable equations for one of the variables.

➢ How to write and solve equations with equivalent ratios to solve problems involving proportional relationships.

Guiding Questions

Think about these questions throughout this chapter:

What is the area?

How can I write it?

What's the relationship?

How can I solve it?

Is there another way?

Chapter Outline

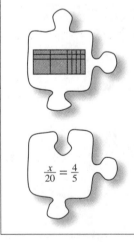

Section 5.1   Using algebra tiles and generic rectangles, you will develop a method to rewrite products, such as $(3x - 2)(4 + x)$. Then, continuing the solving focus of Chapter 3, you will study how to solve one-variable equations containing products and how to solve multi-variable equations for one of the variables.

Section 5.2   Here you will continue your study of proportional situations started in Section 2.2. You will develop algebraic techniques to solve proportions and continue to build intuition about what makes a relationship proportional.

5.1.1 What can I do with rectangles?

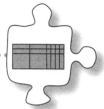

Exploring an Area Model

In Chapter 2, you used tiles to rewrite algebraic expressions involving addition and subtraction. In this chapter, you will use algebra tiles again, but this time you will rewrite expressions using multiplication.

5-1.   Your teacher will put this group of tiles on the overhead:

    a.   Using your own tiles, arrange the same group of tiles into one large rectangle. On your paper, sketch what your rectangle looks like.

    b.   What are the dimensions (length and width) of the rectangle you made? Label your sketch with its dimensions.

    c.   Write a *length · width = area* statement showing the equivalence of the area as the **product** of its length and width and as the **sum** of its parts.

5-2.   Your teacher will assign several of the expressions below. For each expression, build a rectangle using all of the tiles, if possible. Sketch each rectangle, find its dimensions, and write an expression showing the equivalence of the area as a **sum** (like $x^2 + 5x + 6$) and as a **product** (like $(x + 3)(x + 2)$). If it is not possible to build a rectangle, explain why not.

    a. $x^2 + 3x + 2$ b. $6x + 15$

    c. $2x^2 + 7x + 6$ d. $xy + x + y + 1$

    e. $2x^2 + 10x + 12$ f. $2y^2 + 6y$

    g. $y^2 + xy + 2x + 2y$ h. $3x^2 + 4x + 1$

    i. $x^2 + 2xy + y^2 + 3x + 3y + 2$ j. $2xy + 4y + x + 2$

5-3.   Make a rectangle from any number of tiles. Your rectangle must contain at least one of each of the following tiles: x^2, y^2, xy, x, y, and 1. Sketch your rectangle in your Learning Log and write its area as a **product** and as a **sum**. Explain how you know that the product and sum are equivalent. Title this entry "Area as a Product and as a Sum" and label it with today's date.

METHODS AND MEANINGS

Multiplying Algebraic Expressions with Tiles

MATH NOTES

The area of a rectangle can be written two different ways. It can be written as a **product** of its base and height or as a **sum** of its parts. For example, the area of the shaded rectangle at right can be written two ways:

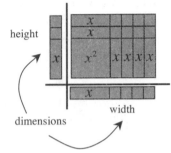

area as a product   area as a sum

$$\underbrace{(x+4)}_{base}\underbrace{(x+2)}_{height} = \underbrace{x^2+6x+8}_{area}$$

Review & Preview

5-4.   For the entire rectangle at right, find the area of each part and then find the area of the whole.

	11	8
7		
3		

5-5.   A tile pattern has 5 tiles in Figure 0 and adds 7 tiles in each new figure. Write the equation of the line that represents the growth of this pattern.

5-6.   Write the area of the rectangle at right as a **product** and as a **sum**. Refer to the Math Notes box for this lesson if you need help.

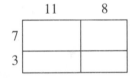

5-7.   Draw Figures 1, 2, and 3 for a tile pattern that could be described by $y = -3x + 10$.

5-8.   Fisher thinks that any two lines must have a point of intersection. Is he correct? If so, explain how you know. If not, produce a **counterexample**. That is, find two lines that do not have a point of intersection and explain how you know.

5-9.   In the last election, candidate A received twice as many votes as candidate B. Candidate C received 15,000 fewer votes than candidate B. If a total of 109,000 votes were cast, how many votes did candidate A receive?

Algebra Connections

5.1.2 How can I rewrite a product?

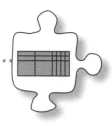

Multiplying Binomials and the Distributive Property

In Lesson 5.1.1, you made rectangles with algebra tiles and found the dimensions of the rectangles. You wrote the area both as a sum and as a product. Today you will **reverse** the process, starting with the product of the dimensions of a rectangle and finding its area as a sum.

5-10. For each of the following rectangles, find the dimensions (length and width) and write the area as the **product** of the dimensions and as the **sum** of the tiles. Remember to combine like terms whenever possible.

a.

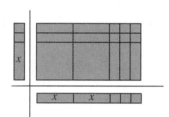

b.

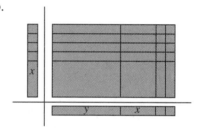

5-11. Your teacher will assign your team four of the expressions below. Use your cornerpiece to build rectangles with the given dimensions. Sketch each rectangle on your paper, label its dimensions, and write an equivalence statement for its area as a **product** and as a **sum**. Be prepared to share your solutions with the class.

a. $(2x)(4x)$

b. $(x+3)(2x+1)$

c. $2x(x+5)$

d. $(2x+1)(2x+1)$

e. $x(2x+y)$

f. $(2x+5)(x+y+2)$

g. $2(3x+5)$

h. $y(2x+y+3)$

5-12.   With the class, examine the solutions you found
         for parts (c), (e), (g), and (h) of problem 5-11.
         As you discuss your observations, you may
         want to focus on these questions:

                Do you see a pattern?

         What happens to the term outside the parentheses?

         What happens to the terms inside the parentheses?

                Does this pattern make sense?

5-13.   Using the patterns your team identified, multiply the following expressions *without*
         using your tiles. Be ready to share your process with the class.

         a. $2x(6x + 5)$ b. $6(4x + 1)$

         c. $3y(4x + 3)$ d. $7y(10x + 11y)$

5-14.   The pattern you used to multiply a one-term expression (like x) by
         a multiple-term expression (like $x + 2$) is called the **Distributive
         Property**. In your Learning Log, describe this pattern. Make up
         your own example and show the pattern in as many ways as you
         can. Title this entry "The Distributive Property" and label it with
         today's date.

───────────  Review & Preview ───────────

5-15.   Examine the rectangles formed with tiles below. For each figure, write its area as a
         product of the base and height and as a **sum** of its parts.

         a.   b.

         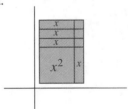   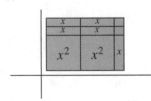

Algebra Connections

5-16.   Find the total area of each rectangle below. Each number inside the rectangle
         represents the area of that smaller rectangle, while each number along the side
         represents the length of that portion of the side.

a.

b.

5-17.   When solving $\frac{x}{6} = \frac{5}{2}$ for x, Nathan noticed that x is divided by 6.

   a.   What can he do to both sides of the equation to get x alone?

   b.   Solve for x. Then check your solution in the original equation.

   c.   Use the same process to solve this equation for x: $\frac{x}{10} = \frac{2}{5}$.

5-18.   Jamila wants to play a game called "Guess My
         Line." She gives you the following hints:
         "Two points on my line are (1, 1) and (2, 4)."

   a.   What is the growth rate of her line?
         A graph of the line may help.

   b.   What is the y-intercept of her line?

   c.   What is the equation of her line?

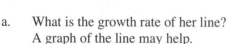

5-19.   A calculator manufacturer offers two different models for students. The company
         has sold 10,000 scientific calculators so far and continues to sell 1500 per month.
         It has sold 18,000 graphical models and continues to sell 1300 of this model each
         month. When will the sales of scientific calculators equal the sales of graphical
         calculators?

5-20.   On graph paper, make an $x \rightarrow y$ table and graph $y = 2x^2 - x - 3$. Find its x- and
         y-intercepts.

5.1.3 How can I generalize the process?

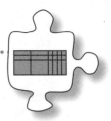

Using Generic Rectangles to Multiply

You have been using algebra tiles and the concept of area to multiply algebraic expressions. Today you will be introduced to a tool that will help you find the product of the dimensions of a rectangle. This will allow you to multiply expressions without tiles.

5-21.   Use the Distributive Property to find each product below.

 a. $6(-3x + 2)$ b. $x(4x - 2)$

 c. $5t(10 - 3t)$ d. $-4(8 - 6k + y)$

5-22.   Write the area as a **product** and as a **sum** for the composite rectangle shown at right.

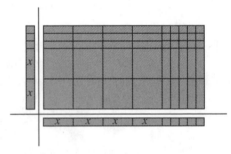

5-23.   Now examine the following diagram. How is it similar to the set of tiles in problem 5-22? How is it different? Talk with your teammates and write down all of your observations.

	$12x$	15
3		
$2x$	$8x^2$	$10x$

$4x$ 5

5-24. Diagrams like the one in problem 5-23 are referred to as **generic rectangles**. Generic rectangles allow you to use an area model to multiply expressions without using the algebra tiles. Using this model, you can multiply with values that are difficult to represent with tiles.

Draw each of the following generic rectangles on your paper. Then find the area of each part and write the area of the whole rectangle as a **product** and as a **sum**.

a.

b.

c.

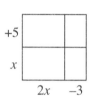

d.

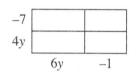

e. How did you find the area of the individual parts of each generic rectangle?

5-25. Multiply and simplify the following expressions using either a generic rectangle or the Distributive Property. For part (a), verify that your solution is correct by building a rectangle with algebra tiles.

a. $(x+5)(3x+2)$

b. $(2y-5)(5y+7)$

c. $3x(6y-11)$

d. $(5w-2p)(3w+p-4)$

5-26.   THE GENERIC RECTANGLE CHALLENGE

Copy each of the generic rectangles below and fill in the missing dimensions and areas. Then write the entire area as a product and as a sum. Be prepared to share your reasoning with the class.

a.

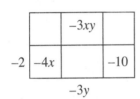

b.

c.

d.

ETHODS AND MEANINGS

The Distributive Property

MATH NOTES

The **Distributive Property** states that for any three terms a, b, and c:

$$a(b + c) = ab + ac$$

That is, when a multiplies a group of terms, such as $(b + c)$, then it multiplies *each* term of the group. For example, when multiplying $2(x + 4)$, the 2 multiplies both the x and the 4. This can be shown with **algebra tiles** or in a **generic rectangle** (see below).

	$2 \cdot x$	$2 \cdot 4$

2

      x +4

$$2(x + 4) = 2 \cdot x + 2 \cdot 4 = 2x + 8$$

The 2 multiplies each term.

5-27.   Use a generic rectangle to multiply the following expressions. Write each solution both as a sum and as a product.

   a. $(2x+5)(x+6)$ b. $(m-3)(3m+5)$

   c. $(12x+1)(x-5)$ d. $(3-5y)(2+y)$

5-28.   Solve each equation below for x. Then check your solutions.

   a. $\frac{x}{8}=\frac{3}{4}$ b. $\frac{2}{5}=\frac{x}{40}$ c. $\frac{1}{8}=\frac{x}{12}$ d. $\frac{x}{10}=\frac{12}{15}$

5-29.   Copy and complete each of the Diamond Problems below. The pattern used in the Diamond Problems is shown at right.

   a.   b.   c.   d.

5-30.   Review what you know about graphs by answering the following questions.

   a.   Find the equation of the line graphed at right.

   b.   What are its x- and y-intercepts?

   c.   On your own graph paper, graph the line.

   d.   On the same set of axes, graph a line *parallel* to the line graphed at right, but through the *origin* $(0, 0)$. Find the equation of this new line.

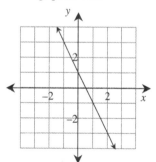

5-31.   Mailboxes Plus sends packages overnight for $5 plus $0.25 per ounce. United Packages charges $2 plus $0.35 per ounce. Mr. Molinari noticed that his package would cost the same to mail using either service. How much does his package weigh?

5-32.   Decide if the statement below is true or false. **Justify** your response.

   "The expression $(x+3)(x-1)$ is equivalent to $(x-1)(3+x)$."

5.1.4 What if an equation has a product?

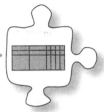

Solving Equations With Multiplication

Now that you know how to multiply algebraic expressions, you can solve equations that involve multiplication.

5-33. Review what you learned in Lesson 5.1.3 by multiplying each expression below. First decide if you will multiply each expression using the Distributive Property or using a generic rectangle. Remember to simplify your result.

a. $(6x-11)(2x+5)$ b. $-2x(15x-3)$

c. $(6-y)(y+2)$ d. $16(3-m^2)$

5-34. How can you represent $3(2x+1)$ with algebra tiles? Work with your team to build this expression.

a. Build an equation mat to represent the equation $3(2x+1)=8x-5$. Solve this equation and record your steps algebraically.

b. Check that your solution is correct by substituting your answer into the original equation.

5-35. **Multiple Choice:** Which equations below are represented by the diagram at right? Be prepared to defend your answer.

a. $3(x+1)-3-2(x+3)=-2(x+6)$

b. $3x-1-3-2x+6=-2x+12$

c. $3x+3-3-2x-6=-2x-12$

5-36. Copy one of the correct equations from problem 5-35 and solve for x. Be sure to record all of your steps. Check your solution by substituting your answer into your equation.

5-37. Your teacher will assign you several of the equations below. Work with a partner to solve the equations using algebra tiles and an equation mat. Check your solution by substituting your answer into the original equation.

    a. $3(x-4)=15$ b. $1-2(3x-5)=11$

    c. $5(y-4)=10$ d. $-2(x-2)=11$

    e. $6(x+4)=3(5x+2)$ f. $5-x(x+3)=-(x+5)(x+1)$

5-38. Now work with your team to solve each of these equations without using tiles. You may want to draw generic rectangles to help you rewrite the products.

    a. $2(y-2)=-6$ b. $43=4(x+6)-1$

    c. $(x+3)(x+4)=(x+1)(x+2)$ d. $2(x+1)+3=3(x-1)$

METHODS AND MEANINGS

Checking a Solution

MATH NOTES

To check a solution to an equation, substitute the solution into the equation and verify that it makes the two sides of the equation equal.

For example, to verify that $x=10$ is a solution to the equation $3(x-5)=15$, substitute 10 into the equation for x and then verify that the two sides of the equation are equal.

As shown at right, $x=10$ is a solution to the equation $3(x-5)=15$.

$$3(10-5)\overset{?}{=}15$$
$$3(5)\overset{?}{=}15$$
$$15=15 \quad ✔ \quad \textit{Correct!}$$

What happens if your answer is incorrect? To investigate this, test any solution that is not correct. For example, try substituting $x=2$ into the same equation. The result shows that $x=2$ is not a solution to this equation.

$$3(2-5)\overset{?}{=}15$$
$$3(-3)\overset{?}{=}15$$
$$-9\neq15 \quad$$ 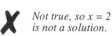 $\textit{Not true, so } x = 2$ $\textit{is not a solution.}$

5-39.   Which equation below has *no* solution? Explain how you know.

a. $4(x+1) = 2x + 4$ b. $9 - 5x + 2 = 4 - 5x$

5-40.   Rena says that if $x = -5$, the equation below is true. Her friend, Dean, says the answer is $x = 3$. Who is correct? **Justify** your conclusion.

$$9(x + 4) = 1 + 2x$$

5-41.   Find the rule for the pattern represented at right.

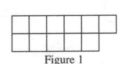

Figure 1

5-42.   Harry the Hungry Hippo is munching on the lily pads in his pond. When he got to the pond, there were 20 lily pads, but he is eating 4 lily pads an hour. Heinrick the Hungrier Hippo found a better pond with 29 lily pads! He eats 7 lily pads every hour.

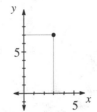

a.   If Harry and Heinrick start eating at the same time, when will their ponds have the same number of lily pads remaining?

b.   How many lily pads will be left in each hole at that time?

5-43.   Graph each equation below on the same set of axes and label the point of intersection with its coordinates.

$$y = 2x + 3 \qquad\qquad y = x + 1$$

5-44.   Shooter Magee is the Wolverines' best free-throw shooter. He normally makes three out of every four shots. In an upcoming charity event, Shooter will shoot 500 free throws. If he makes over 400 baskets, the school wins $1000. Should the Wolverines expect to win the cash for the school? Show and organize your work.

Algebra Connections

5.1.5 How can I change it to $y = mx + b$ form?

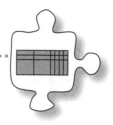

Working With Multi-Variable Equations

So far in this course, you have used your equation mat to find solutions for all types of linear equations with one variable. Today you will learn how to **apply** these skills to solving linear equations with two variables. As you work today, keep the following questions in mind:

> What is a solution to an equation? What does it look like?

> What is the growth factor?

> What is the y-intercept?

5-45.   You now have a lot of experience working with equations that compare two quantities. For example, while working with the height of a tree, you found the relationship $y = 4x + 5$, which compared x (the number of years after it was planted) with y (its height in feet). For this tree:

a.   What was its starting height? How can you tell from the equation?

b.   What was its growth rate? That is, how many feet did the tree grow per year? **Justify** your answer.

5-46.   CHANGING FORMS

You could find the growth rate and starting value for $y = 4x + 5$ quickly because the equation is in $y = mx + b$ form. But what if the equation is in a different form? Explore this situation below.

a.   The line $-6x + 2y = 10$ is written in **standard form**. Can you tell what the growth rate of the line is? Its y-intercept? Predict these values.

b.   The equation $-6x + 2y = 10$ is shown on the equation mat at right. Set up this equation on your equation mat using tiles. Using only "legal" moves, rearrange the tiles to get y by itself on the left side of the mat. Record each of your moves algebraically.

c.   Now use your result from part (b) to find the growth factor and y-intercept of the line $-6x + 2y = 10$. Did your result match your prediction in part (a)?

5-47. Your teacher will assign you one of the linear equations listed below. For your equation:

- Use algebra tiles to set up the equation on your equation mat.

- Using only "legal" moves, rearrange your tiles to create an equation that starts with "$y = ...$" Be sure to record all of your moves algebraically and be prepared to share your steps with the class.

- What is the growth factor of your line? What is the y-intercept? How can you tell?

a. $2x + y = 3x - 7$ b. $x + 2y = 3x + 4$

c. $3y + 2 = 2y - 5x$ d. $2(y - 3) = 2x - 6$

e. $5 - 3(x + 1) = 2y - 3x + 2$ f. $x - (y + 2) = 2(2x + 1)$

5-48. Solve each of the following equations for the indicated variable. Use your equation mat if it is helpful. Write down each of your steps algebraically.

a. Solve for y: $2(y - 3) = 4$

b. Solve for x: $2x + 5y = 10$

c. Solve for y: $6x + 3y = 4y + 11$

d. Solve for x: $3(2x + 4) = 2 + 6x + 10$

e. Solve for x: $y = -3x + 6$

f. Solve for p: $m = 8 - 2(p - m)$

g. Solve for y: $x^2 + 4y = (x + 6)(x - 2)$

h. Solve for q: $4(q - 8) = 7q + 5$

METHODS AND MEANINGS

Linear Equations

MATH NOTES

A **linear equation** is an equation that forms a line when it is graphed. This type of equation may be written in several different forms. Although these forms look different, they are equivalent; that is, they all graph the same line.

STANDARD FORM: An equation in $ax + by = c$ form, such as $-6x + 3y = 18$.

$y = mx + b$ **FORM:** An equation in $y = mx + b$ form, such as $y = 2x - 6$.

You can quickly find the **growth factor** and **y-intercept** of a line in $y = mx + b$ form. For the equation $y = 2x - 6$, the growth factor is 2, while the y-intercept is $(0, -6)$.

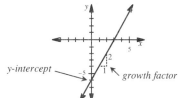

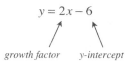

growth factor   y-intercept

5-49.   Use what you know about $y = mx + b$ to graph each of the following equations quickly on the same set of axes.

   a. $y = 3x + 5$ b. $y = -2x + 10$ c. $y = 1.5x$

5-50.   Multiply each of the following expressions. Show all of your work.

   a. $(x + 3)(4x + 5)$ b. $(-2x - 4)(3x + 4)$

   c. $(3y - 8)(-x + y)$ d. $(y - 4)(3x + 5y - 2)$

5-51.   Solve each of the following equations for the indicated variable. Show all of your steps.

a. $y = 2x - 5$ for x

b. $p = -3w + 9$ for w

c. $2m - 6 = 4n + 4$ for m

d. $3x - y = -2y$ for y

5-52.   Find the rule for the following tile pattern.

Figure 2   Figure 3   Figure 4

5-53.   Consider these two equations:

$$y = 3x - 2$$
$$y = 4 + 3x$$

a.   Graph both equations on the same set of axes.

b.   Solve this system using the Equal Values Method.

c.   Explain how the answer to part (b) agrees with the graph you made in part (a).

5-54.   Joe drove 100 miles from San Francisco to Gilroy and used 4 gallons of gas. How much gas should he expect to use for a 3000-mile trip to New York City? Be sure to **justify** your reasoning.

$5.1.6$ What kinds of equations can I solve now?

Solving Equations Without Manipulatives

So far, you have developed your equation-solving skills in three major sections of this course (Sections 2.1, 3.2, and 5.1). Today you will practice solving equations while moving away from using algebra tiles. At the end of the lesson, you will summarize everything you know about solving equations.

5-55. Your teacher will explain the way you are working today on the problems below. As you work, be sure to record all of your steps carefully. Check your solutions, if possible.

a. Solve for x: $5(4x+3)=75$

b. Solve for y: $x-2y=4$

c. Solve for x: $-6=-6(3x-8)$

d. Solve for y: $3x+6y=24$

e. Solve for x: $2-3(2x-1)=17$

f. Solve for y: $5+2(x+y)=11$

g. Solve for x: $y=-3x+4$

h. Solve for x: $x(2x-1)=2x^2+5x-12$

i. Solve for w: $2(v-3)=1-(w+4)$

j. Solve for x: $4x(x+1)=(2x-3)(2x+5)$

5-56. SUMMARY OF SOLVING EQUATIONS

Write a letter to Clarissa, a new student in class, explaining everything you have learned about how to solve equations. Clarissa does not have algebra tiles, so you will need to show her how to solve *without* the tiles. Make up examples that show all of the different equation-solving skills you have. Be sure to explain your ideas to her thoroughly so she will know what to do on her own.

5-57. Solve each of the following equations. Be sure to show your work carefully and check your answers.

    a. $2(3x-4)=22$ b. $6(2x-5)=-(x+4)$

    c. $2-(y+2)=3y$ d. $3+4(x+1)=159$

5-58. Find the dimensions of the generic rectangle at right. Then write an equivalency statement (length · width = area) of the area as a product and as a sum.

x^2	$-5x$
$3x$	-15

5-59. Consider the rule $y=\frac{1}{3}x-2$.

    a. Without graphing, find the zero of $y=\frac{1}{3}x-2$. Remember that a zero of a rule is an input that makes the output zero.

    b. Make a table and graph $y=\frac{1}{3}x-2$ on graph paper.

    c. How could you find the zero of $y=\frac{1}{3}x-2$ with your graph from part (b)? What about with the table? Explain.

5-60. One number is five more than a second number. The product of the numbers is 3300. Find the two numbers.

5-61. Ms. B and Ms. D are writing problems for an algebra book. Ms. B started with 10 problems already written, and she can write 6 problems an hour. Ms. D had no problems written, but she writes 10 problems an hour.

    a. When will Ms. B have the same number of problems written as Ms. D?

    b. How many problems will they each have written at that time?

5-62. How many yearbooks should your school order? Your student government surveyed three homeroom classes, and 55 of 90 students said that they would definitely buy a yearbook. If your school has 2000 students, approximately how many books should be ordered? Show and organize your work.

5.2.1 How can I write proportions?

Setting Up and Solving Proportions

In Chapter 2, you studied proportional situations and used several strategies to solve problems involving such situations. Since then, you have learned to set up and solve equations to solve many types of problems. Today you will investigate methods for using equations to solve proportion problems.

5-63.   Use what you know about solving equations to solve for x. Remember to check your solution to each equation. Be prepared to share your method with the class.

   a. $\frac{x}{2} = 9$ b. $\frac{x}{18} = \frac{2}{3}$ c. $\frac{3}{2} = \frac{x+3}{5}$ d. $\frac{7}{3} = \frac{4}{x}$

5-64.   POLITICAL POLL

Mr. Mears is running for mayor of Atlanta. His campaign managers are eager to determine how many citizens of Atlanta will vote for him in the upcoming election. They decided to pay a respected, impartial statistical company to survey potential voters (a process called "polling") in order to find out how many people will probably vote for Mr. Mears.

One afternoon, pollsters called 100 random potential voters in Atlanta to ask them how they would vote in the election. During that survey, 68 people indicated that they would vote for Mr. Mears.

   a.   If the pollsters had instead called 50 randomly selected potential voters, predict how many people would have said that they would vote for Mr. Mears.

   b.   Is this relationship proportional? Why or why not?

   c.   Carina decided to organize the information in a table like the one shown at right. She wants to figure out how many people will probably vote for Mr. Mears if 350,125 people vote in the election. Help her determine how many votes Mr. Mears will probably receive. Then complete her table on your paper. Be prepared to share your method with the class.

Number of Potential Voters	Number of Votes Expected for Mr. Mears
50	
100	68
350,125	

5-65. Carina noticed a pattern in her table. If she makes a **ratio** (a fraction) of the two numbers of potential voters and another ratio of the two numbers of votes for Mr. Mears, the two ratios are equal! See her notes below:

	Number of Potential Voters	Number of Votes Expected for Mr. Mears
	50	34
	100	68

$$\frac{50 \text{ number of voters}}{100 \text{ number of voters}} = \frac{1}{2} \qquad \frac{34 \text{ votes for Mears}}{68 \text{ votes for Mears}} = \frac{1}{2}$$

a. Carina wonders what would happen if she created ratios with numbers in the same row. Write two ratios using the values in the rows circled at right. Are your ratios equal?

Number of Potential Voters	Number of Votes Expected for Mr. Mears
50	34
100	68

b. What about diagonally? Will the ratios be equal? Set up some ratios and determine if they are equal.

c. Why are some ratios equal and others not?

d. Carina's neighborhood has 527 potential voters. If her neighborhood reflects the entire city, how many neighbors will probably vote for Mr. Mears? Since she does not know the answer to this question, she placed an x in the table at right.

Number of Potential Voters	Number of Votes Expected for Mr. Mears
50	34
100	68
527	x

Write an equation using two equal ratios and solve for x. Then answer her question.

5-66. Make a table and set up an equation for each proportional situation below.

a. In two minutes, Stacie can write her name 17 times. How long will it take her to write her name 85 times?

b. Eight of 29 students in your class want to attend the Winter Ball. If your class represents the entire school, how many of the 1490 students will probably attend the dance?

METHODS AND MEANINGS

Ratios and Proportions

A **ratio** is a way to compare two related numbers, such as 68 expected votes for Mr. Mears out of 100 people surveyed. It can be written with a colon, such as 68:100, or it can be written as a fraction, such as:

$$\frac{68 \text{ votes for Mr. Mears}}{100 \text{ people surveyed}}$$

A ratio can compare any two quantities, such as comparing the number of boys and girls in your class (such as 17 boys:18 girls), or comparing the heights of two people (such as $\frac{62 \text{ inches}}{65 \text{ inches}}$).

An equation that sets two ratios equal is called a **proportion**. For example, the proportion below is an equation made up of two equal ratios:

$$\frac{68 \text{ votes for Mr. Mears}}{100 \text{ people surveyed}} = \frac{34 \text{ votes for Mr. Mears}}{50 \text{ people surveyed}}$$

Review & Preview

5-67.   Chi loves to read. He can speed-read 40 pages in 3 minutes. How long should it take him to read *The Scarlet Letter*, a 265-page novel?

5-68.   GETTING IN SHAPE

Frank weighs 160 pounds and is on a diet to gain two pounds a week so that he can make the football team. John weighs 208 pounds and is on a diet to lose three pounds a week so that he can be on the wrestling team in a lower weight class.

a.   If Frank and John can meet these goals with their diets, when will they weigh the same, and how much will they weigh at that time?

b.   Clearly explain your method.

5-69.   Below are two pairs of equal ratios. For each pair, find two more ratios that are
          equal.

   a.   b. $\frac{13}{20} = \frac{65}{100} = \frac{?}{?} = \frac{?}{?}$

          $\frac{1}{5} = \frac{10}{50} = \frac{?}{?} = \frac{?}{?}$

5-70.   Find each of the following products by drawing and labeling a generic rectangle or
          by using the Distributive Property.

   a. $(x+5)(x+4)$ b. $2y(y+3)$

5-71.   Simplify the expressions below. You may want to draw or visualize algebra tiles to
          help you rewrite these problems.

   a. $(2x^2 + 3x + 5) + (x^2 + 2x + 8)$ b. $(3x^2 + 8x + 1) + (2x^2 + 8x + 4)$

   c. $(3x^2 + 5x + 7) - (4x^2 + x + 1)$ d. $(x^2 + 9x + 8) - (x^2 + 4x + 8)$

   e. $(7x^2 + x + 10) - (3x^2 + 12x + 12)$

5.2.2 What strategy can I use to solve?

$\frac{x}{20} = \frac{4}{5}$

Practice With Proportions

In the last lesson, you used equations to solve problems involving proportional situations.
Today you will practice writing and solving these special equations, called **proportions**, while
you help a student set up a recycling program for her school. As you work, focus on these
questions:

          What information can you use to answer this question?

          How can you use that information to write an equation?

5-72.   Solve for x. Remember to check your solution to each equation.

   a. $7.5 = \frac{x}{4}$ b. $\frac{x}{20} = \frac{4}{5}$ c. $\frac{x-4}{12} = \frac{7}{3}$ d. $\frac{100}{30} = \frac{4}{3x}$

5-73.   RECYCLING CLUB

Elsie is starting a recycling club at her school and hopes to use the money earned from recycling cans to buy recycling bins for the school.

Elsie first needs to figure out how much the cans that can be collected at her school will weigh, so she starts by weighing the cans in her recycling bin at home. She finds that 50 cans weigh 0.77 kg. The next day, Elsie counts cans at school and finds that her fellow students throw away 1240 cans each day.

a.   Put all of Elsie's information into a table like the one shown at right. Let x represent anything Elsie does not know yet.

# of Cans	Weight (kg)

b.   Write and solve a **proportion** (an equation setting two ratios equal) from your table. How much do all of the school's cans weigh?

c.   Elsie's school just got a new soda machine in the cafeteria. Now the students at her school consume 2070 cans a day. Add this information to your table, and then use a proportion to find out how much all of those cans weigh.

5-74.   In order to buy recycling bins for her school, Elsie plans to collect empty aluminum cans in big plastic bags and drive them to a local recycling center. Elsie wants to figure out how many days she will need to use plastic bags before she can buy the recycling bins.

a.   The recycling center pays 25 cents per kg for aluminum cans. If her school recycles 2070 cans each day, how much money will Elsie earn each day by recycling?

b.   Elsie has a friend at a local store who can get her 6 recycling bins for $14.99. Elsie thinks her school needs 30 recycling bins. Set up and solve a proportion to find out how much money Elsie needs in order to buy all of the bins for her school. Remember to check your answer.

c.   Now put it all together: Assuming Elsie recycles about 2070 cans each day, for how many days will Elsie have to recycle before she can buy her school new recycling bins?

5-75.   Jeremy enlarged the shape at right to create a similar shape. The
        side that was originally 34 units long became 51 units long. How
        long is the side that was originally 10 units long?

5-76.   Beth's favorite toy is a 4-inch-long scale model of a popular convertible. The full-
        sized convertible is 184 inches long and 74 inches wide. Use a proportion to find the
        width of Beth's model.

Ⓛ OOKING DEEPER

Rational Numbers and Closure

Any number that can be written in the form $\frac{a}{b}$ (with a and b being
integers and b not being zero) is called a **rational number**.

For example, -5, $2\frac{3}{4}$, and $0.\overline{6}$ are all rational numbers, as illustrated below.

$$-5 = \frac{-5}{1} \qquad\qquad 2\frac{3}{4} = \frac{11}{4} \qquad\qquad 0.\overline{6} = \frac{2}{3}$$

A set of numbers is called **closed** under an operation (like addition or
multiplication) when using that operation with some of those numbers always
results in one of those kinds of numbers. For example, odd numbers are
closed under multiplication since $(odd) \cdot (odd) = odd$, but are not closed under
addition since $(odd) + (odd) \neq odd$. The **closure properties** of rational
numbers state that for all rational numbers a and b, $a + b$ and $a \cdot b$ are both
rational numbers.

Review & Preview

5-77.   Solve each equation below for the indicated variable, if possible. Show all steps.

   a.   Solve for x: $2x + 22 = 12$ b.   Solve for y: $2x - y = 3$

   c.   Solve for x: $2x + 15 = 2x - 15$ d.   Solve for y: $6x + 2y = 10$

Algebra Connections

5-78.   Janelle came to bat 464 times in 131 games. At this rate, how many times should she expect to have at bat in a full season of 162 games?

5-79.   Jung's car travels 32 miles per gallon of gas. For each question below, write an equation, and then solve it.

      a.   How far will Jung's car go on 8 gallons of gas?

      b.   If Jung drives 118 miles, how much gas will be used?

5-80.   The graph at right contains the lines for $y = x + 2$ and $y = 2x - 1$.

      a.   Using the graph, what is the solution to this system?

      b.   Solve the system algebraically to confirm your answer to part (a).

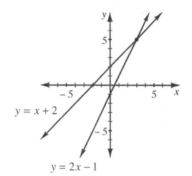

5-81.   The Math Notes box for this lesson explains that the set (or group) of odd numbers is closed under multiplication because (odd)(odd) = odd. However, the set of odd numbers is *not* closed under addition because (odd) + (odd) ≠ odd.

      a.   Examine the set of all even numbers. Is this set closed under addition? Show how you know.

      b.   Is the set of even numbers closed under multiplication? Show how you know.

5-82.   For each generic rectangle below, find the dimensions (length and width). Then write the area as a **product** of the dimensions and as a **sum**.

      a.   b.

$2x^2$	$10x$

$2x^2$	$10x$
$3x$	15

5.2.3 How can I use proportionality?

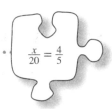

Applying Proportions

5-83.   ESTIMATING FISH POPULATIONS TEAM CHALLENGE

Fish biologists need to keep track of fish populations in the waters they monitor. They want to know, for example, how many striped bass there are in San Francisco Bay. This number changes throughout the year, however, as fish move in and out of the bay to spawn. Therefore, biologists need a way to gather current data fairly quickly and inexpensively.

Your team will be given a "lake" (paper bag) with "fish" (beans). How many fish are in your lake?

Your Task: Determine the number of fish in your lake as accurately as possible *without* actually counting the fish. Then count the fish and find out how accurate your method was. Be ready to share your process and solution with the class.

Discussion Points

What are you supposed to find? Explain in your own words.

How do you think fish biologists determine the population of fish in a lake?

What information can you gather to help you answer this question?

What tools will you need?

Can you use a proportion to determine the number of fish in your lake?
Why or why not?

Further Guidance

5-84.   Since it is impossible to count every animal, biologists use a process called "tag and recapture" to help them estimate the size of a population. Tag and recapture involves collecting a sample of animals, tagging them, and releasing them back into the wild. Later, biologists collect a new sample of the animals and count the number in the sample, distinguishing between first-time captures and recaptures. Then they use the data to estimate the population size.

Your team's task is to use the tag-and-recapture process to estimate the number of "fish" (beans) in your "lake" (paper bag).

a.   How many fish do you think are in your lake? Estimate.

b.   Use the "net" (small cup) to collect an initial sample. Carefully count the number of fish in the sample and record the data on your paper.

c.   In order to tag the fish, replace each fish in the sample with a fish of a different color. Add these tagged fish to the lake. Be careful not to let any of the fish jump out onto the floor! (Put the original fish from your sample aside. Do not return them to the lake, or else this will increase the number of fish in the lake.)

d.   Gently shake the bag to mix the fish thoroughly. Then collect another sample. Count the number of tagged and untagged fish in this new sample and record the information on your paper. Then return the entire sample to the lake.

e.   Look over the data you have collected. How many tagged fish are in the lake? How many tagged fish were in the second sample? What was the total number of fish in the second sample? Use this data to determine the total number of fish in the lake.

f.   Repeat the process outlined in parts (c) and (d) to get a second estimate of the total number of fish in the lake. Is this second estimate close to the first?

g.   **Extension:** Your solutions represent two estimates for the fish population of your lake. While it is important to get an accurate count, each time you net a sample, it costs the taxpayers $500 for your time and equipment. So far, your samples have cost a total of $1000. If you think your estimate is accurate at this point, record it on the class chart with your cost. If you think you should try another sample for better accuracy, do the same steps as before. Draw as many samples as you need, but remember that each sample costs $500.

h.   Count the fish in your lake to find the actual population. Then record your team's data on the class chart. Use the average of your estimates to represent your overall estimate of fish in the lake.

i.   Was your estimate close? Was it better than your estimate from part (a)? If not, what might have thrown it off? Is this method of counting populations accurate? Why or why not?

———— *Further Guidance section ends here.* ————

METHODS AND MEANINGS

Using Generic Rectangles to Multiply

A generic rectangle can be used to find products because it helps to organize the different areas that make up the total rectangle. For example, to multiply $(2x + 5)(x + 3)$, a generic rectangle can be set up and completed as shown below. Notice that each product in the generic rectangle represents the area of that part of the rectangle.

	$2x$	$+5$
x	$2x^2$	$5x$
$+3$	$6x$	15

$$(2x + 5)(x + 3) = 2x^2 + 11x + 15$$

area as a product   area as a sum

Note that while a generic rectangle helps organize the problem, its size and scale is not important.

5-85.   Find each of the following products by drawing and labeling a generic rectangle or by using the Distributive Property.

a. $(x + 2)(x + 8)$

b. $(2m + 30)(m + 20)$

c. $x(y + 10)$

d. $(2x + 3)(3x + 4)$

5-86.   Did you know that the Statue of Liberty was a gift
         from France? It was shipped to New York and
         reassembled on an island in New York Harbor. It was
         finished in 1886. The distance from the base to the
         torch is 152 feet. The gift store sells a scale model of
         the statue measuring 18 inches (1.5 feet) tall.

    a.   If the length of the index finger on the real statue
         is eight feet, what is its length on the scale
         model?

    b.   Alex wanted to know the length of the right arm
         on the statue. He measured the model, and the
         right arm was five inches long. What is the
         length of the arm on the statue?

5-87.   Solve each of the following equations for x. Then check each solution.

    a. $\frac{x}{16} = \frac{7}{10}$ b. $\frac{6}{15} = \frac{3}{x}$ c. $\frac{2x}{5} = \frac{12}{8}$ d. $-8 = \frac{2}{x}$

5-88.   Graph the lines $y = -4x + 3$ and $y = x - 7$ on the same set of axes. Then find their
         point of intersection.

5-89.   Change each equation below into $y = mx + b$ form.

    a. $y - 4x = -3$ b. $3y - 3x = 9$

    c. $3x + 2y = 12$ d. $2(x - 3) + 3y = 0$

Chapter 5 Closure What have I learned?

Reflection and Synthesis

The activities below offer you a chance to reflect on what you have learned during this chapter. As you work, look for concepts that you feel very comfortable with, ideas that you would like to learn more about, and topics you need more help with. Look for **connections** between ideas as well as **connections** with material you learned previously.

①   TEAM BRAINSTORM

With your team, brainstorm a list for each of the following topics. Be as detailed as you can. How long can you make your list? Challenge yourselves. Be prepared to share your team's ideas with the class.

Topics: What have you studied in this chapter? What ideas and words were important in what you learned? Remember to be as detailed as you can.

Connections: What topics, ideas, and words that you learned *before* this chapter are **connected** to the new ideas in this chapter? Again, make your list as long as you can.

② MAKING CONNECTIONS

The following is a list of the vocabulary used in this chapter. The words that appear in bold are new to this chapter. Make sure that you are familiar with all of these words and know what they mean. Refer to the glossary or index for any words that you do not yet understand.

area	dimensions	**Distributive Property**
generic rectangles	growth	"legal" moves
linear equation	product	**proportion**
ratio	similar	solution
solve	**standard form**	starting value
sum	$y = mx + b$	

Make a concept map showing all of the **connections** you can find among the key words and ideas listed above. To show a **connection** between two words, draw a line between them and explain the **connection**, as shown in the example below. A word can be **connected** to any other word as long as there is a **justified connection**. For each key word or idea, provide a sketch that illustrates the idea (see the example below).

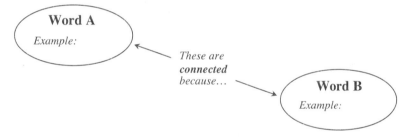

Your teacher may provide you with vocabulary cards to help you get started. If you use the cards to plan your concept map, be sure either to re-draw your concept map on your paper or to glue the vocabulary cards to a poster with all of the **connections** explained for others to see and understand.

While you are making your map, your team may think of related words or ideas that are not listed above. Be sure to include these ideas on your concept map.

③ SUMMARIZING MY UNDERSTANDING

This section gives you an opportunity to show what you know about certain math topics or ideas. Your teacher will give you directions for exactly how to do this.

④ WHAT HAVE I LEARNED?

This section will help you evaluate which types of problems you have seen with which you feel comfortable and those with which you need more help. This section appears at the end of every chapter to help you check your understanding. Even if your teacher does not assign this section, it is a good idea to try the problems and find out for yourself what you know and what you need to work on.

Solve each problem as completely as you can. The table at the end of the closure section has answers to these problems. It also tells you where you can find additional help and practice on problems like these.

CL 5-90. Two brothers, Martin and Morris, are in their backyard. Morris is taking down a wall on one side of the yard while Martin is building a wall on the other side. Martin starts from scratch and lays 2 bricks every minute. Meanwhile, Morris takes down 3 bricks each minute from his wall. It takes Morris 55 minutes to finish tearing down his wall.

  a. How many bricks were originally in the wall that Morris started tearing down?

  b. Represent this situation with equations, tables, and a graph.

  c. When did the two walls have the same number of bricks?

CL 5-91. Rewrite each of these products as a sum.

  a. $6x(2x + y - 5)$ b. $(2x - 11)(x + 4)$

  c. $(7x)(2xy)$ d. $(x - 2)(3 + y)$

CL 5-92. Find the missing areas and dimensions for each generic rectangle below. Then write each area as a sum and as a product.

  a.

            b.

CL 5-93. For each equation below, solve for x.

  a. $(x - 1)(x + 7) = (x + 1)(x - 3)$ b. $2x - 5(x + 4) = -2(x + 3)$

CL 5-94. For each equation below, solve for y.

      a. $6x - 2y = 4$ b. $6x + 3y = 4x - 2y + 8$

      c.   Find the growth factors and y-intercepts for the equations in parts (a) and (b).

CL 5-95. For every 42 berries Samantha picks, her dog Clepto eats 7 berries. Samantha picked 462 berries last Saturday.

      a.   How many berries did Clepto eat last Saturday? Answer this question by writing and solving a proportion.

      b.   After Clepto was finished eating, how many berries did Samantha take home on Saturday?

CL 5-96. Solve for each variable.

      a. $\frac{x}{7} = \frac{3}{10}$ b. $\frac{8}{m} = \frac{3}{22}$ c. $\frac{11}{5} = \frac{2p}{3}$

CL 5-97. Kirstin enlarged her favorite picture at right on her computer so that the enlarged figure was similar to her original drawing. If the measurements of the original and new figure are as shown in the diagram at right, find x. Show all work.

CL 5-98. Find x and y for the system of equations at right:

$$y = 3x - 5$$
$$y = -x + 23$$

CL 5-99. Check your answers using the table at the end of the closure section. Which problems do you feel confident about? Which problems were hard? Use the table to make a list of topics you need help on and a list of topics you need to practice more.

This course focuses on five different **Ways of Thinking**: reversing thinking, justifying, generalizing, making connections, and applying and extending understanding. These are some of the ways in which you think while trying to make sense of a concept or to solve a problem (even outside of math class). During this chapter, you have probably used each Way of Thinking multiple times without even realizing it!

So far, each chapter of this course has focused on a different Way of Thinking, as you can see in the table below.

Chapter 1	**making connections**
Chapter 2	**justifying**
Chapter 3	**generalizing**
Chapter 4	**reversing thinking**

This closure activity will focus on the fifth Way of Thinking: **applying and extending**. Read the description of this Way of Thinking at right.

Think about the topics that you have learned during this chapter. When did you broaden your understanding of a concept? When did you apply an idea to solve a real-life problem? You may want to flip through the chapter to refresh your memory about the problems that you have worked on. Discuss any ideas you have with the rest of the class.

Once your discussion is complete, examine some of the ways you have **applied** and **extended** your understanding as you answer the questions below.

Applying and Extending

To extend understanding means to increase or expand what you know about an idea. You think this way when you try to apply your knowledge in new ways or consider new possibilities. An application is often the answer to a question like, *"How can I use this?"* When you catch yourself thinking, *"What if…"*, you are usually trying to extend your understanding.

a. One way you **applied** your understanding of area was to use an area model to multiply expressions. For example, the area of the rectangle at right represents the product $(4x + 3)(2x - 7)$.

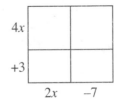

    i.   Copy and complete the generic rectangle and write its area as a sum.

Continues on next page →

⑤   *Continued from previous page.*

      ii.   Now **apply** your understanding to find two more products similar to $(4x + 3)(2x - 7)$. In other words, create your own products in the form $(ax + b)(cx + d)$ and use an area model to multiply.

      iii.   Now **extend** this idea: What if one of the expressions being multiplied has three terms? How can a generic rectangle be used to multiply two expressions such as $(x - 3)(3y + 2x + 1)$? Discuss this with your team. Then create and complete a generic rectangle for $(x - 3)(3y + 2x + 1)$ and write its area as a sum.

      iv.   Part (*iii*) was an **extension** because it considered a new "What if…?" question that came from the study of multiplying expressions. Now, as a team, write your own "What if…?" questions that come from this work. Be ready to share your questions with the class.

   b.   Now examine how you can **apply** proportional reasoning to solve different problems. With your team, answer the questions below.

      i.   The math club is sponsoring a math contest, and to prepare, Clarisse needs to sharpen 568 pencils. Luckily, the club has an electric pencil sharpener! When Clarisse started to sharpen the first 8 pencils, she noticed that it took her 2.5 minutes. Assuming she can continue sharpening pencils at the same rate, how long will it take her to sharpen the rest of the pencils? Write and solve a proportion to answer this question.

      ii.   To pay for trophies, the math club will sell 176 raffle tickets for $1 each. The club will randomly select 22 tickets to award prizes. If the club sponsor, Mr. Wallis, bought 40 tickets, will he probably win a prize? If so, how many prizes do you predict he would win? Show how you found our answer.

      iii.   Now, with your team, create at least two problems that would require someone to **apply** proportional reasoning to solve. Be creative! Be ready to share your problems with the class.

Answers and Support for Closure Activity #4
What Have I Learned?

Problem	Solution	Need Help?	More Practice
CL 5-90.	a. $55(3) = 165$ bricks	Lesson 5.1.5 Math Notes box	Problems 5-19, 5-31, 5-42, 5-45, 5-61, and 5-68

b. Martin's rule: $y = 2x$

Morris's rule: $y = 165 - 3x$

Martin's table:

Min.	Bricks
0	0
1	2
2	4
...	...
56	112
57	114

Morris's table:

Min.	Bricks
0	165
1	162
2	159
...	...
54	3
55	0

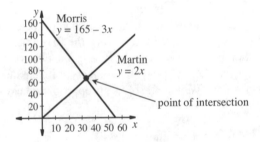

c. After 33 hours, they will each have 66 bricks.

Problem	Solution	Need Help?	More Practice
CL 5-91.	a. $12x^2 + 6xy - 30x$ b. $2x^2 - 3x - 44$ c. $14x^2y$ d. $3x + xy - 6 - 2y$	Lessons 5.1.1 and 5.1.3 Math Notes boxes	Problems 5-11, 5-13, 5-21, 5-25, 5-27, 5-33, 5-50, 5-70, and 5-85

Problem	Solution	Need Help?	More Practice

CL 5-92.

a. $(2x+1)(1+8x) = 16x^2 + 10x + 1$

	$8x$	$16x^2$	$8x$
	1	$2x$	1
		$2x$	1

b. $(2y-3)(4x+5) =$
$8xy - 12x + 10y - 15$

	5	$10y$	-15
	$4x$	$8xy$	$-12x$
		$2y$	-3

Need Help?: Lessons 5.1.1, 5.1.3, and 5.2.3 Math Notes boxes

More Practice: Problems 5-16, 5-24, 5-26, 5-58, and 5-82

CL 5-93.

a. $x = \frac{1}{2}$

b. $x = -14$

Need Help?: Lesson 5.1.3 Math Notes box, Lesson 5.1.4

More Practice: Problems 5-34, 5-37, 5-38, 5-48, 5-55, and 5-57

CL 5-94.

a. $y = 3x - 2$

b. $y = -\frac{2}{5}x + \frac{8}{5}$

c. part (a): $m = 3, b = -2$

   part (b): $m = -\frac{2}{5}, b = \frac{8}{5}$

Need Help?: Lesson 5.1.5

More Practice: Problems 5-46, 5-47, 5-48, 5-51, 5-55, 5-77, and 5-89

CL 5-95.

a. 77 berries

b. 385 berries

Need Help?: Lesson 5.2.1 Math Notes box

More Practice: Problems 5-54, 5-62, 5-66, 5-67, 5-75, 5-76, 5-78, 5-79, and 5-86

Problem	Solution	Need Help?	More Practice
CL 5-96.	a. $x = \frac{21}{10}$ or 2.1 b. $x = \frac{176}{3}$ or $58\frac{2}{3}$ c. $p = \frac{33}{10}$ or 3.3	Section 5.2	Problems 5-17, 5-28, 5-63, 5-72, and 5-87
CL 5-97.	$x = \frac{35}{3} \approx 11.7$	Lesson 5.2.1 Math Notes box	Problems 5-54, 5-62, 5-66, 5-67, 5-75, 5-76, 5-78, 5-79, and 5-86
CL 5-98.	$x = 7$ $y = 16$	Lesson 4.2.1 Math Notes box, Lesson 4.2.3, problem 4-86, and Lesson 4.2.4 Math Notes box	Problems 5-43, 5-53, 5-80, and 5-88

6

SYSTEMS OF EQUATIONS

CHAPTER 6 — Systems of Equations

In Chapter 4, you studied the **connections** between the multiple representations of data and learned how to write equations from situations. You also developed a way to solve a system of equations. In this chapter, you will learn how to solve word problems by writing an equation (or a system of equations). Also, unlike previous chapters, where you were limited to certain kinds of systems of equations, in this chapter you will learn how to solve *any* system of linear equations, regardless of its form.

Along the way, you will develop new ways to solve different forms of systems and will learn how to recognize when one method may be most efficient. By the end of this chapter, you will know multiple ways to find the point of intersection of two lines and will be able to solve systems that arise from different contexts.

Guiding Questions

Think about these questions throughout this chapter:

What is a solution?

How can I represent it algebraically?

How can I solve it?

Is there another way?

How can I check my answer?

In this chapter, you will learn:

> What a solution of a system of equations represents.

> How to solve contextual word problems by writing and solving equations.

> How to recognize systems of equations that have no solution or infinite solutions.

> How to solve different forms of systems quickly and efficiently.

Chapter Outline

Section 6.1 In this section, you will write and solve mathematical sentences (such as one- and two-variable equations) to solve contextual word problems.

Section 6.2 You will develop methods to solve systems of equations in different forms. You will learn which equations will result in lines when graphed. You will also find ways to know which solving method is most efficient and accurate.

Section 6.3 Section 6.3 provides an opportunity for you to review and **extend** what you learned in Chapters 1 through 6. You will make important **connections** between solving equations, multiple representations, proportional reasoning, and systems of equations.

6.1.1 How can I write it using algebra?

$$b+g=23$$

Mathematical Sentences

Spoken and written languages use *sentences* to convey information. A sentence has a subject and verb, follows the rules of grammar, and is structured with punctuation. Likewise, algebra uses **mathematical sentences**, such as $b + g = 23$, which also convey information and follow structural rules.

During this lesson, you will explore various mathematical sentences and learn how to interpret their meanings. Then you will write mathematical sentences of your own.

6-1. How can variables give you new information? Suppose Mr. Titelbaum's class has b boys and g girls.

    a. Mr. Titelbaum noticed that $b + g = 23$. What does that tell you about his class?

    b. If $b = g - 3$, what statement can you make about the number of boys and girls?

    c. How many girls are in Mr. Titelbaum's class? Explain how you know.

6-2. The local commuter train has three passenger cars. When it is sold out, each passenger car can hold p people.

    a. In addition to the passengers, the train has 8 employees. Write an expression that represents the total number of people on this commuter train.

    b. When it is sold out, the train has a total of 176 people on board. Write an equation that represents this fact.

    c. Solve your equation to determine how many people a passenger car can hold. Be sure to check your solution when you are finished.

MATHEMATICAL SENTENCES

A **mathematical sentence** uses variables and mathematical operations to represent information. For example, if you know that b represents the number of boys in a class and g represents the number of girls in the same class, then the mathematical sentence "$b + g = 23$" states that if you add the number of boys to the number of girls, you get a result of 23. In other words, there are 23 students in the class.

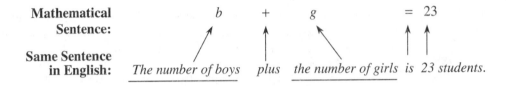

Mathematical Sentence: $\qquad b \qquad + \qquad g \qquad\qquad = 23$

Same Sentence in English: *The number of boys   plus   the number of girls   is   23 students.*

While many mathematical sentences contain more than one variable (such as $b + g = 23$ above), some only contain one variable. For example, if p represents the maximum number of people in a train's passenger car, then the mathematical sentence $3p + 8 = 176$ states that a train with 3 passenger cars and 8 additional people will have 176 people in all. This is shown below.

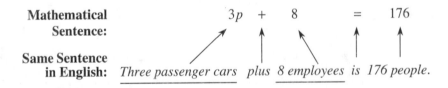

Mathematical Sentence: $\qquad 3p \quad + \quad 8 \qquad = \qquad 176$

Same Sentence in English: *Three passenger cars   plus   8 employees   is   176 people.*

Mathematical sentences convey information once you understand what each variable represents. Sometimes the structure of the equation or the letter of the variable can reveal its possible meaning. With your team, study the two mathematical sentences below and decide what each could be trying to communicate. Be prepared to share your description with the class.

a. $0.25q + 0.05n = 5.00$ b. $l + w + l + w = 30$

         Algebra Connections

6-4.   Mathematical sentences are easier to understand when everyone knows what the variables represent. For example, if you knew that l in part (b) of problem 6-3 represented the length of one side of a rectangle, then it would have been easier to understand that the mathematical sentence $l + w + l + w = 30$ could have been stating that the perimeter of a rectangle is 30 units.

A statement that describes what the variable represents is called a "**let" statement**. It is called this because it often is stated in the form "Let $l = ...$". While solving the problems below, examine how "let" statements are used.

a.   Let m = the number of students at Mountain View High School and let $m - 100$ = the number of students at neighboring Ferguson High School. Which school has more students? How can you tell?

b.   Based on the "let" statements in part (a) above, translate this mathematical sentence into English: $m + (m - 100) = 5980$.

c.   A book called *How I Love Algebra* has only three chapters. Let p = the number of pages in Chapter 1, $p + 12$ = the number of pages in Chapter 2, and $\frac{p}{2}$ = the number of pages in Chapter 3. Which is the longest chapter? Which is the shortest?

d.   Using the definitions in part (c) above, write and solve a mathematical sentence that states that *How I Love Algebra* has 182 pages. How many pages are in Chapter 1?

6-5.   With your team, practice translating words into mathematical symbols. For each problem below, write an expression or equation that best represents the given situation.

a.   Turner rode his bike m miles. If Carolyn rode 10 less than twice the number of miles that Turner rode, how many miles did Carolyn ride?

b.   Your teacher spent $9.50 on 5 boxes of chalk and 2 boxes of overhead pens. If c represents the price of a box of chalk and p represents the price of a box of overhead pens, write an equation to represent this purchase.

c.   Each fruit basket comes with a apples, p pears, and b bananas. Wendi orders 4 fruit baskets and gets 84 pieces of fruit. Write an equation that represents this order.

6-6. In your Learning Log, write your own mathematical sentence. Be sure to state what any variables represent. Title this entry "Writing Mathematical Sentences" and include today's date.

6-7. Solve the problem below using a Guess and Check table. *Note: Be sure to put your work in a safe place, because you will need it for the next lesson.*

The perimeter of a triangle is 31 cm. Sides #1 and #2 have equal length, while Side #3 is one centimeter shorter than twice the length of Side #1. How long is each side?

6-8.   Write expressions to represent the quantities described below.

    a.   If Thompson Valley High School has x students and if Erwin Middle School has 342 fewer students, how many students does Erwin Middle School have?

    b.   If w represents the width of a rectangle and if its length is twice its width, how long is the rectangle?

    c.   When Mr. Van Exel bought his laptop, he paid $400 more than three times the amount he paid for his camera. If he paid c dollars for his camera, then how much did he pay for his laptop?

6-9.   Solve the system of equations below using the Equal Values Method.

$$a = 12b + 3$$
$$a = -2b - 4$$

6-10.   Ms. Cai's class is studying a tile pattern. The rule for the tile pattern is $y = 10x - 18$. Kalil thinks that Figure 12 of this pattern will have 108 tiles. Is he correct? **Justify** your answer.

6-11.   Angel is picking blackberries in her backyard for a delicious pie. She can pick 9 blackberries in 2 minutes. If she needs 95 blackberries for the pie, how long will it take her to pick the berries?

6-12.   Juan thinks that the graph of $6y + 12x = 4$ is a line.

    a.   Solve Juan's equation for y.

    b.   Is this equation **linear**? That is, is its graph a line? Explain how you know.

    c.   What are the growth factor and y-intercept of this graph?

6.1.2 How can I use variables to solve problems?

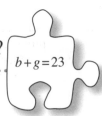

$b+g=23$

Solving Word Problems by Writing Equations

In Lesson 6.1.1, you examined mathematical sentences (equations that convey related information). Today you will learn more ways to translate written information into algebraic symbols and will then solve the equations that represent the relationships.

6-13.   Match each mathematical sentence on the left with its translation on the right.

a. $2z+12=30$

b. $12z+5(z+2)=30$

c. $z+(z-2)+5(z-2)=30$

d. $z+12z=30$

1.   A zoo has two fewer elephants than zebras and five times more monkeys than elephants. The total number of elephants, monkeys, and zebras is 30.

2.   Zola earned $30 by working two hours and receiving a $12 bonus.

3.   Thirty ounces of metal is created by mixing zinc with silver. The number of ounces of silver needed is twelve times the number of ounces of zinc.

4.   Eddie, who earns $5 per hour, worked two hours longer than Zach, who earns $12 per hour. Together they earned $30.

6-14.   In Lesson 6.1.1, you examined how to translate words into mathematical symbols to form expressions and equations. However, you can also use Guess and Check tables to help you write mathematical sentences. Find your solution for problem 6-7, reprinted below.

The perimeter of a triangle is 31 cm. Sides #1 and #2 have equal length, while Side #3 is one centimeter shorter than twice the length of Side #1. How long is each side?

a.   Add a row to your Guess and Check table. If x represents the length of Side #1, then what is the length of Side #2? Side #3? Fill in the columns for Sides #1, #2, and #3 with these variable expressions.

b.   Write a mathematical sentence that states that the perimeter is 31 cm.

c.   If you have not done so already, solve the equation you found in part (b) and determine the length of each side. Does this answer match the one you got for problem 6-7?

6-15. For the following word problems, write one or two equations and then solve the problem. You may choose to use a Guess and Check table to help you set up equations, although it is not required. Regardless of your method, be sure to define your variable(s) with appropriate "let" statements.

a. Herman and Jacquita are each saving money to pay for college. Herman currently has $15,000 and is working hard to save $1000 per month. Jacquita only has $12,000 but is saving $1300 per month. In how many months will they have the same amount of savings?

b. There are 21 animals on Farmer Cole's farm – all sheep and chickens. If the animals have a total of 56 legs, how many of each type of animal lives on his farm?

c. When ordering supplies, Mr. Williams accidentally ordered 12 more than twice his usual number of pencils. When the order arrived, he received 60 pencils! How many pencils does Mr. Williams usually order?

d. George bought some CDs at his local store. He paid $15.95 for each CD. Nora bought the same number of CDs from a store online. She paid $13.95 for each CD, but had to pay $8 for shipping. In the end, both George and Nora spent the exact same amount of money buying their CDs! How many CDs did George buy?

e. After the math contest, Basil noticed that there were four extra-large pizzas that were left untouched. In addition, another three slices of pizza were uneaten. If there were a total of 51 slices of pizza left, how many slices does an extra-large pizza have?

6-16.   Solve for x. Check your solutions, if possible.

   a. $-2(4-3x)-6x=10$

   b. $\frac{x-5}{-2}=\frac{x-1}{-3}$

6-17.   On the same set of axes, graph the two rules shown at right. $y=-x+2$
         Then find the point(s) of intersection, if one (or more) exists. $y=3x+6$

6-18.   Evaluate the expression $6x^2-3x+1$ for $x=-2$.

6-19.   The basketball coach at Washington High School normally starts each game with the
         following five players:

                   Melinda, Samantha, Carly, Allison, and Kendra

         However, due to illness, she needs to substitute Barbara for Allison and Lakeisha for
         Melinda at this week's game. What will be the starting roster for this upcoming
         game?

6-20.   When Ms. Shreve solved an equation in class, she checked her
         solution and it did not make the equation true! Examine her work
         below and find her mistake. Then find the correct solution.

$$5(2x-1)-3x=5x+9$$
$$10x-5-3x=5x+9$$
$$7x-5=5x+9$$
$$12x=4$$
$$x=\frac{1}{3}$$

6-21.   Determine if the statement below is true or false. **Justify** your conclusion.

$$2(3+5x)=6+5x$$

6.1.3 How can I solve the system?

Solving Problems by Writing Equations

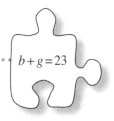

$b + g = 23$

In Lessons 6.1.1 and 6.1.2, you created mathematical sentences that represented word problems. But how can you tell if you can use one variable or two? And is one method more convenient than another? Today you will compare the different ways to represent a word problem with mathematical symbols.

You will also explore how to use the Equal Values Method to solve systems containing equations that are not in $y = mx + b$ form.

6-22. ONE EQUATION OR TWO?

Review what you learned in Lesson 6.1.2 by answering the questions below.

a. Solve the problem below using Guess and Check.

Elsie took all of her cans and bottles from home to the recycling plant. The number of cans was one more than four times the number of bottles. She earned 10¢ for each can and 12¢ for each bottle, and ended up earning $2.18 in all. How many cans and bottles did she recycle?

b. Use your Guess and Check table to help you write an equation that represents the information in part (a). Be sure to define your variable.

c. If you have not done so already, solve your equation from part (b). Does this solution match your answer to part (a)? If not, look for and correct any errors.

d. How can this problem be represented using two variables? With your team, write two mathematical sentences that represent this problem. Be sure to state what your variables represent. You do not need to solve the system.

e. Show that your solution from part (a) makes both equations in part (d) true.

6-23.   Renard thinks that writing two equations for problem 6-22 was easy, but he's not sure if he knows how to solve the system of equations. He wants to use two equations with two variables to solve this problem:

> Ariel bought several bags of caramel candy and taffy. The number of bags of taffy was 5 more than the number of bags of caramels. Taffy bags weigh 8 ounces each, and caramel bags weigh 16 ounces each. The total weight of all of the bags of candy was 400 ounces. How many bags of candy did she buy?

a.   Renard lets t = the number of taffy bags and c = the number of caramel bags. Help him write two equations to represent the information in the problem.

b.   Now Renard is stuck. He says, "If both of the equations were in the form 't = something,' I could use the Equal Values Method to find the solution." Help him change the equations into a form he can solve.

c.   Solve Renard's equations to find the number of caramel and taffy bags that Ariel bought. Check to make sure your solution works.

6-24.   When you write equations to solve word problems, you sometimes end up with two equations like Renard's or like the system shown at right. Notice that the second equation is solved for y, but the first is not. Change the first equation into $y = mx + b$ form, and then solve this system of equations. Discuss with your team how you can make sure your solution is correct.

$$2y + 8x = 10$$
$$y = 5x + 23$$

6-25.   Solve each system below by first changing each equation so that it is in $y = mx + b$ form. Check that your answer makes both equations true.

a. $x - 2y = 4$
       $y = -\frac{1}{2}x + 4$

b. $x + 2y = 14$
       $-x + 3y = 26$

6-26.   Write expressions to represent the quantities described below.

a.   Geraldine is 4 years younger than Tom. If Tom is t years old, how old is Geraldine? Also, if Steven is twice as old as Geraldine, how old is he?

b.   150 people went to see "Ode to Algebra" performed in the school auditorium. If the number of children that attended the performance was c, how many adults attended?

c.   The cost of a new CD is $14.95, and the cost of a video game is $39.99. How much would c CDs and v video games cost?

6-27. Nina has some nickels and 9 pennies in her pocket. Her friend, Maurice, has twice as many nickels as Nina. Together, these coins are worth 84¢. How many nickels does Nina have? Solve using any method, but show all of your work.

6-28. To count the number of endangered falcons in the local county, Fernando first tagged each of the 8 falcons he saw one day. Then, days later, he counted 11 falcons and noticed that only 3 were tagged. What is a good estimate of how many falcons exist in his county? Show how you know.

6-29. As Sachiko solved the equation $(x+2)+3=9$, she showed her work in the table below. Copy the table and provide justification for each step.

Statement	Reason
1. $(x+2)+3=9$	Given
2. $x+(2+3)=9$	
3. $x+5=9$	
4. $x+5-5=9-5$	
5. $x=4$	

6-30. A **prime number** is defined as a number with exactly two integer factors: itself and 1. Jeannie thinks that all prime numbers are odd. Is she correct? If so, state how you know. If not, provide a counterexample.

6-31. In an "If…then…" statement, the "if" portion is called the **hypothesis**, while the "then" portion is called the **conclusion**. For example, in the statement "*If* $x=3$, *then* $x^2=9$," the hypothesis is "$x=3$" while the conclusion is "$x^2=9$."

Identify the hypothesis and conclusion of each of the following statements. Then decide if you think the statement is true or not. **Justify** your decision.

a. If $-x=8$ then $x=-8$.

b. If $3x+y=-11$, then $6x+2y=-22$.

c. If Tomas runs at a constant rate of 4 meters every five seconds, then he will run 50 meters in 1 minute.

6.2.1 How can I solve the system?

Solving Systems of Equations Using Substitution

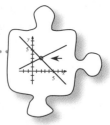

In Chapter 4, you learned that a set of two or more equations that go together is called a **system of equations**. In Lesson 6.1.3, you helped Renard develop a method for solving a system of equations when one of the equations was not solved for a variable. Today you will develop a more efficient method of solving systems that are too messy to solve with the Equal Values Method.

6-32. Review what you learned in Lesson 6.1.3 as you solve the system of equations below. Check your solution.

$$y = -x - 7$$
$$5y + 3x = -13$$

6-33. AVOIDING THE MESS

A new method, called the **Substitution Method**, can help you solve the system in problem 6-32 without getting involved in messy fractions. This method is outlined below.

a. If $y = -x - 7$, then does $-x - 7 = y$? That is, can you switch the y and the $-x - 7$? Why or why not?

$$y = \boxed{-x - 7}$$
$$5y + 3x = -13$$

b. Since you know that $y = -x - 7$, can you switch the y in the second equation with $-x - 7$ from the top equation? Why or why not?

$$y = \boxed{-x - 7}$$
$$5\,\boxed{y} + 3x = -13$$

c. Once you replace the y in the second equation with $-x - 7$, you have an equation with only one variable, as shown below. This is called **substitution** because you are substituting for (replacing) y with an expression that it equals. Solve this new equation for x and then use that result to find y in either of the original equations.

$$5(-x - 7) + 3x = -13$$

242

6-34.   Use the Substitution Method to solve the systems of equations below.

a. $y = 3x$
     $2y - 5x = 4$

b. $x - 4 = y$
     $-5y + 8x = 29$

c. $2x + 2y = 18$
     $x = 3 - y$

d. $c = -b - 11$
     $3c + 6 = 6b$

6-35.   When Mei solved the system of equations below, she got the solution $x = 4$, $y = 2$. *Without solving the system yourself*, can you tell her whether this solution is correct? How do you know?

$$4x + 3y = 22$$
$$x - 2y = 0$$

6-36.   HAPPY BIRTHDAY!

You've decided to give your best friend a bag of marbles for her birthday. Since you know that your friend likes green marbles better than red ones, the bag has twice as many green marbles as red. The label on the bag says it contains a total of 84 marbles.

How many green marbles are in the bag? Write an equation (or system of equations) for this problem. Then solve the problem using any method you choose. Be sure to check your answer when you are finished.

6-37.   Solve each equation for the variable. Check your solutions, if possible.

a. $8a + a - 3 = 6a - 2a - 3$

b. $8(3m - 2) - 7m = 0$

c. $\frac{x}{2} + 1 = 6$

d. $4t - 2 + t^2 = 6 + t^2$

6-38.   The Fabulous Footballers scored an incredible 55 points at
         last night's game. Interestingly, the number of field goals
         was 1 more than twice the number of touchdowns. The
         Fabulous Footballers earned 7 points for each touchdown
         and 3 points for each field goal.

a.   **Multiple Choice:** Which system of equations
      below best represents this situation? Explain your
      reasoning. Assume that t represents the number of
      touchdowns and f represents the number of field goals.

   i. $t = 2f + 1$ ii. $f = 2t + 1$
         $7t + 3f = 55$ $7t + 3f = 55$

   iii. $t = 2f + 1$ iv. $f = 2t + 1$
         $3t + 7f = 55$ $3t + 7f = 55$

b.   Solve the system you selected in part (a) and determine how many touchdowns
      and field goals the Fabulous Footballers earned last night.

6-39.   Yesterday Mica was given some information
         and was asked to find a linear equation. But
         last night her cat destroyed most of the
         information! At right is all she has left:

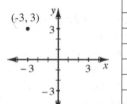

x	y
-3	
-2	1
-1	
0	
1	
2	
3	

a.   Complete the table and graph the line that
      represents Mica's rule.

b.   Mica thinks the equation for this graph could be $2x + y = -3$. Is she correct?
      Explain why or why not. If not, find your own algebraic rule to match the
      graph and $x \rightarrow y$ table.

6-40.   Kevin and his little sister, Katy, are trying to solve the system of equations shown
         below. Kevin thinks the new equation should be $3(6x - 1) + 2y = 43$, while Katy
         thinks it should be $3x + 2(6x - 1) = 43$. Who is correct and why?

$$y = 6x - 1$$
$$3x + 2y = 43$$

6-41.   Create a table and graph the rule $y = 10 - x^2 + 3x$. Label its x- and y-intercepts.

6-42.   Maurice thinks that $x = -2$ is a solution to $x^2 - 3x - 8 = 0$. Is he correct? Explain.

Algebra Connections

6.2.2 How does a graph show a solution?

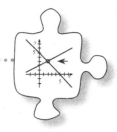

Making Connections: Systems, Solutions, and Graphs

In this chapter you have practiced writing mathematical sentences to represent situations. Often, these sentences give you a system of equations, which you can solve using substitution. Today you will start to represent these situations in an additional way: on a graph. You will also examine more closely what makes a solution to a two-variable equation.

6-43.   THE HILLS ARE ALIVE

The Alpine Music Club is going on its annual music trip. The members of the club are yodelers, and they like to play the xylophone. This year they are taking their xylophones on a gondola to give a performance at the top of Mount Monch.

The gondola conductor charges $2 for each yodeler and $1 for each xylophone. It costs $40 for the entire club, including the xylophones, to ride the gondola. Two yodelers can share a xylophone, so the number of yodelers on the gondola is twice the number of xylophones.

How many yodelers and how many xylophones are on the gondola?

Your Task:

- Represent this problem with a system of equations. Solve the system and explain how its solution relates to the yodelers on the music trip.

- Represent this problem with a graph. Identify how the solution to this problem appears on the graph.

Discussion Points

How can the given information be represented with equations?

What is a solution to a two-variable equation?

How can this problem be represented on a graph?

How does the solution appear on the graph?

Further Guidance

6-44.   Start by focusing on one aspect of the problem: the cost to ride the gondola. The conductor charges $2 for each yodeler and $1 for each xylophone. It costs $40 for the entire club, with instruments, to ride the gondola.

a.   Write an equation with two variables that represents this information. Be sure to define your variables.

b.   Find a combination of xylophones and yodelers that will make your equation from part (a) true. Is this is the only possible combination?

c.   List five additional combinations of xylophones and yodelers that could ride the gondola if it costs $40 for the trip. With your team, decide on a good way to organize and share your list.

d.   Jon says, "I think there could be 28 xylophones and 8 yodelers on the gondola." Is he correct? Use the equation you have written to explain why or why not.

e.   Helga says, "Each correct combination we found is a *solution* to our equation." Is this true? Explain what it means for something to be a solution to a two-variable equation.

6-45.   Now consider the other piece of information: The number of yodelers is twice the number of xylophones.

a.   Write an equation (mathematical sentence) that expresses this piece of information.

b.   List four different combinations of xylophones and yodelers that will make this equation true.

c.   Put the equation you found in part (a) together with your equation from problem 6-44 and use substitution to solve this system of equations.

d.   Is the answer you found in part (c) a solution to the first equation you wrote (the equation in part (a) of problem 6-44)? How can you check? Is it a solution to the second equation you wrote (the equation in part (a) of this problem)? Why is this a solution to the *system* of equations?

6-46.   The solution to "The Hills are Alive" problem can also be represented graphically.

    a.   On graph paper, graph the equation you wrote in part (a) of problem 6-44. The points you listed for that equation may help. What is the shape of this graph? Label your graph with its equation.

    b.   Explain how each point on the graph represents a solution to the equation.

    c.   Now graph the equation you wrote in part (a) of problem 6-45 on the same set of axes. The points you listed for that equation may help. Label this graph with its equation.

    d.   Find the intersection point of the two graphs. What is special about this point?

    e.   With your team, find as many ways as you can to express the solution to "The Hills are Alive" problem. Be prepared to share all the different forms you found for the solution with the class.

Further Guidance section ends here.

6-47.   Consider this system of equations:

$$2x + 2y = 18$$
$$y = x - 3$$

    a.   Use substitution to solve this system.

    b.   With your team, decide how to fill in the rest of the table at right for the equation $2x + 2y = 18$.

x	y
–2	11
–1	
0	
1	
2	
3	

    c.   Use your table to make an accurate graph of the equation $2x + 2y = 18$.

    d.   Now graph $y = x - 3$ on the same set of axes. Find the point of intersection.

    e.   Does the point of intersection you found in part (a) agree with what you see on your graph?

6-48.   If you had an equation with three variables, how would you write its solutions?

6-49.   What is a solution to a two-variable equation? Answer this question in complete sentences in your Learning Log. Then give an example of a two-variable equation followed by two different solutions to it. Finally, make a list of all of the ways to represent solutions to two-variable equations. Title your entry "Solutions to Two-Variable Equations" and label it with today's date.

METHODS AND MEANINGS

The Substitution Method

The **Substitution Method** is a way to change two equations with two variables into one equation with one variable. It is convenient to use when only one equation is solved for a variable.

For example, to solve the system:

$$x = -3y + 1$$
$$4x - 3y = -11$$

Use substitution to rewrite the two equations as one. In other words, replace x with $(-3y + 1)$ to get $4(-3y + 1) - 3y = -11$. This equation can then be solved to find y. In this case, $y = 1$.

$$x = \boxed{-3y + 1}$$

$$4(\;\;\;) - 3y = -11$$

$$4(-3y + 1) - 3y = -11$$

To find the point of intersection, substitute to find the other value.

$$-12y + 4 - 3y = -11$$
$$-15y + 4 = -11$$

Substitute $y = 1$ into $x = -3y + 1$ and write the answer for x and y as an ordered pair.

$$-15y = -15$$
$$y = 1$$

To test the solution, substitute $x = -2$ and $y = 1$ into $4x - 3y = -11$ to verify that it makes the equation true. Since $4(-2) - 3(1) = -11$, the solution must be correct.

$$x = -3(1) + 1 = -2$$

$$(-2, 1)$$

Review & Preview

6-50.   Camila is trying to find the equation of a line that passes through the points $(-1, 16)$ and $(5, 88)$. Does the equation $y = 12x + 28$ work? **Justify** your answer.

6-51.   Solve the systems of equations below using the method of your choice. Check your solutions, if possible.

a. $y = 7 - 2x$
      $2x + y = 10$

b. $3y - 1 = x$
      $4x - 2y = 16$

6-52.   Hotdogs and corndogs were sold at last night's football game. Use the information below to write mathematical sentences to help you determine how many corndogs were sold.

    a.   The number of hotdogs sold was three fewer than twice the number of corndogs. Write a mathematical sentence that relates the number of hotdogs and corndogs. Let h represent the number of hotdogs and c represent the number of corndogs.

    b.   A hotdog costs $3 and a corndog costs $1.50. If $201 was collected, write a mathematical sentence to represent this information.

    c.   How many corndogs were sold? Show how you found your answer.

6-53.   Examine the balanced scales in Figures 1 and 2 shown below. Figure 1 shows that two candies balance three dice. Figure 2 shows that one rubber ball balances two jacks.

Figure 1

Figure 2

Figure 3

    Determine what could be placed on the right side of the scale in Figure 3 to balance with the left side. **Justify** your solution in complete sentences.

6-54.   Rianna thinks that if $a = b$ and if $c = d$, then $a + c = b + d$. Is she correct?

6-55.   For each of the following generic rectangles, find the dimensions (length and width) and write the area as the product of the dimensions and as a sum.

    a.

$3y^2$	$-12y$

    b.

$3y^2$	$-12y$
$5y$	-20

6.2.3   Can I solve without substituting?

Solving Systems Using Elimination

In this chapter, you have learned the Substitution Method for solving
systems of equations. In Chapter 4, you learned the Equal Values Method.
But are these methods the best to use for all types of systems? Today you will develop
a new solution method that can save time for systems of equations in standard form.

6-56.   Jeanette is trying to find the intersection point of these two
equations:

$$2x + 3y = -2$$
$$5x - 3y = 16$$

She has decided to use substitution to find the point of
intersection. Her plan is to solve the first equation for y, and then to substitute the
result into the second equation. Use Jeanette's idea to solve the system.

6-57.   AVOIDING THE MESS: THE ELIMINATION METHOD

Your class will now discuss a new method, called the
Elimination Method, to find the solution to Jeanette's
problem without the complications and fractions of the
previous problem. Your class discussion is outlined
below.

a.   Verify that each equation mat at right represents
one of Jeanette's equations.

$$2x + 3y = -2$$
$$5x - 3y = 16$$

b.   Can these two equations be merged onto one
equation mat as shown below? That is, can the left sides and right sides of two
equations be added together to create a new equation? Why or why not?

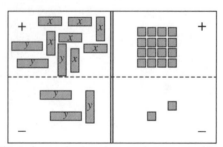

This is the result when the equations are combined.

Problem continues on next page →

6-57. *Problem continued from previous page.*

    c.   Write a new equation for the result of merging Jeanette's equations. Simplify and then solve this new equation for the remaining variable. Notice that you now have only one equation with one variable. What happened to the y-terms?

    d.   Use your solution for x to find y. Check to be sure your solution makes both original equations true.

    e.   How can you record this process on paper? That is, when solving this type of system, how can you show that you are combining the equations?

    f.   Now use the Elimination Method to solve the system of equations at right for x and y. Check your solution.

$$2x - y = -2$$
$$-2x + 3y = 10$$

6-58.   Pat was in a fishing competition at Lake Pisces. She caught some bass and some trout. Each bass weighed 3 pounds, and each trout weighed 1 pound. Pat caught a total of 30 pounds of fish. She got 5 points in the competition for each bass, but since trout are endangered in Lake Pisces, she lost 1 point for each trout. Pat scored a total of 42 points.

    a.   Write a system of equations representing the information in this problem.

    b.   Is this system a good candidate for the Elimination Method? Why or why not?

    c.   Solve this system to find out how many bass and trout Pat caught. Be sure to record your work and check your answer by substituting your solution into the original equations.

6-59.   ANNIE NEEDS YOUR HELP

Annie was all ready to "push together" the two equations below to eliminate the x-terms when she noticed a problem: Both x-terms are positive!

$$2x + 7y = 13$$
$$2x + 3y = 5$$

With your team, figure out something you could do that would allow you to put these equations together and eliminate the x-terms. As you try out different ideas, ask your teacher for some algebra tiles and an equation mat if you think they will help. Once you have figured out a method, solve the system and check your solution. Be ready to share your method with the class.

6-60.   Find the point of intersection of each pair of lines below. If you use an equation mat, be sure to record your process on paper. Otherwise, show your steps algebraically. Check each solution when you are finished.

a. $2y - x = 5$
      $-3y + x = -9$

b. $2x - 4y = 14$
      $4y - x = -3$

c. $3x + 4y = 1$
      $2x + 4y = 2$

METHODS AND **M**EANINGS

Systems of Linear Equations

A **system of linear equations** is a set of two or more linear equations that are given together, such as the example at right:

$$y = 2x$$
$$y = -3x + 5$$

If the equations come from a real-world context, then each variable will represent some type of quantity in both equations. For example, in the system of equations above, y could stand for a number of dollars in *both* equations.

To represent a system of equations graphically, you can simply graph each equation on the same set of axes. The graph may or may not have a **point of intersection**, as shown circled at right.

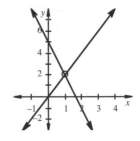

Sometimes two lines have *no* points of intersection. This happens when the two lines are parallel. It is also possible for two lines to have an *infinite* number of intersections. This happens if they are simply the same equation in different forms. Such lines are said to **coincide**.

Also notice that the point of intersection lies on *both* graphs in the system of equations. This means that the point of intersection is a **solution** to *both* equations in the system. For example, the point of intersection of the two lines graphed above is (1, 2). This point of intersection makes both equations true, as shown at right.

$$y = 2x \qquad y = -3x + 5$$
$$(2) = 2(1) \qquad (2) = -3(1) + 5$$
$$2 = 2 \qquad 2 = -3 + 5$$
$$2 = 2$$

The point of intersection makes both equations true; therefore the point of intersection is a solution to both equations. For this reason, the point of intersection is sometimes called a **solution to the system of equations**.

6-61. Find the point of intersection of each pair of lines, if one exists. If you use an equation mat, be sure to record your process on paper. Check each solution, if possible.

a. $x = -2y - 3$
$4y - x = 9$

b. $x + 5y = 8$
$-x + 2y = -1$

c. $4x - 2y = 5$
$y = 2x + 10$

6-62. Jai was solving the system of equations below when something strange happened.

$$y = -2x + 5$$
$$2y + 4x = 10$$

a. Solve the system. Explain to Jai what the solution should be.

b. Graph the two lines on the same set of axes. What happened?

c. Explain how the graph helps to explain your answer in part (a).

6-63. On Tuesday the cafeteria sold pizza slices and burritos. The number of pizza slices sold was 20 less than twice the number of burritos sold. Pizza sold for $2.50 a slice and burritos for $3.00 each. The cafeteria collected a total of $358 for selling these two items.

a. Write two equations with two variables to represent the information in this problem. Be sure to define your variables.

b. Solve the system from part (a). Then determine how many pizza slices were sold.

6-64. A local deli sells 6-inch sub sandwiches for $2.95. It has decided to sell a "family sub" that is 50 inches long. How much should it charge? Show all work.

6-65. Represent the tile pattern below with a table, a rule, and a graph.

 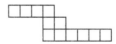

Figure 1   Figure 2   Figure 3

6-66. Use generic rectangles to multiply each of the following expressions.

a. $(x + 2)(x - 5)$

b. $(y + 2x)(y + 3x)$

c. $(3y - 8)(-x + y)$

d. $(x - 3y)(x + 3y)$

$6.2.4$ How can I eliminate a variable?

More Elimination

In Lesson 6.2.3, you learned how to use the Elimination Method to solve systems of equations. In this method, you combined two equations in a way that made one variable disappear. This method is particularly useful for solving systems of equations where neither equation is in $y = mx + b$ form.

Today you will practice using the Elimination Method while learning to deal with various complications that systems of equations sometimes present. As you solve these systems, ask your teammates these questions:

> How can you create one equation with only one variable?
>
> How can you eliminate one variable?
>
> How do you know your solution is correct?

6-67.   Which system of equations below would be easiest to solve using the Elimination Method? Once you have explained your decision, use the Elimination Method to solve this system of equations. (You do not need to solve the other system!) Record your steps and check your solution.

 a. $5x - 4y = 37$
   $-8x + 4y = -52$

 b. $4 - 2x = y$
   $3y + x = 11$

6-68.   Rachel is trying to solve this system:

$$2x + y = 10$$
$$3x - 2y = 1$$

 a.   Combine these equations. What happened?

 b.   Is $2x + y = 10$ the same line as $4x + 2y = 20$? That is, do they have the same solutions? Are their graphs the same? **Justify** your conclusion! Be ready to share your reasoning with the class.

 c.   Since you can rewrite $2x + y = 10$ as $4x + 2y = 20$, perhaps this equivalent form of the original equation can help solve this system. Combine $4x + 2y = 20$ and $3x - 2y = 1$. Is a variable eliminated? If so, solve the system for x and y. If not, brainstorm another way to eliminate a variable. Be sure to check your solution.

 d.   Why was the top equation changed? Would a variable have been eliminated if the bottom equation were multiplied by 2 on both sides? Test this idea.

Algebra Connections

6-69.   For each system below, determine:

- Is this system a good candidate for the Elimination Method? Why or why not?

- What is the best way to get one equation with one variable? Carry out your plan and solve the system for both variables.

- Is your solution correct? Verify by substituting your solution into both original equations.

a. $5m + 2n = -10$
      $3m + 2n = -2$

b. $6a - b = 3$
      $b + 4a = 17$

c. $7x + 4y = 17$
      $3x - 2y = -15$

d. $-18x + 3y = -12$
      $6x - y = 4$

6-70.   A NEW CHALLENGE

Carefully examine this system:

$$4x + 3y = 10$$
$$9x - 4y = 1$$

With your team, propose a way to combine these equations so that you eventually have one equation with one variable. Be prepared to share your proposal with the class.

MᴇTHODS AND Mᴇᴀɴɪɴɢs

MATH NOTES

Coefficients and Constants

A **coefficient** is the numerical part of a term that includes a variable. For example, in the expression below, the coefficient of $7x^2$ is the number 7, the coefficient of $4x$ is 4, and the coefficient of $-y$ is -1. Note that the 9 in the expression below is called a **constant**. A constant is a term that does not include a variable.

$$7x^2 + 4x - y + 9$$

6-71.   Solve these systems of equations using any method. Check each solution, if possible.

a. $2x + 3y = 9$
       $-3x + 3y = -6$

b. $x = 8 - 2y$
       $y - x = 4$

c. $y = -\frac{1}{2}x + 7$
       $y = x - 8$

d. $9x + 10y = 14$
       $7x + 5y = -3$

6-72.   For each line below, make a table and graph. What do you notice?

a. $y = \frac{2}{3}x - 1$

b. $2x - 3y = 3$

6-73.   **Consecutive numbers** are integers that are in order without skipping, such as 3, 4, and 5. Find three consecutive numbers with a sum of 54.

6-74.   Identify the hypothesis and conclusion for each of the following statements. Then decide if the statement is true or false. Justify your decision. You may want to review the meanings of hypothesis and conclusion from problem 6-31.

a.   If $y = \frac{2}{3}x - 5$, then the point (6, –1) is a solution.

b.   If Figure 2 of a tile pattern has 13 tiles and Figure 4 of the same pattern has 15 tiles, then the pattern grows by 2 tiles each figure.

c.   If $(3x + 1)(x - 2) = 4$, then $3x^2 - 5x - 2 = 4$.

6-75.   Aimee thinks the solution to the system below is (–4, –6). Eric thinks the solution is (8, 2). Who is correct? Explain your reasoning.

$$2x - 3y = 10$$
$$6y = 4x - 20$$

6-76.   Figure 3 of a tile pattern has 11 tiles, while Figure 4 has 13 tiles. If the tile pattern grows at a constant rate, how many tiles will Figure 50 have?

Algebra Connections

6.2.5 What is the best method?

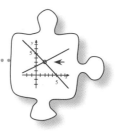

Choosing a Strategy for Solving Systems

When you have a system of equations to solve, how do you know which method to use? Focus today on how to choose a strategy that is the most convenient, efficient, and accurate for a system of equations.

6-77. Erica works in a soda-bottling factory. As bottles roll past her on a conveyer belt, she puts caps on them. Unfortunately, Erica sometimes breaks a bottle before she can cap it. She gets paid 4 cents for each bottle she successfully caps, but her boss deducts 2 cents from her pay for each bottle she breaks.

Erica is having a bad morning. Fifteen bottles have come her way, but she has been breaking some and has only earned 6 cents so far today. How many bottles has Erica capped and how many has she broken?

a. Write a system of equations representing this situation.

b. Solve the system of equations using *two* different methods: substitution and elimination. Demonstrate that each method gives the same answer.

6-78. For each system below, decide which strategy to use. That is, which method would be the most efficient, convenient, and accurate: the Substitution Method, the Elimination Method, or the Equal Values Method? Do not solve the systems yet! Be prepared to **justify** your reasons for choosing one strategy over the others.

a. $x = 4 - 2y$
$3x - 2y = 4$

b. $3x + y = 1$
$4x + y = 2$

c. $x = -5y + 2$
$x = 3y - 2$

d. $2x - 4y = 10$
$x = 2y + 5$

e. $y = \frac{1}{2}x + 4$
$y = -2x + 9$

f. $-6x + 2y = 76$
$3x - y = -38$

g. $5x + 3y = -6$
$2x - 9y = 18$

h. $x - 3 = y$
$2(x - 3) - y = 7$

6-79.   Your teacher will assign you a variety of systems from problem 6-78 to solve. With
your team, use the best strategy to solve each system assigned by your teacher. Be
sure to check your solution.

6-80.   In your Learning Log, write down everything you know about
solving systems of equations. Include examples and explain your
reasoning. Title this entry "Solving Systems of Equations" and
label it with today's date.

Ⓜ ETHODS AND MEANINGS

Intersection, Parallel, and Coincide

When two lines lie on the same flat surface (called a plane), they may
intersect (cross each other) once, an infinite number of times, or never.

For example, if the two lines are **parallel**, then they never
intersect. Examine the graph of two parallel lines at right.
Notice that the distance between the two lines is constant.

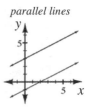

parallel lines

However, what if the two lines lie exactly on top of each
other? When this happens, we say that the two lines
coincide. When you look at two lines that coincide, they
appear to be one line. Since these two lines intersect each
other at all points along the line, coinciding lines have an
infinite number of intersections.

intersecting lines

While some systems contain lines that are parallel and
others coincide, the most common case for a system of
equations is when the two lines intersect once, as shown at
right.

6-81.   Solve the following systems of equations using any method. Check each solution, if possible.

   a. $-2x + 3y = 1$
          $2x + 6y = 2$

   b. $y = \frac{1}{3}x + 4$
          $x = -3y$

   c. $3x - y = 7$
          $y = 3x - 2$

   d. $x + 2y = 1$
          $3x + 5y = 8$

6-82.   The Math Club is baking pies for a bake sale. The fruit-pie recipe calls for twice as many peaches as nectarines. If it takes a total of 168 pieces of fruit for all of the pies, how many nectarines are needed?

6-83.   Candice is solving this system:

$$2x - 1 = 3y$$
$$5(2x - 1) + y = 32$$

   a.   She notices that each equation contains the expression $2x - 1$. Can she substitute $3y$ for $2x - 1$? Why or why not?

   b.   Substitute $3y$ for $2x - 1$ in the second equation to create one equation with one variable. Then solve for x and y.

6-84.   Examine the diagram at right. The smaller triangle is similar to the larger triangle. Write and solve a proportion to find x.

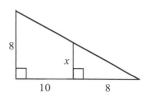

6-85.   Figure 2 of a tile pattern is shown at right. If the pattern grows linearly and if Figure 5 has 15 tiles, then find a rule for the pattern.

Figure 2

6-86.   Given the hypothesis that line l is parallel to line m and that line m is parallel to line n, what can you conclude? Justify your conclusion.

6.3.1 What can I do now?

Pulling It All Together

This lesson contains many problems that will require you to use the algebra content you have learned so far in new ways. It will require you to use all five Ways of Thinking (justifying, making connections, applying and extending, reversing thinking, and generalizing) and will help you solidify your understanding.

Your teacher will describe today's activity. As you solve the problems below, remember to make **connections** between all of the different subjects you have studied in Chapters 1 through 6. If you get stuck, think of what the problem reminds you of. Decide if there is a different way to approach the problem. Most importantly, discuss your ideas with your teammates.

6-87. Brianna has been collecting insects and measuring the lengths of their legs and antennae. Below is the data she has collected so far.

	Ant	Beetle	Grasshopper
Length of Antenna (x)	2 mm	6 mm	20 mm
Length of Leg (y)	4 mm	10 mm	31 mm

a. Graph the data Brianna has collected. Put the antenna length on the x-axis and leg length on the y-axis.

b. Brianna thinks that she has found an algebraic rule relating antenna length and leg length: $4y - 6x = 4$. If x represents the length of the antenna and y represents the leg length, could Brianna's rule be correct? If not, find your own algebraic rule relating antenna length and leg length.

c. If a ladybug has an antenna 1 mm long, how long does Brianna's rule say its legs will be? Use both the rule and the graph to **justify** your answer.

6-88.   Barry is helping his friend understand how to solve systems of equations. He wants to give her a problem to practice. He wants to give her a problem that has two lines that intersect at the point (–3, 7). Help him by writing a system of equations that will have (–3, 7) as a solution and demonstrate how to solve it.

6-89.   Examine the generic rectangle at right. Determine the missing attributes and then write the area as a product and as a sum.

6-90.   One evening, Gemma saw three different phone-company ads. TeleTalk boasted a flat rate of 8¢ per minute. AmeriCall charges 30¢ per call plus 5¢ per minute. CellTime charges 60¢ per call plus only 3¢ per minute.

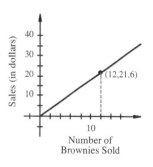

a.   Gemma is planning a phone call that will take about 5 minutes. Which phone plan should she use and how much will it cost?

b.   Represent each phone plan with a table and a rule. Then graph each plan on the same set of axes, where x represents time in minutes and y represents the cost of the call in cents. If possible, use different colors to represent the different phone plans.

c.   How long would a call need to be to cost the same with TeleTalk and AmeriCall? What about AmeriCall and CellTime?

d.   Analyze the different phone plans. How long should a call be so that AmeriCall is cheapest?

6-91.   Lashayia is very famous for her delicious brownies, which she sells at football games. The graph at right shows the relationship between the number of brownies she sells and the amount of money she earns.

a.   How much should she charge for 10 brownies? Be sure to demonstrate your reasoning.

b.   During the last football game, Lashayia made $34.20. How many brownies did she sell? Show your work.

6-92.   How many solutions does each equation below have? How can you tell?

    a. $4x - 1 + 5 = 4x + 3$

    b. $6t - 3 = 3t + 6$

    c. $6(2m - 3) - 3m = 2m - 18 + m$

    d. $10 + 3y - 2 = 4y - y + 8$

6-93.   Anthony has the rules for three lines: A, B, and C. When he solves a system with lines A and B, he gets no solution. When he solves a system with lines B and C, he gets infinite solutions. What solution will he get when he solves a system with lines A and C? **Justify** your conclusion.

6-94.   Complete the Guess and Check table below and find a solution. Then write a possible word problem that would fit the table.

Stevie	Joan	Julio	Total	31.50? Check
3	5	8.50	16.50	Too low
10	19	22.50	51.50	Too high
7.50	14	17.50	39.00	Too high

6-95.   Normally, the longer you work for a company, the higher your salary per hour. Hector surveyed the people at his company and placed his data in the table below.

Number of Years at Company	1	3	6	7
Salary per Hour	$7.00	$8.50	$10.75	$11.50

    a.   Use Hector's data to estimate how much he makes, assuming he has worked at the company for 12 years.

    b.   Hector is hiring a new employee who will work 20 hours a week. How much should the new employee earn for the first week?

6-96.   Dexter loves to find shortcuts. He has proposed a few new moves to help simplify and solve equations. Examine his work below. For each, decide if his move is "legal." That is, decide if the move creates an equivalent equation. **Justify** your conclusions using the "legal" moves you already know.

a.
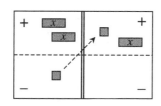

b.
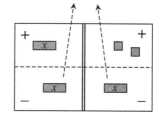

c.
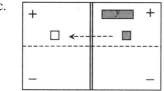

d.

6-97.   Solve the problem below using *two different methods*.

The Math Club sold roses and tulips this year for Valentine's Day. The number of roses sold was 8 more than 4 times the number of tulips sold. Tulips were sold for $2 each and roses for $5 each. The club made $414.00. How many roses were sold?

6-98.   Use substitution to find where the two parabolas below intersect. Then confirm your solution by graphing both on the same set of axes.

$$y = x^2 + 5$$
$$y = x^2 + 2x + 1$$

METHODS AND MEANINGS

MATH NOTES

The Elimination Method for Solving Systems of Equations

One method of solving systems of equations is the **Elimination Method**. This method involves adding or subtracting both sides of two equations to eliminate a variable. Equations can be combined this way because balance is maintained when equal amounts are added to both sides of an equation. For example, if $a = b$ and $c = d$, then if you add a and c you will get the same result as adding b and d. Thus, $a + c = b + d$.

Consider the system of linear equations shown at right. Notice that when both sides of the equations are added together, the sum of the x-terms is zero and so the x-terms are eliminated. (Be sure to write both equations so that x is above x, y is above y, and the constants are similarly matched.)

$$3x + 2y = 14$$
$$-3x + 5y = 14$$
$$\frac{7y}{7} = \frac{28}{7}$$
$$y = 4$$

Now that you have one equation with one variable ($7y = 28$), you can solve for y by dividing both sides by 7. To find x, you can substitute the answer for y into one of the original equations, as shown at right. You can then test the solution for x and y by substituting both values into the other equation to verify that $-3x + 5y = 14$.

$$3x + 2(4) = 14$$
$$3x + 8 = 14$$
$$3x = 6$$
$$x = 2$$

$$-3(2) + 5(4) = 14 \checkmark$$

Since $x = 2$ and $y = 4$ is a solution to both equations, it can be stated that the two lines cross at the point (2, 4).

6-99.   Find the point of intersection for each set of equations below using any method. Check your solutions, if possible.

    a. $6x - 2y = 10$
             $3x - 5 = y$

    b. $6x - 2y = 5$
             $3x + 2y = -2$

    c. $5 - y = 3x$
             $y = 2x$

    d. $y = \frac{1}{4}x + 5$
             $y = 2x - 9$

6-100.   Consider the equation $-6x = 4 - 2y$.

a.   If you graphed this equation, what shape would the graph have? How can you tell?

b.   Without changing the form of the equation, find the coordinates of three points that must be on the graph of this equation. Then graph the equation on graph paper.

c.   Solve the equation for y. Does your answer agree with your graph? If so, how do they agree? If not, check your work to find the error.

6-101.   A tile pattern has 10 tiles in Figure 2 and increases by 2 tiles for each figure. Find a rule for this pattern and then determine how many tiles are in Figure 100.

6-102.   Make a table and graph the rule $y = -x^2 + x + 2$ on graph paper. Label the x-intercepts.

6-103.   Mr. Greer solved an equation below. However, when he checked his solution, it did not make the original equation true. Find his error and then find the correct solution.

$$4x = 8(2x - 3)$$
$$4x = 16x - 3$$
$$-12x = -3$$
$$x = \frac{-3}{-12}$$
$$x = \frac{1}{4}$$

6-104.   Thirty coins, all dimes and nickels, are worth $2.60. How many nickels are there?

6-105. **Multiple Choice:** Martha's equation has the graph shown at right. Which of these are solutions to Martha's equation? (Remember that more than one answer may be correct.)

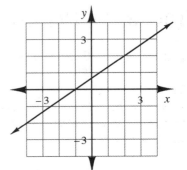

    a. $(-4, -2)$

    b. $(-1, 0)$

    c. $x = 0$ and $y = 1$

    d. $x = 2$ and $y = 2$

6-106. Copy and complete the table below. Then write the corresponding rule.

IN (x)	2	10	6	7	−3	0	−10	100	x
OUT (y)	−7				18	3			

6-107. Solve the following equations for x, if possible. Check your solutions.

    a. $-(2 - 3x) + x = 9 - x$ b. $\frac{6}{x+2} = \frac{3}{4}$

    c. $5 - 2(x + 6) = 14$ d. $\frac{1}{2}x - 4 + 1 = -3 - \frac{1}{2}x$

6-108. Using the variable x, write an equation that has no solution. Explain how you know it has no solution.

6-109. Given the hypothesis that $2x - 3y = 6$ and $x = 0$, what can you conclude? **Justify** your conclusion.

6-110. **Multiple Choice:** Which equation below could represent a tile pattern that grows by 3 and has 9 tiles in Figure 2?

    a. $3x + y = 3$ b. $-3x + y = 9$

    c. $-3x + y = 3$ d. $2x + 3y = 9$

Chapter 6 Closure   What have I learned?

Reflection and Synthesis

The activities below offer you a chance to reflect on what you have learned during this chapter. As you work, look for concepts that you feel very comfortable with, ideas that you would like to learn more about, and topics you need more help with. Look for **connections** between ideas as well as **connections** with material you learned previously.

①   TEAM BRAINSTORM

With your team, brainstorm a list for each of the following topics. Be as detailed as you can. How long can you make your list? Challenge yourselves. Be prepared to share your team's ideas with the class.

Topics: What have you studied in this chapter? What ideas and words were important in what you learned? Remember to be as detailed as you can.

Connections: What topics, ideas, and words that you learned *before* this chapter are **connected** to the new ideas in this chapter? Again, make your list as long as you can.

②   MAKING CONNECTIONS

The following is a list of the vocabulary used in this chapter. The words that appear in bold are new to this chapter. Make sure that you are familiar with all of these words and know what they mean. Refer to the glossary or index for any words that you do not yet understand.

coefficients	**coincide**	**Elimination Method**
Equal Values Method	equation	graph
"let" statement	linear equation	**mathematical sentence**
ordered pair	**parallel**	point of intersection
situation	solution	standard form
Substitution Method	system of equations	variable
$y = mx + b$		

Make a concept map showing all of the **connections** you can find among the key words and ideas listed above. To show a **connection** between two words, draw a line between them and explain the **connection**, as shown in the example below. A word can be **connected** to any other word as long as there is a **justified connection**. For each key word or idea, provide a sketch that illustrates the idea (see the example on the following page).

Continues on next page →

②   *Continued from previous page.*

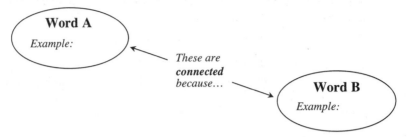

Your teacher may provide you with vocabulary cards to help you get started. If you use the cards to plan your concept map, be sure either to re-draw your concept map on your paper or to glue the vocabulary cards to a poster with all of the **connections** explained for others to see and understand.

While you are making your map, your team may think of related words or ideas that are not listed here. Be sure to include these ideas on your concept map.

③   SUMMARIZING MY UNDERSTANDING

This section gives you an opportunity to show what you know about certain math topics or ideas. Your teacher will give you directions for exactly how to do this. Your teacher may give you a "GO" page to work on. The "GO" stands for "Graphic Organizer," a tool you can use to organize your thoughts and communicate your ideas clearly.

④   WHAT HAVE I LEARNED?

This section will help you evaluate which types of problems you have seen with which you feel comfortable and those with which you need more help. Even if your teacher does not assign this section, it is a good idea to try these problems and find out for yourself what you know and what you need to work on.

Solve each problem as completely as you can. The table at the end of the closure section has answers to these problems. It also tells you where you can find additional help and practice on problems like these.

CL 6-111. Solve these systems of equations using any method.

a. $y = 3x + 7$
      $y = -4x + 21$

b. $3x - y = 17$
      $-x + y = -7$

c. $x = 3y - 5$
      $2x + 12y = -4$

d. $2x - 3y = -16$
      $-4x + 2y = -4$

CL 6-112. Bob climbed down a ladder from his roof, while Rob climbed up another ladder next to him. Each ladder had 30 rungs. Their friend Jill recorded the following information about Bob and Rob:

> Bob went down 2 rungs every second.
>
> Rob went up 1 rung every second.

At some point, Bob and Rob were at the same height. Which rung were they on?

CL 6-113. Solve for x.

a. $6x - 11 = 4x + 12$

b. $2(3x - 5) = 6x - 4$

c. $(x - 3)(x + 4) = x^2 + 4$

d. $\frac{x}{25} = \frac{7}{10}$

CL 6-114. Solve the equations in parts (a) and (b) for y. Then name the growth factor and the y-intercept of each equation in part (c).

a. $-6x - 2y = 8$

b. $2x^2 + 2y = 4x + 2x^2 - 7$

c.   For each of the two solved equations, find the y-intercept and growth factor. **Justify** your answers.

CL 6-115. Florida ecologists sampled Lake George to estimate the number of rainbow trout in the lake. Out of 156 fish, 18 were rainbow trout. About how many rainbow trout should they expect to find in a sample of 500 fish?

CL 6-116. As treasurer of his school's 4H club, Kenny wants to buy gifts for all 18 members. He can buy t-shirts for $9 and sweatshirts for $15. The club has only $180 to spend. If Kenny wants to spend all of the club's money, how many of each type of gift can he buy?

a.   Write a system of equations representing this problem.

b.   Solve your system of equations and figure out how many of each type of gift Kenny should buy.

CL 6-117. Simplify each expression.

a. $3(x^2 - 7x) + 5xy - (x - 4xy) - 2x^2 + 21x$

b. $3y - (4x + 7) - y + 11 + (2x - y + 12)$

CL 6-118. Rewrite each expression below as a product and as a sum.

    a. $(x+7)(2x-5)$ b. $5x(y-7)$ c. $(3x-7)(x^2-2x+11)$

CL 6-119. Each part (a) through (d) below represents a different tile pattern. For each, find the growth factor and the number of tiles in Figure 0.

    a.

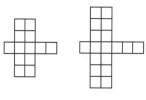

        Figure 2   Figure 3   Figure 4

    b.

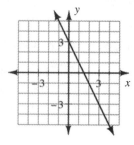

    c. $y = 3x - 14$

    d.

x	-3	-2	-1	0	1	2	3
y	18	13	8	3	-2	-7	-12

CL 6-120. Check your answers using the table at the end of the closure section. Which problems do you feel confident about? Which problems were hard? Use the table to make a list of topics you need help on and a list of topics you need to practice more.

⑤   HOW AM I THINKING?

This course focuses on five different **Ways of Thinking**: reversing thinking, justifying, generalizing, making connections, and applying and extending understanding. These are some of the ways in which you think while trying to make sense of a concept or to solve a problem (even outside of math class). During this chapter, you have probably used each Way of Thinking multiple times without even realizing it!

Review each of the Ways of Thinking that are described in the closure sections of Chapters 1 through 5. Then choose three of these Ways of Thinking that you remember using while working in this chapter. For each Way of Thinking that you choose, show and explain where you used it and how you used it. Describe why thinking in this way helped you solve a particular problem or understand something new. (For instance, explain why you wanted to **generalize** in this particular case, or why it was useful to see these particular **connections**.) Be sure to include examples to demonstrate your thinking.

Answers and Support for Closure Activity #4
What Have I Learned?

Problem	Solution	Need Help?	More Practice
CL 6-111.	a. $x = 2$, $y = 13$ b. $x = 5$, $y = -2$ c. $x = -4$, $y = \frac{1}{3}$ d. $x = \frac{11}{2}$, $y = 9$	Lessons 6.2.2, 6.2.3, and 6.3.1 Math Notes boxes	Problems 6-24, 6-25, 6-32, 6-34, 6-51, 6-56, 6-61, 6-62, 6-71, and 6-81
CL 6-112.	They were on the 10th rung.	Lessons 6.2.2, 6.2.3, and 6.3.1 Math Notes boxes	Problems 6-38, 6-43, 6-52, 6-58, 6-77, 6-90, and 6-97
CL 6-113.	a. $x = 11.5$ b. no solution c. $x = 16$ d. $x = 17.5$	Lesson 5.1.3 Math Notes box, Lesson 5.1.4	Problems 6-16, 6-37, and 6-107
CL 6-114.	a. $y = -3x - 4$ b. $y = 2x - \frac{7}{2}$ c. (a) y-intercept: (0, –4), growth: –3 (b) y-intercept: (0, –3.5), growth: 2	Lesson 5.1.5, Lesson 5.1.5 Math Notes box	Problems 6-12 and 6-100
CL 6-115.	approximately 58 rainbow trout	Lesson 5.2.1, Lesson 5.2.1 Math Notes box	Problems 6-11, 6-28, and 6-64
CL 6-116.	a. $9x + 15y = 180$, $x + y = 18$ b. 15 t-shirts, 3 sweatshirts	Lessons 6.2.2, 6.2.3, and 6.3.1 Math Notes boxes	Problems 6-38, 6-43, 6-52, 6-58, 6-77, 6-90, and 6-97

Problem	Solution	Need Help?	More Practice
CL 6-117.	a. $x^2 + 9xy - x$ b. $y - 2x + 16$	Lessons 2.1.5 and 5.1.3 Math Notes boxes	Problems 4-6, 3-15, and 3-75
CL 6-118.	a. $2x^2 + 9x - 35$ b. $5xy - 35x$ c. $3x^3 - 13x^2 + 47x - 77$	Lessons 5.1.3 and 5.2.3 Math Notes boxes	Problems 6-66 and 6-103
CL 6-119.	a. growth: 5, Figure 0: 3 tiles b. growth: –2, Figure 0: 3 tiles c. growth: 3, Figure 0: –14 tiles d. growth: –5, Figure 0: 3 tiles	Sections 3.1 and 4.1, Lesson 4.1.7 Math Notes box	Problems 6-10, 6-76, 6-85, 6-101, and 6-110

Additional Topics 1.1

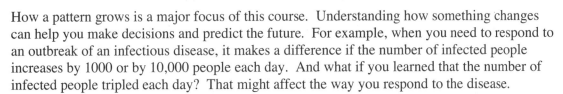

Investigating the Growth of Patterns

This lesson is designed to follow Lesson 1.1.4.

How a pattern grows is a major focus of this course. Understanding how something changes can help you make decisions and predict the future. For example, when you need to respond to an outbreak of an infectious disease, it makes a difference if the number of infected people increases by 1000 or by 10,000 people each day. And what if you learned that the number of infected people tripled each day? That might affect the way you respond to the disease.

Today you will work with your study team to analyze this and other situations that involve different types of relationships. As you work together, ask each other the following questions to start and continue productive mathematical discussions.

What is the pattern? How is it changing? How can you describe it?

How does it grow (or get smaller)?

How can we organize the data?

AT-1. DATA LABS

Today your team will collect and analyze data from three labs, which are described below. At each station, read the directions carefully, and collect and record your data. While you may visit the stations in any order, do not split your team members between stations. Instead, make sure you visit each station as a team so that every team member understands what the data represents and how each pattern is changing.

Once your data is collected, move on to problems AT-2 and AT-3 to analyze your data.

Lab A: Hot Tub Design

Perry is designing a hot tub that he will locate behind his house. He has 36 square designer tiles to use for the bottom of his hot tub. He wants to use all of the tiles, but he does not yet know how he will arrange them to form the hot tub. If his hot tub will be rectangular, how many different rectangles with an area of 36 square units does he have to choose from?

Use the square tiles provided to find as many rectangular configurations as you can. Remember to record the length and the width of each rectangle you find. Assume that Perry's yard is big enough to accommodate any rectangular design you create and that it matters which dimension is the width and which is the length.

Problem continues on next page →

Problem continued from previous page.

Lab B: Local Crisis

Health officials in Parsnipville are concerned about the recent outbreak of the flu. While scientists are working hard to find a vaccine, the town leaders are turning to you to predict how many people will be sick over time. They hope to find a vaccine in a week. Here are the facts: The epidemic started when Velma and Stanley returned from their exotic vacation with symptoms of the flu. Then, each day, the number of sick people has multiplied by three. The town of Parsnipville has 3800 citizens.

Use the beans (or other material) provided by your teacher to represent the people infected with the flu. Start with two beans to represent Velma and Stanley. Then carefully replace each bean with three beans to represent the growth of the disease. Collect (and record) data for the first few days until you understand how the disease is growing.

Lab C: Sign On the Dotted Line

Certain legal documents, such as those used when buying property, sometimes require up to 50 signatures! How long do you think that might take? To find out, collect data as one person of your team signs his or her first name. Have a team member use a stop watch to time how long it takes to sign his or her first name 2, 3, 5, 7, and 10 times. In order to collect good, clean data, be sure to have your team member practice signing his or her first name before you start.

AT-2.   REPRESENTING DATA

In problem AT-1, you collected data for three different situations. Now your team will work together to find ways of representing the data to help answer questions in problem AT-3. Obtain an AT2 Resource Page from your teacher.

a.   For each lab, complete the corresponding table below on the resource page. Use patterns to complete your table for any values in the top row not already included in your data from problem AT-1. Some entries are started for you.

Lab A: Hot Tub Design

Width of Hot Tub	1	2	3	4	6	9	12	18	36
Length of Hot Tub	36								

Lab B: Local Crisis

Day	0	1	2	3	4	5	6	7
# of Infected People	2							

Lab C: Sign On the Dotted Line

# of Signatures	0	1	2	3	4	5	6	7	8	9	10
Time (in seconds)											

Problem continues on next page →

AT-2. *Problem continued from previous page.*

    b.   Now plot your data from each lab on the set of axes provided on the resource page. Note that some data points may not fit on the given axes. Then describe each graph. What does each graph look like? Should the points be connected?

    c.   For each graph, find the point where $x = 4$ and label it with its coordinate. Then explain what that point represents in each context.

AT-3.   ANALYSIS

    Graphs and tables not only represent data, but they also allow you to answer questions about the data. Use your tables and graphs on the resource page from problem AT-2 to answer the questions below.

    a.   Which data appears to be linear? That is, when graphed, which data forms a line? Explain why it makes sense for this context to have a linear graph.

    b.   The town of Parsnipville will have a vaccine on Day 7. Since the town has 3800 citizens, how many people will need the vaccine on that day? Is it easier to answer this question with your graph or with your table? Explain.

    c.   Now that Perry knows his options for the design of his hot tub, he wants to pick the hot tub that has the smallest perimeter. What do you recommend?

    d.   Why isn't there a point when $x = 0$ for your graph for Lab A? Could there be? Explain.

METHODS AND **M**EANINGS

MATH NOTES

Direct and Inverse Variation

There are several special relationships that you will study in this course. One of these is called **direct variation** (also called **direct proportion**). The data you gathered in the "Sign on the Dotted Line" lab (in problem AT-1) is an example of direction variation.

Another relationship you will study about in this course is **inverse variation** (also called **inverse proportion**). The data collected in the "Hot Tub Design" lab (in problem AT-1) is an example of inverse variation.

While direct and inverse variation will be formally defined in a later lesson, examples of graphs of both types of variation are shown at right.

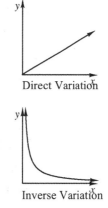

Direct Variation

Inverse Variation

AT-4.   Consider the situation described below.

   a.   Meredith lives 24 blocks from her friend's house. If she travels 1 block every
          minute, how many minutes will it take her to reach her friend's house? What if
          she travels 2 blocks every minute? Show how you calculated each answer.

   b.   Copy and complete the table below to represent the amount of time it would
          take Meredith to get to her friend's house.

Speed (in blocks per minute)	1	2	3	4	6	8	10	12	24
Time to Get to Her Friend's House (in mins)									

   c.   What happens to the time it takes to get to her friend's house as Meredith's
          speed increases? Explain.

AT-5.   In December of 2003, the average price for a gallon of regular gas in the United
          States was $1.50.

   a.   At that time, what did it cost to buy 12 gallons of gas?

   b.   Gerald paid $12.60 for a tank of gas. How many gallons did he buy?

   c.   At right is a graph of this situation. Predict how
          the line would change to represent the average
          cost of gas in December of 2005, when gas cost
          $2.20 per gallon on average.

   d.   Review the Math Notes box for this lesson.
          Does the cost of gas vary directly with the
          number of gallons or inversely? Explain how
          you know.

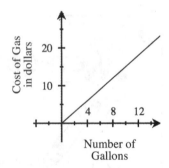

AT-6.   Marilee has a collection of three football jerseys with the numbers 2, 5, and 14 on
          them. One way to represent a set (or collection) of numbers on the jerseys is with
          set notation. Using set notation, Marilee's set of jerseys numbers can be written
          $\{2, 5, 14\}$. The "curly" brackets indicate that it is the set of objects that are listed
          inside the brackets.

   a.   If she decides to pack only one jersey for a trip, one choice is $\{2\}$. What other
          choices could she make? Use set notation to represent your solutions.

   b.   How many ways could she choose two jerseys? Use set notation to list all the
          ways Marilee could select two jerseys to take on her trip.

Algebra Connections

AT-7. Consider the statement, "The sum of two odd numbers is odd." Is this statement true or false? Explain your reasoning. If the statement is false, produce a **counterexample** (an example that shows at least one exception).

AT-8. If a and b are any positive integers, decide if each statement below is sometimes true, always true, or never true. **Explain** how you made your decision.

    a. $a + b = b + a$ b. $a - b = b - a$

    c. $a \cdot b = b \cdot a$ d. $a \div b = b \div a$

Additional Topics 1.2

Algebraic Properties

This lesson is designed to follow Lesson 2.1.9.

One of the Ways of Thinking used in this course is **justifying**. Up until now, you have justified your conclusions using explanations and reasoning to convince others. Another way to demonstrate valid conclusions is to use algebraic properties (sometimes referred to as "laws"). During this lesson, you will use the Commutative, Associative, Identity, and Inverse Properties of addition and multiplication to justify conclusions and determine if other conclusions are valid.

AT-9. Use algebra tiles and an expression comparison mat to show that the expressions below are equivalent.

$$3 + (2x^2 + 3x) \text{ and } (3 + 2x^2) + 3x$$

    a.   State the algebraic property that justifies that they are equivalent.

    b.   Use the same property to rewrite the expression $(4 + y) + 2y$. Then simplify the expression as much as possible.

    c.   What if the terms are not being added? Does the Associative Property still hold? Use algebra tiles and an expression comparison mat to compare $2x^2 - (3x - 8)$ with $(2x^2 - 3x) - 8$. Are these expressions equivalent? Explain.

    d.   Your work for part (c) answered the question "What if the terms are not being added?" What is another question you could ask about the Associative Property? Create another test for the Associative Property that will help you better understand the conditions under which it holds true. Be creative. When you are finished, be prepared to share your results with your class.

AT-10.   When finding the perimeter of the shape at right for part (b) of
         problem 2-13, Kiet and Corvell saw the shape differently. Their
         resulting expressions are shown below.

> Kiet: $2 + 2x + 2$ Corvell: $2 + x + 3 + x - 1$

    a.   Examine each expression. Is each expression valid for the perimeter of the
         shape? **Justify** your conclusion.

    b.   Show that the expressions are equivalent. What algebraic properties can be
         used to demonstrate that Kiet's expression is equivalent to Corvell's
         expression?

AT-11.   Examine the work below of a
         student simplifying the
         expression $9 - (3 - 5y)$. Is the
         work valid? If so, **justify** your
         conclusion by naming the
         algebraic properties. If not,
         explain which statement (or
         statements) is incorrect and
         provide a valid strategy to simplify the expression.

> **Note:** This stoplight icon will
> appear periodically throughout
> the text. Problems with this icon
> display common errors that can
> be made. Be sure not to make the
> same mistakes yourself!

    a. $9 - (3 - 5y)$
    b. $(9 - 3) - 5y$
    c. $(6 + 3 - 3) - 5y$
    d. $(6 + 0) - 5y$
    e. $6 - 5y$

AT-12.   Using algebra tiles, Brad and Donis each used different steps to simplify the
         expression $-5 + 2x + 8$. Their work is show below. For each student's work, justify
         each step by naming the property that was used or other valid reasoning. Then
         compare their strategies.

Donis's work		Brad's work	
Statement	**Reason**	**Statement**	**Reason**
1. $-5 + 2x + 8$	Given	1. $-5 + 2x + 8$	Given
2. $2x + 8 + (-5)$	a.	2. $-5 + 2x + 5 + 3$	e.
3. $2x + 3 + 5 + (-5)$	b.	3. $-5 + 5 + 2x + 3$	f.
4. $2x + 3 + 0$	c.	4. $0 + 2x + 3$	g.
5. $2x + 3$	d.	5. $2x + 3$	h.

AT-13.　Determine if the following statements are always true, sometimes true, or never true. **Justify** your conclusion.

a.　$3x^2 + 7 = 7 + 3x^2$

b.　$2x - 1 = 5$

c.　$-(-18) = 18$

d.　$-2 + 8 = -10$

e.　A rectangle with perimeter of 10 units has an area of 6 square units.

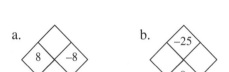

AT-14.　Using the pattern shown at right, copy and complete the following Diamond Problems. Then answer parts (e) and (f) below.

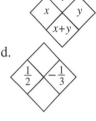

a. 　　b.　c.　d.

e.　What property guarantees that (a) and (c) have the same solutions? Justify your answer.

f.　Use the same property to find another solution to (b) above.

AT-15.　Examine the work below that shows one way to simplify the expression $-8 + 0 + (1 \cdot 5x + 13)$. Is the work valid? If so, **justify** your conclusion by naming the algebraic property for each step. If not, explain which statement (or statements) is incorrect and provide a valid strategy to simplify the expression.

a.　$-8 + 0 + (1 \cdot 5x + 13)$
b.　$-8 + (1 \cdot 5x + 13)$
c.　$-8 + (5x + 13)$
d.　$-8 + (13 + 5x)$
e.　$(-8 + 13) + 5x$
f.　$(-8 + 8 + 5) + 5x$
g.　$5 + 5x$

AT-16.   Review the algebraic properties found in the Math Notes boxes for Chapter 2. Then identify which property is being used below.

    a. $1 \cdot (3y) = 3y$ b. $16 + 2x = 2x + 16$

    c. $-4 + 4 = 0$ d. $3 + (6 + 2x) = (3 + 6) + 2x$

    e. $18x^2 + 0 = 18x^2$ f. $\frac{3}{4} \cdot \frac{4}{3} = 1$

AT-17.   Decide if the following statements are true or false. **Justify** your conclusion.

    a. $\frac{1}{2}(18) = 18 \div 2$ b.   If $a + 2 = b$, then $a + 3 = b + 1$

    c. $10 - 2 \cdot 5 = 40$ d.   If $2x - 5 = 7$, then $x = 6$

AT-18.   The set of integers can be represented with the notation below.

$$\{..., -3, -2, -1, 0, 1, 2, 3, ...\}$$

Note that the "…" symbol indicates that the numbers continue to follow the pattern without end. Use set notation to represent the set of numbers described below.

    a.   The set of even numbers

    b.   The set of natural numbers (i.e., integers greater than or equal to zero)

AT-19.   Decide if the following statements are always, sometimes, or never true. Explain your answer.

    a.   When a number is squared, the result is always positive.

    b.   The product of two negative numbers is positive.

    c.   If a and b are integers, then $\frac{a}{b}$ is an integer.

    d.   If the number x is an even integer, then $x + 2$ must be odd.

Additional Topics 1.3

Modeling Data

This lesson is designed to follow Lesson 3.2.4.

To find out if a roller coaster was safe, you collected data comparing a person's reach height with his or her height and found out that this data is roughly linear. What other types of graphs and rules can model a situation? Today you will examine a new situation in which data can help to answer a question.

AT-20.   BIRTHDAY PARTY

Kate is planning to ride her bike across town to attend her grandmother's 65th birthday party. The distance between her home and the party is 10 blocks. Assume that Kate will ride her bike at a constant rate.

   a.   If Kate takes 10 minutes to ride to the party, how fast does she need to travel in blocks per minute (bpm)? Explain how you found your answer.

   b.   How fast does Kate need to travel if she takes 5 minutes to ride from home to the party? 2 minutes? 1 minute?

   c.   Complete the table below. What is the relationship between the input (time it takes her to get from home to the party) and her corresponding speed?

Traveling Time (min)	¼	½	1	2	4	5	10	15	20
Speed (blocks per min)									

   d.   Examine the data in the table. Is it linear? How can you tell?

AT-21.   GRAPHING THE DATA

Return to your data from part (c) of problem AT-20. Carefully graph the points on graph paper. As you graph, answer the questions below. You may answer the questions in any order.

   •   What scale should you use so that you can plot all of the points and so that your graph is as large as possible?

   •   Can Kate's traveling time be exactly zero minutes? Why or why not? Adjust your graph to reflect your conclusion.

   •   Is the graph linear? If not, describe the shape formed by the data.

   •   What happens to Kate's speed as her traveling time increases?

   •   Does it make sense to connect the data? Why or why not?

   •   Have you seen this type of graph before? If so, in what circumstances (i.e., what was the situation or problem in which this type of graph appeared)?

AT-22.   WRITING A RULE

While graphing your data in problem AT-21, you may have noticed that you graphed a similar relationship in problem 3-103. Find your graph and table from problem 3-103 to learn more about this type of relationship.

a.   List four different points from the table in problem 3-103 in (x, y) form.

b.   What is the relationship between the x- and y-coordinates of each point from part (a)? How can you write this relationship algebraically?

c.   The relationship in problem 3-103 is an example of **inverse variation**. Any relationship for which the product of the x- and y-values is a constant is an example of inverse variation. The rule for this type of relationship is often written as $y = \frac{\text{constant}}{x}$ or as $xy = \text{constant}$. In the case of problem 3-103, the rule could be written as $y = \frac{24}{x}$ or $xy = 24$.

Examine your data from the Birthday Party, problem AT-20. Does the product of the corresponding x- and y-values remain constant? If so, write a rule in the form $y = \frac{\text{constant}}{x}$.

d.   If Kate wants to get to her grandmother's party in 3 minutes, how fast does she need to travel? Confirm your answer using your graph and your rule. Which representation provides the most accurate answer?

AT-23.   EXTENSION

Obtain a grapher from your teacher.

a.   Enter the points of your data from part (c) of problem AT-20 into your grapher and plot the data. Choose an appropriate viewing window that will allow you to see all of the data points.

b.   Now graph the rule from part (c) of problem AT-22 on top of the data. Does your rule seem to "fit" the data? If not, adjust your rule by changing the constant to find a better fit.

METHODS AND MEANINGS

More on Direct and Inverse Variation

When the product of each input and its corresponding output is a constant, the relationship is said to **vary inversely**. The relationship between Kate's traveling time and her speed in problem AT-20 is an example of inverse variation.

If the product of x and y equals a constant (not equal to 0), then x **and** y **vary inversely**. Formally, x and y vary inversely (or, said differently, x and y are **inversely proportional**) *if* $xy = k$ *or* $y = \frac{k}{x}$ for a constant $k \neq 0$.

An example, $y = \frac{12}{x}$, is graphed at right. In the case of the Birthday Party problem (AT-20), negative values of x and y are inappropriate. However, the rule $y = \frac{12}{x}$ does allow for negative and positive values for x and y, thus producing a portion of the graph in Quadrant III. Also note that the graph has no y-intercept, since $12 \div 0$ is undefined.

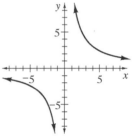

Example of
Inverse Variation

Another type of relationship is called **direct variation**. If the graph of a set of points is linear and passes through the point (0, 0), then y **varies directly with** x. Formally, x and y vary directly (or, said differently, are **directly proportional**) if for a constant k, not equal to zero, $y = kx$.

An example of direct variation, $y = \frac{1}{2}x$, is graphed at right. Notice that this example includes the portion of $y = \frac{1}{2}x$ in Quadrant III. However, in some direct variation situations, this portion of the graph may not make sense.

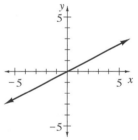

Example of
Direct Variation

AT-24.   On graph paper, draw at least three different rectangles with an area of 36 square units.

a.   Complete the table below for rectangles with an area of 36 square units.

Base	1	2	3	4	6	9	12	18	36	x
Height										

b.   Based on the data in the table, what type of relationship do x and y have? How can you tell?

c.   Write the rule you described in part (b) in algebraic symbols.

d.   Use the points in your table to graph this rule on graph paper.

AT-25.   In problems AT-20 and AT-24, you considered situations involving inverse variation. But what if y varies *directly* with x? Consider the situation where y is twice the value of x.

a.   How can you write this relationship algebraically? How is this rule different than an inverse variation relationship? You may want to review the Math Notes box from this lesson for more information.

b.   Create a table for this relationship.

c.   On graph paper, graph this relationship. Describe the resulting shape.

AT-26.   The amount of money Rachelle earns for babysitting varies directly with the number of hours she works. This means that the amount of money she earns is proportional to how many hours she works.

a.   If Rachelle earns $42 after babysitting 7 hours, how much does she earn per hour? How much should she earn if she babysits for 5 hours? Show how you found your answers.

b.   Rachelle decided to raise her rate to $9 per hour. How much will Rachelle earn if she babysits 3 hours? How many hours would she need to work to earn $45?

AT-27.   During a trip to the Midwest, Mr. Presley spent the same amount each day. He kept records of his available money and created the graph at right.

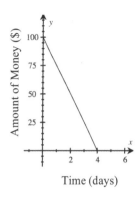

a.   How much money did Mr. Presley have at the start of his trip? How can you tell?

b.   How much did Mr. Presley spend each day? Explain how you know.

c.   What if Mr. Presley started with $150 but followed the same spending pattern. How would that change his graph? Explain.

d.   What if Mr. Presley spent less per day? Predict how that would change his graph.

AT-28.   Use your pattern-finding skills to copy and complete the table below.

IN (x)	−1	½	1	2	3	4	5	10
OUT (y)	−20	40	20	10				

a.   Explain any patterns you found in your table. How did you find each y-value?

b.   Examine the data in the table. Without graphing the data, predict whether the graph would be linear or not. **Justify** your conclusion.

c.   Write a rule for the data in the table. Use your rule to find y when x = 100.

Glossary

absolute value   The absolute value of a number is the distance of the number from zero. Since the absolute value represents a distance, without regard to direction, it is always non-negative. Thus the absolute value of a negative number is its opposite, while the absolute value of a non-negative number is just the number itself. The absolute value of x is usually written "$|x|$". For example, $|-5| = 5$ and $|22| = 22$. (p. 389)

Additive Identity Property   The Additive Identity Property states that adding zero to any expression leaves the expression unchanged. That is, $a + 0 = a$. For example, $-2xy^2 + 0 = -2xy^2$. (p. 53)

Additive Inverse Property   The Additive Inverse Property states that for every number a there is a number $-a$ such that $a + (-a) = 0$. For example, the number 5 has an additive inverse of -5; $5 + (-5) = 0$. The additive inverse of a number is often called its opposite. For example, 5 and -5 are opposites. (p. 72)

Additive Property of Equality   The Additive Property of Equality states that equality is maintained if the same amount is added to both sides of an equation. That is, if $a = b$, then $a + c = b + c$. For example, if $y = 3x$, then $y + 1.5 = 3x + 1.5$. (p. 249)

algebra tiles   An algebra tile is a manipulative whose area represents a constant or variable quantity. The algebra tiles used in this course consist of large squares with dimensions x-by-x and y-by-y; rectangles with dimensions x-by-1, y-by-1, and x-by-y; and small squares with dimensions 1-by-1. These tiles are named by their areas: x^2, y^2, x, y, xy, and 1, respectively. The smallest squares are called "unit tiles." In this text, shaded tiles will represent positive quantities while unshaded tiles will represent negative quantities. (p. 41)

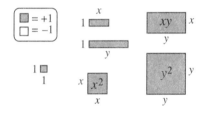

area   For this course, area is the number of square units needed to fill up a region on a flat surface. In later courses, the idea will be extended to cones, spheres, and more complex surfaces. (p. 5)

Area = 15 square units

Associative Property of Addition   The Associative Property of Addition states that if a sum contains terms that are grouped, the sum can be grouped differently with no effect on the total. That is, $a + (b + c) = (a + b) + c$. For example, $3 + (4 + 5) = (3 + 4) + 5$. (p. 53)

Associative Property of Multiplication   The Associative Property of Multiplication states that if a product contains terms that are grouped, the product can be grouped differently with no effect on the result. That is, $a(bc) = (ab)c$. For example, $2 \cdot (3 \cdot 4) = (2 \cdot 3) \cdot 4$. (p. 53)

asymptote   A line that a graph of a curve approaches as closely as you wish. An asymptote is often represented by a dashed line on a graph. For example, the graph at right has an asymptote at $y = -3$. (p. 472)

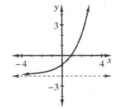

average   See "mean."

axes   In a coordinate plane, two number lines that meet at right angles at the origin $(0, 0)$. The x-axis runs horizontally and the y-axis runs vertically. See the example at right. (p. 10)

b   When the equation of a line is expressed in $y = mx + b$ form, the constant b gives the y-intercept of the line. For example, the y-intercept of the line $y = -\frac{1}{3}x + 7$ is 7. (p. 149)

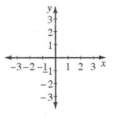

base (1) When working with an exponential expression in the form a^b, a is called the base. For example, 2 is the base in 2^5. (5 is the exponent, and 32 is the value.) (Also see "exponent.") (p. 452) (2) When working with geometric figures, the term "base" may be applied to a side of a triangle, rectangle, parallelogram, or trapezoid. "Base" may also be applied to the face of a prism, cylinder, pyramid, or cone.

binomial   An expression that is the sum or difference of exactly two terms, each of which is a monomial. For example, $-2x + 3y^2$ is a binomial. (pp. 193, 329)

boundary line or curve   A line or curve on a two-dimensional graph that divides the graph into two regions. A boundary line or curve is used when graphing inequalities with two variables. For example, the inequality $y < \frac{2}{3}x + 2$ is graphed at right. The dashed boundary line has equation $y = \frac{2}{3}x + 2$. A boundary line is also sometimes called a "dividing line." (p. 393)

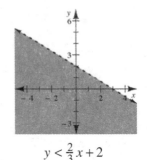

$$y < \frac{2}{3}x + 2$$

boundary point   The endpoint of a ray or segment on a number line where an inequality is true. For strict inequalities (that is, inequalities involving < or >), the point is not part of the solution. We find boundary points by solving the equality associated with our inequality. For example, the solution to the equation $2x + 5 = 11$ is $x = 3$, so the inequality $2x + 5 \geq 11$ has a boundary point at 3. The solution to that inequality is illustrated on the number line at right. A boundary point is also sometimes called a "dividing point." (p. 386)

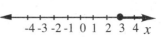

closure properties of rational numbers   The closure properties of rational numbers state that the product or sum of two rational numbers is a rational number. For example, $\frac{1}{2}$ and $\frac{3}{4}$ are both rational numbers; $\frac{1}{2} + \frac{3}{4}$ is $\frac{5}{4}$; and $\frac{5}{4}$ is a rational number. Also, 2.2 and 0.75 are both rational numbers; $2.2 \cdot 0.75$ is 1.65; and 1.65 is a rational number. (p. 214)

coefficient (numerical)   A number multiplying a variable or product of variables. For example, -7 is the coefficient of $-7xy^2$. (p. 255)

coincide   Two graphs coincide if they have all their points in common. For example, the graphs of $y = 2x + 4$ and $3y = 6x + 12$ coincide; both graphs are lines with a slope of 2 and a y-intercept of 4. When the graphs of two equations coincide, those equations share all the same solutions and have an infinite number of intersection points. (p. 252)

combining like terms   Combining two or more like terms simplifies an expression by summing constants and summing those variable terms in which the same variables are raised to the same power. For example, combining like terms in the expression $3x + 7 + 5x - 3 + 2x^2 + 3y^2$ gives $8x + 4 + 2x^2 + 3y^2$. When working with algebra tiles, combining like terms involves putting together tiles with the same dimensions. (p. 57)

common denominator   A common denominator of a group of fractions is an expression that has the denominators of each of the fractions as a factor. For example, if we are simplifying the sum $\frac{2}{x+3} + \frac{5x}{7} + \frac{3x-8}{2}$, we might use $14(x + 3)$ as a common denominator for all three terms. (p. 503)

common factor   A common factor is a factor that is the same for two or more terms. For example, x^2 is a common factor of $3x^2$ and $-5x^2y$. (p. 338)

Commutative Property of Addition   The Commutative Property of Addition states that if two terms are added, the order can be reversed with no effect on the total. That is, $a + b = b + a$. For example, $7 + 12 = 12 + 7$. (p. 45)

Commutative Property of Multiplication   The Commutative Property of Multiplication states that if two expressions are multiplied, the order can be reversed with no effect on the result. That is, $ab = ba$. For example, $5 \cdot 8 = 8 \cdot 5$. (p. 45)

complete graph   A complete graph includes all the necessary information about a line or a curve. To be complete, a graph must have the following components: (1) the x-axis and y-axis labeled, clearly showing the scale; (2) the equation of the graph written near the line or curve; (3) the line or curve extended as far as possible on the graph with arrows if the line or curve continues beyond the axes; (4) the coordinates of all special points, such as x- and y-intercepts, shown in (x, y) form. (p. 120)

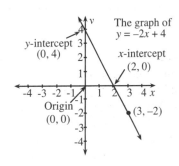

completing the square   In this course, we use completing the square to convert a quadratic equation in standard form into perfect square form. To complete the square, we add (or subtract) a constant to (or from) both sides of the equation so that the quadratic expression can be factored into a perfect square. For example, when given the quadratic equation $x^2 - 6x + 4 = 0$, we can complete the square by adding 5 to both sides. The resulting equation, $x^2 - 6x + 9 = 5$, has a left-hand side we can factor, resulting in the perfect square form quadratic equation $(x - 3)^2 = 5$. (p. 444)

conclusion   In an "If...then..." statement, the "then" portion is called the conclusion. For example, in the statement "*If* $x = 3$, *then* $x^2 = 9$," the conclusion is "$x^2 = 9$." (Also see "hypothesis.") (p. 241)

consecutive numbers   Integers that are in order without skipping any of them. For example, 8, 9, and 10 are consecutive numbers. (p. 256)

congruent   Two shapes are congruent if they have exactly the same size and shape. For example, the two triangles at right are congruent.

constant   A symbol representing a value that does not change. For example, in the equation $y = 2x + 5$, the number 5 is a constant. (p. 255)

continuous graph   A graph whose points are connected with an unbroken line or curve is called a continuous graph. A continuous graph can be traced with a pencil without ever lifting the pencil to move from one point on the graph to another point. For example, the graphs shown below are both continuous. (Also see "discrete.") (p. 102)

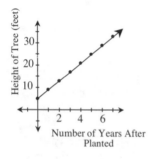
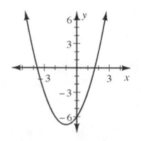

coordinate(s)   The number corresponding to a point on the number line or an ordered pair (x, y) that corresponds to a point in a two-dimensional coordinate system. In an ordered pair, the x-coordinate appears first and the y-coordinate appears second. For example, the point (3, 5) has an x-coordinate of 3. (pp. 8, 10)

coordinate plane   A flat surface defined by two number lines meeting at right angles at their zero points. A coordinate plane is also sometimes called a "Cartesian Plane." (p. 10)

coordinate system   A system of graphing ordered pairs of numbers on a coordinate plane. An ordered pair represents a point, with the first number giving the horizontal position relative to the x-axis and the second number giving the vertical position relative to the y-axis. For example, the diagram at right shows the point (3, 5) graphed on a coordinate plane. (p. 8)

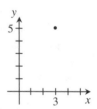

counterexample   An example showing that a statement has at least one exception; that is, a situation in which the statement is false. For example, the number 4 is a counterexample to the hypothesis that all even numbers are greater than 7. (p. 192)

deductive reasoning   See "justify."(p. 448)

degree   (1) The degree of a monomial is the sum of the exponents of its variables. For example, $3x^2y^5$ has degree 7, because the sum of the exponents (5+2) is 7.   (2) The degree of a polynomial in one variable is the degree of the term with the highest exponent. For example, $3x^5 - 4x^2 - x + 7$ has degree 5, because the highest exponent to which x is raised is 5. (3) The degree of a polynomial in more than one variable is the highest sum of the exponents among the terms. For example, $2x^5y^3 - 4x^2y^4z^3 - xy^5 + 3y^2z - 12$ has degree 9, because the sum of the exponents in the second term is 9 and no term has a higher exponent sum.

dependent variable   When one quantity depends for its value on one or more others, it is called the dependent variable. For example, we might relate the speed of a car to the amount of force you apply to the gas pedal. Here, the speed of the car is the dependent variable; it depends on how hard you push the pedal. The dependent variable appears as the output value in an $x \rightarrow y$ table, and is usually placed relative to the vertical axis of a graph. We often use the letter y for the dependent variable. When working with functions or relations, the dependent variable represents the output value. (Also see "independent variable.") (pp. 110, 473)

difference of squares   A polynomial that can be factored as the product of the sum and difference of two terms. The general pattern is $x^2 - y^2 = (x + y)(x - y)$. Most of the differences of squares found in this course are of the form $a^2x^2 - b^2 = (ax + b)(ax - b)$, where a and b are nonzero real numbers. For example, the difference of squares $4x^2 - 9$ can be factored as $(2x + 3)(2x - 3)$. (p. 497)

dimensions   The dimensions of a flat region or space tell how far it extends in each direction. For example, the dimensions of a rectangle might be 16 cm wide by 7 cm high. (p. 22)

discrete graph   A graph that consists entirely of separated points is called a discrete graph. For example, the graph shown at right is discrete. (Also see "continuous.") (p. 102)

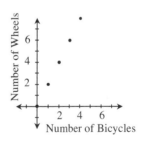

discriminant   For quadratic equations in standard form $ax^2 + bx + c = 0$, the discriminant is $b^2 - 4ac$. If the discriminant is positive, the equation has two roots; if the discriminant is zero, the equation has one root; if the discriminant is negative, the equation has no real-number roots. For example, the discriminant of the quadratic equation $2x^2 - 4x - 5$ is $(-4)^2 - 4(2)(-5) = 56$, which indicates that that equation has two roots (solutions).

Distributive Property   We use the Distributive Property to write a product of expressions as a sum of terms. The Distributive Property states that for any numbers or expressions a, b, and c, $a(b + c) = ab + ac$. For example, $2(x + 4) = 2 \cdot x + 2 \cdot 4 = 2x + 8$. We can demonstrate this with algebra tiles or in a generic rectangle. (p. 198)

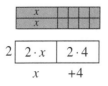

dividing line   See "boundary line."

dividing point   See "boundary point."

domain   The set of all input values for a relation or function. For example, the domain of the function graphed at right is $x \geq -3$. (p. 473) For variables, the domain is the set of numbers the variable may represent. (Also see "range.")

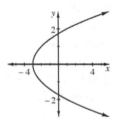

Elimination Method   A method for solving a system of equations. The key step in using the Elimination Method is to add or subtract both sides of two equations to eliminate one of the variables. For example, the two equations in the system at right can be added together to get the simplified result $7x = 14$. We can solve this equation to find x, then substitute the x-value back into either of the original equations to find the value of y. (pp. 250, 264)

$$5x + 2y = 10$$
$$2x - 2y = 4$$

equal   Two quantities are equal when they have the same value. For example, when $x = 4$, the expression $x + 8$ is equal to the expression $3x$ because their values are the same. (p. 68)

Equal Values Method   A method for solving a system of equations. To use the Equal Values Method, take two expressions that are each equal to the same variable and set those expressions equal to each other. For example, in the system of equations at right, $-2x + 5$ and $x - 1$ each equal y. So we write $-2x + 5 = x - 1$, then solve that equation to find x. Once we have x, we substitute that value back into either of the original equations to find the value of y. (p. 176)

$$y = -2x + 5$$
$$y = x - 1$$

equation   A mathematical sentence in which two expressions appear on either side of an "equals" sign (=), stating that the two expressions are equivalent. For example, the equation $7x + 4.2 = -8$ states that the expression $7x + 4.2$ has the value –8. In this course, an equation is often used to represent a rule relating two quantities. For example, a rule for finding the area y of a tile pattern with figure number x might be written $y = 4x - 3$. (p. 68)

equation mat   An organizing tool used to visually represent two equal expressions using algebra tiles. For example, the equation mat at right represents the equation $2x - 1 - (-x + 3) = 6 - 2x$. (p. 69)

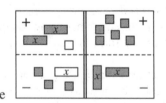

equivalent   Two expressions are equivalent if they have the same value. For example, $2 + 3$ is equivalent to $1 + 4$. (p. 19)   Two equations are equivalent if they have all the same solutions. For example, $y = 3x$ is equivalent to $2y = 6x$. Equivalent equations have the same graph. (p. 205)

evaluate   To evaluate an expression, substitute the value(s) given for the variable(s) and perform the operations according to the order of operations. For example, evaluating $2x + y - 10$ when $x = 4$ and $y = 3$ gives the value 1. (p. 49)

exponent   In an expression of the form a^b, b is called the exponent. For example, in the expression 2^5, 5 is called the exponent. (2 is the base, and 32 is the value.) The exponent indicates how many times to use the base as a multiplier. For example, in 2^5, 2 is used 5 times: $2^5 = 2 \cdot 2 \cdot 2 \cdot 2 \cdot 2 = 32$. For exponents of zero, the rule is: for any number $x \neq 0$, $x^0 = 1$. For negative exponents, the rule is: for any number $x \neq 0$, $x^{-n} = \frac{1}{x^n}$, and $\frac{1}{x^{-n}} = x^n$. (Also see "laws of exponents.") (p. 452)

expression   An expression contains one or more numbers and/or variables. Each part of the expression separated by addition or subtraction signs is called a "term." For example, each of these is an expression: $6xy^2$, 24, $2.5q - 7$, $\frac{y-3}{4+x}$. (p. 47)

expression comparison mat   An expression comparison mat puts two expression mats side-by-side so they can be compared to see which represents the greater value. For example, in the expression comparison mat at right, the left-hand mat represents –3, while the right-hand mat represents –2. Since $-2 > -3$ the expression on the right is greater. (p. 55)

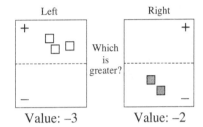

expression mat   An organizing tool used to visually represent an expression with algebra tiles. An expression mat has two regions, a positive region at the top and a negative region at the bottom. The tiles on the expression mat at right represent a value of -3. (p. 47)

Value: –3

factor   (1) In arithmetic: When two or more integers are multiplied, each of the integers is a factor of the product. For example, 4 is a factor of 24, because $4 \cdot 6 = 24$.   (2) In algebra: When two or more algebraic expressions are multiplied together, each of the expressions is a factor of the product. For example, x^2 is a factor of $-17x^2y^3$, because $(x^2)(-17y^3) = -17x^2y^3$. (3) To factor an expression is to write it as a product. For example, the factored form of $x^2 - 3x - 18$ is $(x - 6)(x + 3)$. (p. 329)

factored completely   A polynomial is factored completely if none of the resulting factors can be factored further using integer coefficients. For example, $-2(x + 3)(x - 1)$ is the completely factored form of $-2x^2 - 4x + 6$. (p. 337)

factored form   A quadratic equation in the form $a(x + b)(x + c) = 0$, where a is nonzero, is said to be in factored form. For example, $-7(x + 2)(x - 1.5) = 0$ is a quadratic equation in factored form. (p. 438)

Fibonacci Sequence The sequence of numbers 1, 1, 2, 3, 5, 8, 13, …. Each term of the Fibonacci sequence (after the first two terms) is the sum of the two preceding terms. (p. 95)

Figure 0   The figure that comes before Figure 1 in a tile pattern. When representing a tile pattern with a graph, the y-intercept of the graph is the number of tiles in Figure 0. When representing a tile pattern with an equation in $y = mx + b$ form, b gives the number of tiles in Figure 0. (p. 142)

F.O.I.L.   An approach for multiplying two binomials. "F.O.I.L." stands for "First, Outer, Inner, Last." It describes the order in which to multiply the terms of two binomials to be sure to get all the products. For example, the equation below shows how to apply the F.O.I.L. method to multiply $(2x + 3)(x - 4)$.

$$(2x + 3)(x - 4) = \underset{firsts}{(2x)(x)} + \underset{outers}{(2x)(-4)} + \underset{inners}{(3)(x)} + \underset{lasts}{(3)(-4)} = 2x^2 - 5x - 12$$

fraction buster   "Fraction busting" is a method of simplifying equations involving fractions that uses the Multiplicative Property of Equality to rearrange the equation so that no fractions remain. To use this method, multiply both sides of an equation by the common denominator of all the fractions in the equation. The result will be an equivalent equation with no fractions. For example, when given the equation $\frac{x}{7} + 2 = \frac{x}{3}$, we can multiply both sides by the "fraction buster" 21. The resulting equation, $3x + 42 = 7x$, is equivalent to the original but contains no fractions. (p. 419)

function   A relation in which for each input value there is one and only one output value. For example, the relation $f(x) = x + 4$ is a function; for each input value (x) there is exactly one output value. In terms of ordered pairs (x, y), no two ordered pairs of a function have the same first member (x). (p. 473)

function notation   When a rule expressing a function is written using function notation, the function is given a name, most commonly "f," "g," or "h." The notation $f(x)$ represents the output of a function, named f, when x is the input. It is pronounced "f of x." For example, $g(2)$, pronounced "g of 2", represents the output of the function g when $x = 2$. If $g(x) = x^2 + 3$, then $g(2) = 7$. (p. 464)

generic rectangle   A type of diagram used to visualize multiplying expressions without algebra tiles. Each expression to be multiplied forms a side length of the rectangle, and the product is the sum of the areas of the sections of the rectangle. For example, the generic rectangle at right can be used to multiply $(2x + 5)$ by $(x + 3)$. (p. 218)

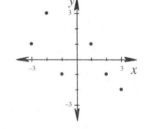

$$(2x + 5)(x + 3) = 2x^2 + 11x + 15$$

area as a product   area as a sum

graph   A graph represents numerical information spatially. The numbers may come from a table, situation (pattern), or rule (equation or inequality). Most of the graphs in this course show points, lines, and/or curves on a two-dimensional coordinate system like the one at right (pp. 8, 10) or on a single axis called a number line (see below). (p. 21) (See "complete graph.")

greater than   One expression is greater than another if its value is larger. We indicate this relationship with the greater than symbol ">". For example, $4+5$ is greater than $1+1$. We write $4+5>1+1$. (pp. 55, 377)

greatest common factor (GCF)   (1) For integers, the greatest positive integer that is a common factor of two or more integers. For example, the greatest common factor of 28 and 42 is 14.   (2) For two or more algebraic monomials, the product of the greatest common integer factor of the coefficients of the monomials and the variable(s) in each algebraic term with the smallest degree of that variable in every term. For example, the greatest common factor of $12x^3y^2$ and $8xy^4$ is $4xy^2$. (3) For a polynomial, the greatest common monomial factor of its terms. For example, the greatest common factor of $16x^4+8x^3+12x$ is $4x$.

growth   One useful way to analyze a mathematical relationship is to examine how the output value grows as the input value increases. We can see this growth on a graph of a linear relationship by looking at the slope of the graph. (p. 142)

growth factor   When two quantities are in a linear relationship, the growth factor describes how much the output value changes when the input value increases by 1. For example, the $x \rightarrow y$ table at right shows a linear relationship with a growth factor of 6. The growth factor is equal to the slope of the line representing a linear relationship. The growth factor is also equal to the value of m when the relationship is represented with an equation in $y=mx+b$ form. (p. 205)

x	y
1	7
2	13
3	19
4	25

growth number   See "growth factor."

Guess and Check   A strategy for solving problems that starts with making a guess and then checking whether that guess is a correct solution to the problem. If the guess is not correct, the checking process helps suggest a closer next guess. The second guess is then checked. This process is repeated until a correct solution is found. Being organized is critical to using Guess and Check successfully. A table is one good way to organize your work. The Guess and Check process leads to writing equations to represent and solve word problems. (pp. 22, 65)

horizontal lines   Horizontal lines are "flat" and run left to right in the same direction as the x-axis. Horizontal lines have equations of the form $y=b$, where b can be any number. For example, the graph at right shows the horizontal lines $y=3$ and $y=-2$. The slope of any horizontal line is 0. The x-axis has the equation $y=0$ because $y=0$ everywhere on the x-axis. (p. 291)

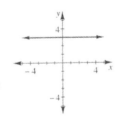

hypothesis   (1) A term scientists use to mean an "educated guess" (or what mathematicians call a conjecture), based on data, patterns, and relationships. For instance, having looked at many multiples of five, you might form a hypothesis that every multiple of five ends in the digit 0 or the digit 5.   (2) In an "If...then..." statement, the "if" portion is called the hypothesis. For example, in the statement "*If* $x=3$, *then* $x^2=9$," the hypothesis is "$x=3$." (Also see "conclusion.") (p. 241)

identity element for addition   0 is the identity element for addition because adding 0 to an expression leaves the expression unchanged. That is, $a + 0 = 0$. (Also see "Additive Identity Property.") (p. 53)

identity element for multiplication   1 is the identity element for multiplication because multiplying an expression by 1 leaves the expression unchanged. That is, $a(1) = a$. (Also see "Multiplicative Identity Property.") (p. 53)

Identity Property of Addition   See "Additive Identity Property."

Identity Property of Multiplication   See "Multiplicative Identity Property."

independent variable   When one quantity changes in a way that does not depend on the value of another quantity, the value that changes independently is represented with the independent variable. For example, we might relate the speed of a car to the amount of force you apply to the gas pedal. Here, the amount of force applied may be whatever the driver chooses, so it represents the independent variable. The independent variable appears as the input value in an $x \rightarrow y$ table, and is usually placed relative to the horizontal axis of a graph. We often use the letter x for the independent variable. When working with functions or relations, the independent variable represents the input value. (Also see "dependent variable.") (pp. 110, 473)

inductive reasoning   Drawing a conclusion based on a pattern. For example, having seen many multiples of 5 that end in the digit 0 or 5, you might use inductive reasoning to make a hypothesis or conjecture that *all* multiples of 5 end in the digit 0 or 5. (p. 448)

inequality   An inequality consists of two expressions on either side of an inequality symbol. For example, the inequality $7x + 4.2 < -8$ states that the expression $7x + 4.2$ has a value less than 8. (p. 352)

inequality symbols   The symbol $\leq$ read from left to right means "less than or equal to." The symbol $\geq$ read from left to right means "greater than or equal to." The symbols $<$ and $>$ mean "less than" and "greater than," respectively. For example, "7<13" means that 7 is less than 13. (p. 377)

input value   The input value is the independent variable in a relation. We substitute the input value into our rule (equation) to determine the output value. For example, if we have a rule for how much your phone bill will be if you talk a certain number of minutes, the number of minutes you talk is the input value. The input value appears first in an $x \rightarrow y$ table, and is represented by the variable x. When working with functions, the input value, an element of the domain, is the value put into the function. (pp. 97, 464)

integers   The set of numbers $\{ \ldots -3, -2, -1, 0, 1, 2, 3, \ldots \}$. (p. 15)

intersection   See "point of intersection."

irrational numbers   The set of numbers that cannot be expressed in the form $\frac{a}{b}$, where a and b are integers and $b \neq 0$. For example, π and $\sqrt{2}$ are irrational numbers. (p. 365)

justify   To use facts, definitions, rules, and/or previously proven statements in an organized way to convince an audience that a claim (or an answer) is valid or true. For example, you might justify your claim that $x = 2$ is a solution to $3x = 6$ by pointing out that when you multiply 3 by 2, you get 6. (p. 88)

lattice points   The points on a coordinate grid where the grid lines intersect. The diagram at right shows two lattice points. The coordinates of lattice points are integers. (p. 283)

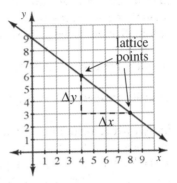

laws of exponents   The laws of exponents we study in this course are: (p. 452)

Law	Examples	
$x^m x^n = x^{m+n}$ for all x	$x^3 x^4 = x^{3+4} = x^7$	$2^5 \cdot 2^{-1} = 2^4$
$\frac{x^m}{x^n} = x^{m-n}$ for $x \neq 0$	$x^{10} \div x^4 = x^{10-4} = x^6$	$\frac{5^4}{5^7} = 5^{-3}$
$(x^m)^n = x^{mn}$ for all x	$(x^4)^3 = x^{4 \cdot 3} = x^{12}$	$(10^5)^6 = 10^{30}$
$x^0 = 1$ for $x \neq 0$	$\frac{y^2}{y^2} = y^0 = 1$	$9^0 = 1$
$x^{-1} = \frac{1}{x}$ for $x \neq 0$	$\frac{1}{x^2} = (\frac{1}{x})^2 = (x^{-1})^2 = x^{-2}$	$3^{-1} = \frac{1}{3}$
$x^{m/n} = \sqrt[n]{x^m}$ for $x \geq 0$	$\sqrt{k} = k^{1/2}$	$y^{2/3} = \sqrt[3]{y^2}$

least common multiple (LCM)   (1) The smallest common multiple of a set of two or more integers. For example, the least common multiple of 4, 6, and 8 is 24. (2) For two or more algebraic monomials, the product of the least common integer multiples of the coefficients of the monomials and the variable(s) in each algebraic term with the greatest degree of that variable in every term. For example, the least common factor of $12x^3y^2$ and $8xy^4$ is $24x^3y^4$. (p. 503)

"legal" moves   When working with an equation mat or expression comparison mat, there are certain "legal" moves you can make with the algebra tiles that keep the relationship between the two sides of the mat intact. For example, removing an x tile from the positive region of each side of an equation mat is a legal move; it keeps the expressions on each side of the mat equal. The legal moves are those justified by the properties of the real numbers. (p. 54)

less than   (1) One expression is less than another if its value is not as large. We indicate this relationship with the less than symbol "<". For example, $1+1$ is less than $4+5$. We write $1+1 < 4+5$. (p. 377) (2) We sometimes say that one amount is a certain quantity less than another amount. For example, a student movie ticket might cost two dollars *less than* an adult ticket. (p. 28)

"let" statement   A "let" statement is written at the beginning of our work to identify the variable that will represent a certain quantity. For example, in solving a problem about grilled cheese sandwiches, we might begin by writing "Let s = the number of sandwiches eaten." It is particularly important to use "let" statements when writing mathematical sentences, so that your readers will know what the variables in the sentences represent. (p. 233)

like terms   Two or more terms that contain the same variable(s), with corresponding variables raised to the same power. For example, $5x$ and $2x$ are like terms. (Also see "combining like terms.") (p. 57)

line of symmetry   A line that divides a shape into two pieces that are mirror images of each other. If you fold a shape over its line of symmetry, the shapes on both sides of the line will match perfectly. A shape with a line of symmetry is shown at right. (p. 342)

line of symmetry

linear equation   An equation in two variables whose graph is a line. For example, $y = 2.1x - 8$ is a linear equation. The standard form for a linear equation is $ax + by = c$, where a, b, and c are constants and a and b are not both zero. Most linear equations can be written in $y = mx + b$ form, which is more useful for determining the line's slope and y-intercept. (p. 205)

looking inside   "Looking inside" is a method of solving one-variable equations containing parentheses or an absolute value symbol. To use "looking inside," we first determine what the value of the entire expression inside the parentheses (or absolute value symbol) must be. We then use that fact to solve for the value of the variable. For example, to use "looking inside" to solve the equation $4(x + 2) = 36$, we first determine that $x + 2$ must equal 9. We then solve the equation $x + 2 = 9$ to find that $x = 7$. (p. 424)

m   When the equation of a line is expressed in $y = mx + b$ form, the constant m gives the slope of the line. For example, the slope of the line $y = -\frac{1}{3}x + 7$ is $-\frac{1}{3}$. (p. 149)

mathematical sentence   A mathematical sentence is an equation that uses variables to represent unknown quantities. For example, the mathematical sentence $b + g = 23$ might represent the fact that the total number of boys and girls in the class is 23. It is helpful to define variables using "let" statements before using them in a mathematical sentence. (Also see " 'let' statement.") (p. 232)

mean   The mean, or average, of several numbers is one way of defining the "middle" of the numbers. To find the average of a group of numbers, add the numbers together then divide by the number of numbers in the set. For example, the average of the numbers 1, 5, and 6 is $(1 + 5 + 6) \div 3 = 4$. (p. 11)

monomial   An expression with only one term. It can be a number, a variable, or the product of a number and one or more variables. For example, 7, $3x$, $-4ab$, and $3x^2y$ are each monomials. (p. 329)

multiple representations   See "representation" and "representations web."

Multiplicative Identity Property   The Multiplicative Identity Property states that multiplying any expression by 1 leaves the expression unchanged. That is, $a(1) = a$. For example, $437x \cdot 1 = 437x$. (p. 53)

Multiplicative Inverse Property   The Multiplicative Inverse Property states that for every nonzero number a there is a number $\frac{1}{a}$ such that $a \cdot \frac{1}{a} = 1$. For example, the number 6 has a multiplicative inverse of $\frac{1}{6}$; $6 \cdot \frac{1}{6} = 1$. The multiplicative inverse of a number is usually called its reciprocal. For example, $\frac{1}{6}$ is the reciprocal of 6. For a number in the form $\frac{a}{b}$, where a and b are non-zero, the reciprocal is $\frac{b}{a}$. (p. 72)

Multiplicative Property of Equality   The Multiplicative Property of Equality states that equality is maintained if both sides of an equation are multiplied by the same amount. That is, if $a = b$, then $a \cdot c = b \cdot c$. For example, if $y = 3x$, then $2(y) = 2(3x)$.

negative   A negative number is a number less than zero. Negative numbers are graphed on the negative side of a number line. (p. 15)

non-commensurate   Two measurements are called non-commensurate if no whole number multiple of one measurement can ever equal a whole number multiple of the other. For example, measures of 1 cm and $\sqrt{2}$ cm are non-commensurate, because no combination of items 1 cm long will ever have exactly the same length as a combination of items $\sqrt{2}$ cm long. (p. 42)

numeral   A symbol that names a number. For example, each of these is a numeral: 22.6, –19, 0.

numerical coefficient   See "coefficient."

opposite   Two numbers are opposites if they are the same distance from zero, but one is positive and one is negative. For example, 5 and –5 are opposites. The opposite of a number is sometimes called its additive inverse, indicating that the sum of a number and its opposite is zero. (p. 72)

order of operations   The specific order in which certain operations are to be carried out to evaluate or simplify expressions. The order is: parentheses (or other grouping symbols), exponents (powers or roots), multiplication and division (from left to right), and addition and subtraction (from left to right). (p. 49)

ordered pair Two numbers written in order as follows: (x, y). The primary use of ordered pairs in this course is to represent points in an x-y coordinate system. The first coordinate (x) represents the horizontal distance and direction from the origin; the second coordinate (y) represents the vertical distance and direction from the origin. For example, the ordered pair (3, 5) represents the point shown in bold at right. (p. 10)

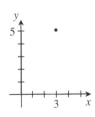

origin The point on a coordinate plane where the *x*- and *y*-axes intersect is called the origin. This point has coordinates $(0, 0)$. The point assigned to zero on a number line is also called the origin. (p. 120)

output value The output value is the dependent variable in a relation. When we substitute the input value into our rule (equation), the result is the output value. For example, if we have a rule for how much your phone bill will be if you talk a certain number of minutes, the amount of your phone bill is the output value. The output value appears second in an $x \rightarrow y$ table, and is represented by the variable *y*. When working with functions, the output value, an element of the range, is the value that results from applying the rule for the function to an input value. (pp. 97, 464)

parabola A parabola is a particular kind of mathematical curve. In this course, a parabola is always the graph of a quadratic function $y = ax^2 + bx + c$ where *a* does not equal 0. The diagram at right shows some examples of parabolas. The highest or lowest point on the graph is called the vertex. (p. 106)

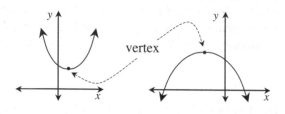

parallel Two or more straight lines on a flat surface that do not intersect (no matter how far they are extended) are parallel. If two lines have the same slope and do not coincide, they are parallel. For example, the graphs of $y = 2x + 3$ and $y = 2x - 2$ are parallel (see diagram at right). When two equations have parallel graphs, the equations have no solutions in common. (p. 252)

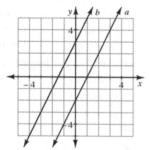

pattern A pattern is a set of things in order that change in a regular way. For example, the numbers 1, 4, 7, 10, ... form a pattern, because each number increases by 3. The numbers 1, 4, 9, 16, ... form a pattern, because they are squares of consecutive integers. (p. 96) In this course, we often look at tile patterns, whose figure numbers and areas we represent with a table, a rule (equation), or a graph. (pp. 18, 93)

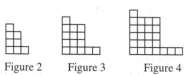

Figure 2   Figure 3   Figure 4

percent A ratio that compares a number to 100. Percents are often written using the "%" symbol. For example, 0.75 is equal to $\frac{75}{100}$ or 75%. (p. 19)

perfect square form A quadratic equation in the form $a(x + b)^2 = c$, where *a* is nonzero, is said to be in perfect square form. For example, $3(x - 12)^2 = 19$ is a quadratic equation in perfect square form. (p. 438)

perfect square trinomials   Trinomials of the form $a^2x^2 + 2abx + b^2$, where a and b are nonzero real numbers, are known as perfect square trinomials and factor as $(ax + b)^2$. For example, the perfect square trinomial $9x^2 - 24x + 16$ can be factored as $(3x - 4)^2$. (p. 497)

perimeter   The distance around a figure on a flat surface. (p. 5)

Perimeter =
$5 + 8 + 4 + 6 = 23$ units

perpendicular   Two lines or segments that meet (intersect) to form a 90° angle. For example, the lines shown on the graph at right are perpendicular. If two perpendicular lines are graphed in an x, y-coordinate system, their slopes are opposite reciprocals. (p. 308)

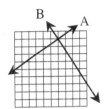

point of intersection   A point of intersection is a point that the graphs of two equations have in common. For example, (3, 4) is a point of intersection of the two graphs shown at right. Two graphs may have one point of intersection, several points of intersection, or no points of intersection. The ordered pair representing a point of intersection gives a solution to the equations of each of the graphs. (pp. 165, 252)

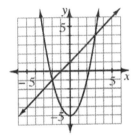

point-slope form   The point-slope form of the equation of a line is $y - k = m(x - h)$, where (h, k) are the coordinates of a point on the line, and m is the slope of the line. For example, a line with slope –4 passing through the point (5, 8) has the equation $y - 8 = -4(x - 5)$. To find the equation of the line in $y = mx + b$ form, we solve the point-slope form equation for y. (p. 314)

polygon   A two-dimensional closed figure of straight line segments ("edges" or "sides") connected end to end. Each side (or edge) intersects only the endpoints of its two adjacent sides (or edges). For example, the shape at right is a polygon.

polynomial   An expression that is the sum or difference of two or more monomials (terms). For example, $x^8 - 4x^6y + 6x^4y^2$ is a polynomial. (p. 329)

power   A number or variable raised to an exponent in the form x^n. See "exponent."

prediction   A rule (equation), table, or graph can be used to make a prediction about the value(s) a quantity will take that we have not yet seen. For example, we might analyze data about the height of a tree in each of its first three years of growth to predict how tall it will be at the end of year 4. (p. 97)

prime number   A positive integer with exactly two factors. The only factors of a prime number are 1 and itself. For example, the numbers 2, 3, 17, and 31 are all prime. 31 has no factors other than 1 and 31. (p. 241)

problem-solving strategies   This course incorporates several problem-solving strategies, specifically, making a guess and checking it, using manipulatives (such as algebra tiles), making systematic lists, collecting data, graphing, drawing a diagram, breaking a large problem into smaller subproblems, working backward, and writing and solving equations. For example, a student given the details of a cell-phone pricing plan and asked how many minutes would cost $29.95 might approach the problem by writing an equation and solving it, making a table of times and prices, graphing the relationship, or guessing and checking various numbers of minutes. (p. 2)

product   The result of multiplying. For example, the product of 4 and 5 is 20; the product of $3a$ and $8b^2$ is $24ab^2$. (p. 28)

proportion   An equation stating that two ratios (fractions) are equal. For example, the equation below is a proportion. A proportion is a useful type of equation to set up when solving problems involving proportional relationships. (p. 211)

$$\frac{68 \text{ votes for Mr. Mears}}{100 \text{ people surveyed}} = \frac{34 \text{ votes for Mr. Mears}}{50 \text{ people surveyed}}$$

quadrants   The coordinate plane is divided by its axes into four quadrants. The quadrants are numbered as shown in the first diagram at right. When graphing data that has no negative values, we sometimes use a graph showing only the first quadrant. (p. 10)

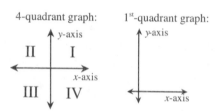

quadratic equation   An equation that can be written in the form $ax^2 + bx + c = 0$, where a, b, and c are real numbers and a is nonzero. A quadratic equation written in this form is said to be in standard form. For example, $3x^2 - 4x + 7.5 = 0$ is a quadratic equation. (p. 348)

quadratic expression   An expression that can be written in the form $ax^2 + bx + c$, where a, b, and c are real numbers and a is nonzero. For example, $3x^2 - 4x + 7.5$ is a quadratic expression. (p. 329)

Quadratic Formula   The Quadratic Formula states that if $ax^2 + bx + c = 0$ and $a \neq 0$, then $x = \frac{-b \pm \sqrt{b^2 - 4ac}}{2a}$. For example, if $5x^2 + 9x + 3 = 0$, then $x = \frac{-9 \pm \sqrt{9^2 - 4(5)(3)}}{2(5)} = \frac{-9 \pm \sqrt{21}}{10}$. (p. 357)

quadrilateral   A polygon with four sides. For example, the shape at right is a quadrilateral. (p. 50)

radical   An expression in the form $\sqrt{a}$, where $\sqrt{a}$ is the positive square root of a. For example, $\sqrt{49} = 7$. (Also see "square root.") (p. 365)

radicand   The expression under a radical sign. For example, in the expression $3+2\sqrt{x-7}$, the radicand is $x-7$.

range   The set of all output values for a function or relation. For example, the range of the function graphed at right is $y>-2$. (Also see "domain.") (p. 473)

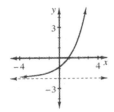

ratio   A ratio compares two quantities by division. A ratio can be written using a colon, but is more often written as a fraction. For example, we might be interested in the ratio of female students in a particular school to the total number of students in the school. This ratio could be written as 1521:2906 or as the fraction shown at right. (p. 211)

$$\frac{1521 \text{ female students}}{2906 \text{ total students}}$$

rational expression   An expression in the form of a fraction in which the numerator and/or denominator contain polynomials. For example, $\frac{x+2}{x^2+8x+12}$ is a rational expression. (pp. 409, 413)

rational numbers   Numbers that can be expressed in the form $\frac{a}{b}$, where a and b are integers and $b \neq 0$. For example, 0.75 is a rational number because it can be expressed in the form $\frac{3}{4}$. (p. 214)

real numbers   Irrational numbers together with rational numbers form the set of the real numbers. For example, the following are all real numbers: 2.78, -13267, 0, $\frac{3}{7}$, π, $\sqrt{2}$. All real numbers are represented on the number line. (p. 365)

reciprocal   The reciprocal of a nonzero number is its multiplicative inverse; that is, the reciprocal of x is $\frac{1}{x}$. For a number in the form $\frac{a}{b}$, where a and b are non-zero, the reciprocal is $\frac{b}{a}$. The product of a number and its reciprocal is 1. For example, the reciprocal of 12 is $\frac{1}{12}$, and $12 \cdot \frac{1}{12} = 1$. (Also see "Multiplicative Inverse Property.") (p. 72)

Reflexive Property   The Reflexive Property states that any expression is always equal to itself. That is, $a = a$. For example, $1627x^2 - 2 = 1627x^2 - 2$.

relation   An equation that relates inputs to outputs. For example, $y = \frac{4x}{x-3}$ and $x^2 + y^2 = 18$ are both relations. The set of input values to a relation is the domain, and the set of output values is the range. A relation can also be thought of as a set of ordered pairs. (p. 473)

representation   A representation expresses a relationship between quantities in a particular way. In this course, we emphasize four different ways of representing a numerical relationship: with a graph, table, situation (pattern), or rule (equation or inequality). (Also see "representations web.") (p. 161)

representations web   The representations web, or just "the web," is an organizational tool we use to keep track of connections between the four representations of numerical relationships emphasized in this course. As we learn how to move from one representation of a particular type of pattern to another, we record this by drawing an arrow on the web. For example, an arrow from "rule" to "graph" in the web might record our ability to draw the graph for a given equation. (Also see "representation.") (p. 161)

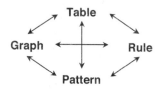

rewriting   To rewrite an equation or expression is to write an equivalent equation or expression. In this course, "rewriting" also refers to a method of solving one-variable equations. In "rewriting," we use algebraic techniques to write an equation equivalent to the original. This will often involve using the Distributive Property to eliminate parentheses. We then solve the equation using various solution methods, including perhaps rewriting again. For example, to solve the equation $4(x+2)=36$ by "rewriting," we use the Distributive Property to rewrite the equation as $4x+8=36$. We then solve this equation to find that $x=7$. (p. 424)

root   A root of an equation is a solution of the equation. For example, the roots of $(x-4)(2x+3)=0$ are $x=4$ and $x=-\frac{3}{2}$. When working with a function $f(x)$, the x-intercepts of the function's graph are the roots of the equation $f(x)=0$. (p. 344)

rule   A rule is an equation or inequality that represents the relationship between two numerical quantities. We often use a rule to represent the relationship between quantities in a table, a pattern, a real-world situation, or a graph. For example, the rule $y=0.4x+25$ might tell us how to find the total cost y in cents of talking on a pay phone for x minutes. (p. 93)

scale on axes   The scale on an axis tells you what number each successive mark on the axis represents. A complete graph has the scale marked with numbers on each axis. Each axis should be scaled so that each interval represents the same amount. (p. 105)

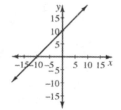

scientific notation   A number is expressed in scientific notation when it is in the form $a \cdot 10^n$, where $1 \le a < 10$ and n is an integer. For example, the number 31,000 can be expressed in scientific notation as $3.1 \cdot 10^4$. (p. 451)

similar figures   Similar figures have the same shape but are not necessarily the same size. For example the two triangles at right are similar. In similar figures, the measures of corresponding angles are equal and the lengths of corresponding sides are proportional. (p. 78)

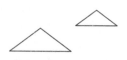

simple radical form   A number $r\sqrt{s}$ is in simple radical form if no square of an integer divides s and s is not a fraction; that is, there are no perfect square factors (square numbers such as 4, 9, 16, etc.) under the radical sign and no radicals in the denominator. For example, $5\sqrt{12}$ is not in simple radical form since 4 (the square of 2) divides 12. But $10\sqrt{3}$ is in simple radical form and is equivalent to $5\sqrt{12}$. (p. 365)

simplify   To simplify an expression is to write a less complicated expression with the same value. A simplified expression has no parentheses and no like terms. For example, the expression $3 - (2x + 7) - 4x$ can be simplified to $-4 - 6x$. When working with algebra tiles, a simplified expression uses the fewest possible tiles to represent the original expression. (p. 55)

slope   A ratio that describes how steep (or flat) a line is. Slope can be positive, negative, or even zero, but a straight line has only one slope. Slope is the ratio $\frac{\text{vertical change}}{\text{horizontal change}}$ or $\frac{\text{change in } y \text{ value}}{\text{change in } x \text{ value}}$, sometimes written $\frac{\Delta y}{\Delta x}$. When the equation of a line is written in $y = mx + b$ form, m is the slope of the line. Some texts refer to slope as the ratio of the "rise over the run." A line has positive slope if it slopes upward from left to right on a graph, negative slope if it slopes downward from left to right, zero slope if it is horizontal, and undefined slope if it is vertical. (p. 291)

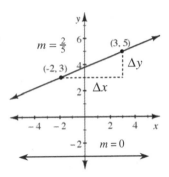

slope-intercept form   See "$y = mx + b$."

slope triangle   A slope triangle is a right triangle drawn on a graph of a line so that the hypotenuse of the triangle is part of the line. The vertical leg length is the change in the y-value (Δy); the horizontal leg length is the change in the x-value (Δx). We use the lengths of the legs in the triangle to calculate the slope ratio $\frac{\Delta y}{\Delta x}$. For example, the diagram at right shows a slope triangle with $\Delta y = 2$, $\Delta x = 4$. The slope of the line in the example is $\frac{2}{4}$, or $\frac{1}{2}$. (Also see "slope.") (p. 282)

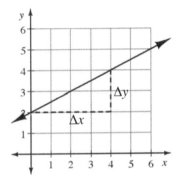

solution   The number or numbers that when substituted into an equation or inequality make the equation or inequality true. For example, $x = 4$ is a solution to the equation $3x - 2 = 10$ because $3x - 2$ equals 10 when $x = 4$. A solution to a two-variable equation is sometimes written as an ordered pair (x, y). For example, $x = 3$ and $y = -2$ is a solution to the equation $y = x - 5$; this solution can be written as $(3, -2)$. (pp. 128, 201, 245, 252)

solve   (1) To find all the solutions to an equation or an inequality (or a system of equations or inequalities). For example, solving the equation $x^2 = 9$ gives the solutions $x = 3$ and $x = -3$. (pp. 68, 119, 170) (2) Solving an equation for a variable gives an equivalent equation that expresses that variable in terms of other variables and constants. For example, solving $2y - 8x = 16$ for y gives $y = 4x + 8$. The equation $y = 4x + 8$ has the same solutions as $2y - 8x = 16$, but $y = 4x + 8$ expresses y in terms of x and some constants. (p. 203)

square numbers   The numbers in the pattern 1, 4, 9, 16, 25, … . That is, the squares of the counting numbers 1, 2, 3, 4, 5, … are known as square numbers.

square root A number a is a square root of b if $a^2 = b$. For example, the number 9 has two square roots, 3 and –3. A negative number has no real square roots; a positive number has two; and zero has just one square root, namely, itself. Other roots, such as cube root, will be studied in other courses. (Also see "radical.") (p. 365)

standard form for a number See "standard notation."

standard form for quadratics A quadratic expression in the form $ax^2 + bx + c$ is said to be in standard form. For example, the following are all expressions in standard form: $3m^2 + m - 1$, $x^2 - 9$, and $3x^2 + 5x$. (p. 335)

standard form of a linear equation The standard form for a linear equation is $ax + by = c$, where a, b, and c are real numbers and a and b are not both zero. For example, the equation $2.5x - 3y = 12$ is in standard form. When you are given the equation of a line in standard form, it is often useful to write an equivalent equation in $y = mx + b$ form to find the line's slope and y-intercept. (p. 205)

standard notation A number written out completely, showing all digits and without use of exponents is written in standard notation. For example, 31,000 is the standard notation for the number expressed by $3.1 \cdot 10^4$. Standard notation is also sometimes called "standard form."

starting value In certain situations, the dependent variable has a starting value where the situation described in a problem begins. For example, if we are measuring the population of a town over time, that population will have some starting value when we begin our measurements. (p. 203)

substitution Replacing one symbol with a number, a variable, or another algebraic expression of the same value. Substitution does not change the value of the overall expression. For example, suppose we are trying to evaluate the expression $13x - 6$ when $x = 4$. Since x has the value 4, we can substitute 4 into the expression wherever x appears, giving us the equivalent expression $13(4) - 6$. (p. 248)

Substitution Method A method for solving a system of equations by replacing one variable with an expression involving the remaining variable(s). For example, in the system of equations at right the first equation tells you that y is equal to $-3x + 5$. We can substitute $-3x + 5$ in for y in the second equation to get $2(-3x + 5) + 10x = 18$, then solve this equation to find x. Once we have x, we substitute that value back into either of the original equations to find the value of y. (pp. 242, 248)

$$y = -3x + 5$$
$$2y + 10x = 18$$

Substitution Property The Substitution Property states that if $a = b$, a can be replaced by b in any expression without changing the value of the expression. For example, if $x = 4$, $13x - 6$ has the same value as $13(4) - 6$.

sum The result of adding two or more numbers. For example, the sum of 4 and 5 is 9. (p. 28)

Symmetric Property of Equality   The Symmetric Property states that if two expressions are equal, it does not matter which is stated first. That is, if $a = b$ then $b = a$. For example, $56 \div 8 = 7$, and $7 = 56 \div 8$.

symmetry   See "line of symmetry."

system of equations   A system of equations is a set of equations with the same variables. Solving a system of equations means finding one or more solutions that make each of the equations in the system true. A solution to a system of equations gives a point of intersection of the graphs of the equations in the system. There may be zero, one, or several solutions to a system of equations. For example, (1.5, –3) is a solution to the system of equations at right; setting $x = 1.5$, $y = -3$ makes both of the equations true. Also, (1.5, –3) is a point of intersection of the graphs of these two equations. (p. 165)

$$y = 2x - 6$$
$$y = -2x$$

system of inequalities   A system of inequalities is a set of inequalities with the same variables. Solving a system of inequalities means finding one or more regions on the coordinate plane whose points represent solutions to each of the inequalities in the system. There may be zero, one, or several such regions for a system of inequalities. For example, the shaded region at right is a graph of the system of inequalities that appears below it. (p. 391)

$$y \le x^2 + x - 6$$
$$y > \tfrac{2}{3} x$$

table   The tables used in this course represent numerical information by organizing it into columns and rows. The numbers may come from a graph, situation (pattern), or rule (equation). Many of the tables in this course are x-y tables like the one shown at right. (pp. 13, 23)

IN (x)	–2	4	1	6	–5
OUT (y)	–6	–2	–3	2	–9

term   A term is a single number, variable, or the product of numbers and variables. In an expression, terms are separated by addition or subtraction signs. For example, in the expression $1.2x - 45 + 3xy^2$, the terms are $1.2x$, -45, and $3xy^2$. (p. 57)

tile pattern   See "pattern."

Transitive Property of Equality   The Transitive Property of Equality states that if $a = b$ and $b = c$, then $a = c$. For example, if $x = 2y$ and $2y = 13$, then x must equal 13.

trend line   A line that represents a set of data. The trend line does not necessarily intersect each data point; it attempts to approximate the data, as in the example at right. Trend lines are often used to make predictions about future, unobserved data points. (p. 279)

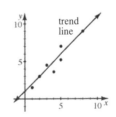

trinomial   A polynomial that is the sum or difference of exactly three terms, each of which is a monomial. For example, $x^2 + 6x + 9$ is a trinomial. (pp. 329)

twice   Two times as much. For example, a twenty-dollar bill has *twice* the value of a ten-dollar bill. (p. 28)

undoing   In this course, "undoing" refers to a method of solving one-variable equations. In "undoing," we undo the last operation that was applied to an expression by applying its inverse operation. We then solve the resulting equation using various solution methods, including perhaps undoing again. For example, in the equation $4(x+2)=36$, the last operation that was applied to the left-hand side was a *multiplication* by 4. So to use "undoing," we *divide* both sides of the equation by 4, giving us $x+2=9$. We then solve the equation $x+2=9$ (perhaps by "undoing" again and subtracting 2 from both sides) to find that $x=7$. (p. 424)

variable   A symbol used to represent one or more numbers. In this course, letters of the English alphabet are used as variables. For example, in the expression $3x-(8.6xy+z)$, the variables are x, y, and z. (p. 41)

vertex (of a parabola)   The vertex of a parabola is the highest or lowest point on the parabola (depending on the parabola's orientation). (p. 106)

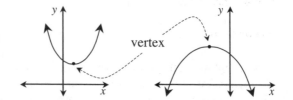

vertical lines   Vertical lines run up and down in the same direction as the y-axis and are parallel to it. All vertical lines have equations of the form $x=a$, where a can be any number. For example, the graph at right shows the vertical lines $x=4$ and $x=-1$. The y-axis has the equation $x=0$ because $x=0$ everywhere on the y-axis. Vertical lines have undefined slope. (p. 291)

Ways of Thinking   This course emphasizes five Ways of Thinking about mathematical ideas: justifying (explaining and verifying your ideas), generalizing (predicting behavior for any situation), making connections (connecting your ideas to other ways of seeing or to past or future learning), reversing thinking (solving problems "backward and forward"), and applying and extending (applying your knowledge to new contexts and extending it to help solve new problems). For example, when confronted with a new type of mathematical problem, you might solve it by reversing your thinking to work backwards or by trying to make connections to problems you have seen before. Once you have a solution, you might be asked to justify your solution or generalize it to a broader class of problems. Finally, you might then apply what you have learned on this problem to the next new type of problem that comes along. (p. 2)

web   See "representations web."

x-axis   See "axes."

x-coordinate   See "coordinate."

x-intercept(s)   The point(s) where a graph intersects the x-axis. A graph may have several x-intercepts, no x-intercepts, or just one. We sometimes report the x-intercepts of a graph with coordinate pairs, but since the y-coordinate is always zero, we often just give the x-coordinates of x-intercepts. For example, we might say that the x-intercepts of the graph at right are (0, 0) and (2, 0), or we might just say that the x-intercepts are 0 and 2. (pp. 119, 301)

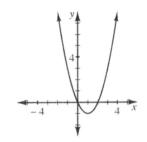

x→y table   An x→y table, like the one at right, represents pairs of values of two related quantities. The input value (x) appears first, and the output value (y) appears second. For example, the x→y table at right tells us that the input value 10 is paired with the output value 18 for some rule. (p. 94)

IN (x)	OUT (y)
	8
0	-2
-4	-10
10	18
-2	
	198
0.5	

y-axis   See "axes."

y-coordinate   See "coordinate."

y-intercept(s)   The point(s) where a graph intersects the y-axis. A function has at most one y-intercept; a relation may have several. The y-intercept of a graph is important because it often represents the starting value of a quantity in a real-world situation. For example, on the graph of a tile pattern the y-intercept represents the number of tiles in Figure 0. We sometimes report the y-intercept of a graph with a coordinate pair, but since the x-coordinate is always zero, we often just give the y-coordinate of the y-intercept. For example, we might say that the y-intercept of the graph at right is (0, 2), or we might just say that the y-intercept is 2. When a linear equation is written in $y = mx + b$ form, b tells us the y-intercept of the graph. For example, the equation of the graph at right is $y = x + 2$ and its y-intercept is 2. (pp. 119, 298, 301)

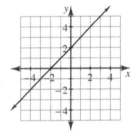

$y = mx + b$ When two quantities x and y have a linear relationship, that relationship can be represented with an equation in $y = mx + b$ form. The constant m is the slope, and b is the y-intercept of the graph. For example, the graph at right shows the line represented by the equation $y = 2x + 3$, which has a slope of 2 and a y-intercept of 3. This form of a linear equation is also called the slope-intercept form. (p. 149)

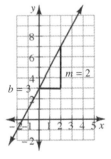

zero   A number often used to represent "having none of a quantity." Zero is neither negative nor positive. Zero is the identity element for addition. (pp. 51, 53, 346, 348)

Zero Product Property   The Zero Product Property states that when the product of two or more factors is zero, one of these factors must equal zero. That is, if $a \cdot b = 0$, then either $a = 0$ or $b = 0$ (or both). For example, if $(x + 4)(2x - 3) = 0$, then either $x + 4 = 0$ or $2x - 3 = 0$ (or both). The Zero Product Property can be used to solve factorable quadratic equations. (p. 349)

List of Symbols

+	plus (addition)		$\sqrt{}$	square root
−	minus (subtraction)		1:5	1 to 5 ratio
·	times (multiplication)		±	plus or minus
÷	divide by (division)		>	greater than
−1	negative one (negative integer)		<	less than
=	equals to		≥	greater than or equal
(x, y)	coordinates of a point		≤	less than or equal to
$y = mx + b$	slope-intercept form of a linear equation		x^2	x squared

1 ▪
1   represents 1

1 ▭ y
    y represents y

1 ▭ x
    x represents x

y ▢ y^2
    y represents y^2

x ▢ x^2
    x represents x^2

x ▭ xy
    y represents xy

Note: For this text, all unshaded tiles will represent negative quantities. For example, the tile ▢ represents −1.

Index
Student Version

Many of the pages referenced here contain a definition or an example of the topic listed, often within the body of a Math Notes box. Others contain problems that develop or demonstrate the topic. It may be necessary to read the text on several pages to fully understand the topic. Also, some problems listed here are good examples of the topic and may not offer any explanation. The page numbers below reflect the pages in the Student Version. References to Math Notes boxes are bolded.

Symbols

$\leq, <, >, \geq$ symbols, 350
Δ (delta), 282, 283
$\pm$ (plus or minus), 357, **358**
$\sqrt{}$ (square root), 365

A

Absolute value, 388, **389**
  solving equations with, **430**
  solving inequalities with, 432
Adding and subtracting rational
  expressions, 499, 502, **503**
Adding integers, **15**
Additive Identity, **53**
Additive Inverse Property, **72**
Algebra tiles, 41, 42, 44, **198**
  building a square, **427**
  multiplying binomials, **192**
  naming, 41
  on an equation mat, 68, **69**
  on an expression comparison mat, 55
  on an expression mat, 47, 52, **60**
  solving equations, 68
  to combine like terms, 42, **57**
  to simplify expressions, 52, **57**, **60**
Algebra, properties of
  Associative Properties, **53**
  Commutative Properties, **45**
  Distributive Property, 194
  Identity Properties, **53**, **410**
  Inverse properties, **72**
  Transitive Property, **448**

All numbers solution, **127**
Apartment problem, the, 22
Applying and extending, 224
Approximate form, 426
Approximating square roots, 365
Area
  as a product, 191, **192**, **218**, 327
  as a sum, 191, **192**, **218**, 327
  of a figure, **5**
  of a rectangle, **5**, 7
  of a square, 336
Associative Property
  of Addition, **53**
  of Multiplication, **53**
Average (mean), 11, 25
Axes, **10**
  independent and dependent, **110**
  scaling, 14, 105, 115
  x- and *y*-axes, **10**

B

b, 149, 150, **298**
Base, **452**
Big Cs problems, 100, 101, 124
Big Race problems, 296, 298, **300**
Binomial, **329**
Boundaries, system of inequalities, 392, **393**
Boundary point, 376, **377**, **386**
Burning Candle problem, the, 512

C

Calculator check, 67
Cartesian plane, **10**
Checking a solution, **201**
Chubby Bunny problems, 169, 170
Closure Properties, **214**, 215
Coefficient, **255**
Coincide, **252**, **258**
Cola Machine problem, 467
Combining like terms, **57**
Common factor, 338
Commutative Property, **45**
Complete Graph, **119**
Completing the square, 436, 437, 438, 440, **444**
    deriving the Quadratic Formula, 510
Conclusion, **241**, 384
Consecutive numbers, 256
Constant, 149, **255**
Continuous, 101, **102**, 147
Coordinates, 8, **10**, 46, **119**
Counterexample, 192, 284
Cube root, 450

D

Decimal, **19**
Deductive reasoning, **448**
Delta, 282, 283
Dependent, 13, **110**, **473**
Deriving the Quadratic Formula, 510
Diamond problems, 6, 16, 331, 332
    factoring, 331, 338
Difference of squares, 497
Dimensions, 7, 27, 46
Discrete, 101, **102**
Distributive Property, 194, **198**
Dividing integers, **24**
Dizzyland problem, 311
Domain, 470, **473**

E

Elimination Method, 250, **264**
Endpoint
    solid, 376, **377**, **386**
    unfilled, 376, **377**, **386**
Equal Values Method, 170, **171**, **176**
Equation of line
    point-slope form, **314**
    slope-intercept form, 150, **298**
    through two points, 310
Equations, 68, **69**
    approximating from data, 279
    equivalent, 411, 416, 418, **419**
    from a pattern, 93, 139
    from a table, 94, 98, 150
    from a situation, 108
    from word problems, **234**
    linear. *See* Linear equations
    proportional, 209, 210, **211**
    quadratic, **335**, 348, **349**
    quadratic application, 360, 364
    quadratic, from a graph, 354
    quadratic, in perfect square form, 426, **427**
    quadratic, solving with the Quadratic Formula, 357, **358**, **361**
    quadratic, solving with the Zero Product Property, **361**
    of a line, 149
    solving. *See* Solving equations
    solving by looking inside, 422, **424**
    solving by rewriting, 411, 414, 415, 416, 418, 422, **424**
    solving by undoing, 422, **424**
    solving with absolute value, **430**
    solving without algebra tiles, **171**
    systems. *See* Systems of equations
Equation mat, 68, **69**
Equivalent, 16
    equations, 399, **416**, 418, **419**
    expressions, 48
    fractions, 212
Estimating Fish problem, 216
Eucalyptus Grove problem, 8

R

Range, 471, **473**
Ratio, 210, **211**
  slope, **291**
Rational expressions, 409
  adding and subtracting, 499, 502, **503**
  multiplying and dividing, 412, **413**
  simplifying, 410, **413**
Rational Numbers, **214**, 365
Ratios, equal, 212
Real numbers, 365
Reasoning
  deductive, **448**
  inductive, **448**
Reciprocal, **72**
Recorder/Reporter, 4
Rectangle
  area, **5**, 7, 191
  area as a product, **218**
  area as a sum, **218**
  building with algebra tiles, 193
  dimensions, **7**, 27, 46, 191
  generic, 197, **198**, **218**
  perimeter, **5**
Regions, 392
Relations, 465, 475
  domain, 470, 471, **473**
  function, 467
  input and output, 464
  range, **473**
  transformations, 479
Representations
  connections between, 139, 152
  multiple, **161**
  numeric, 11, 16, **19**
  web, 144, 159, **161**, 173
Resource Manager, 4
Reversing thinking, 184
Rewriting, solving by, 415, 416, 422, **424**
Rewriting expressions
  Distributive Property, 194, **198**
  multiplying binomials, **192**
  with exponents, **452**
Roots, 450
  of a parabola, 344, 350

Rule, 161
  from a graph, 149, 156
  from a pattern, 100, 139, 143, 148
  from a situation, 108
  from a table, 94, 97, 98, 150
  quadratic, from a graph, 354
  quadratic, from a situation or
    pattern, 345
  quadratic, from a table, 351

S

Saint Louis Gateway Arch problem,
  360
Sampling, 80, 81, 216
Save the Earth problem, 316
Scaling axes, 105, 115
Scatterplot, 163, 278
Scientific notation, 451
Search and Rescue problem, 395
Sierpinski Triangle, **82**
Silent Board Game, 97
Similar figures, **78**, 280
Simplifying expressions, 52, 60, 64
  by combining like terms, **57**
  on an expression mat, **60**
  recording your work, 64
  with algebra tiles, **60**
Slope, 281, 282, 283, **291**, **298**
  as a rate, 293
  negative, 285, 286, **291**
  of parallel lines, 288, 290, 308
  of perpendicular lines, 307, 308
  positive, 286, **291**
  triangles, 282, 285, 286, **298**, **314**
  undefined, **291**
  without a slope triangle, 290
  zero, 286, **291**
Slope-intercept form, 150, **205**, **298**
Solution, **127**
  checking, 118, **201**
  exact and approximate forms, 426
  infinite solutions, **127**
  no solution, **127**
  of a linear equation, 118, 382
  of a one-variable inequality, 376,
    386
  of a system of equations, **252**
  of a system of inequalities, 391,
    399
  of an inequality, 382, 385

THIS BOOK IS THE PROPERTY OF:		Book No._____		
ISSUED TO		Year Used	CONDITION	
			ISSUED	RETURNED
_____		_____		
_____		_____		
_____		_____		
_____		_____		
_____		_____		
_____		_____		
_____		_____		
_____		_____		

PUPILS to whom this texbook is issued must not write on any part of it in any way, unless otherwise instructed by the teacher.